OECD PROCEED

Cleaner Production and Waste Minimisation in OECD and Dynamic Non-Member Economies

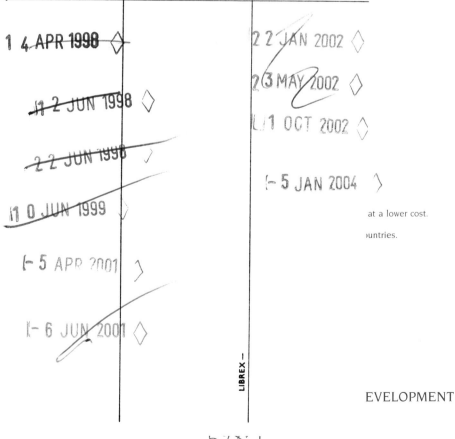
at a lower cost.

ountries.

EVELOPMENT

ORGANISATION FOR ECONOMIC CO-OPERATION AND DEVELOPMENT

Pursuant to Article 1 of the Convention signed in Paris on 14th December 1960, and which came into force on 30th September 1961, the Organisation for Economic Co-operation and Development (OECD) shall promote policies designed:

- to achieve the highest sustainable economic growth and employment and a rising standard of living in Member countries, while maintaining financial stability, and thus to contribute to the development of the world economy;
- to contribute to sound economic expansion in Member as well as non-member countries in the process of economic development; and
- to contribute to the expansion of world trade on a multilateral, non-discriminatory basis in accordance with international obligations.

The original Member countries of the OECD are Austria, Belgium, Canada, Denmark, France, Germany, Greece, Iceland, Ireland, Italy, Luxembourg, the Netherlands, Norway, Portugal, Spain, Sweden, Switzerland, Turkey, the United Kingdom and the United States. The following countries became Members subsequently through accession at the dates indicated hereafter: Japan (28th April 1964), Finland (28th January 1969), Australia (7th June 1971), New Zealand (29th May 1973), Mexico (18th May 1994), the Czech Republic (21st December 1995), Hungary (7th May 1996), Poland (22nd November 1996) and the Republic of Korea (12th December 1996). The Commission of the European Communities takes part in the work of the OECD (Article 13 of the OECD Convention).

FOREWORD

As governments face up to the challenge of implementing sustainable development strategies, increased attention is being focused on the roles of cleaner production, eco-efficiency and waste minimisation in re-orienting production and consumption patterns. Applying a life cycle perspective to products, processes and services is a key characteristic of cleaner production, eco-efficiency and waste minimisation, as well as an emphasis on the links among technological, management/organisational and attitudinal factors.

There is growing interest in applying cleaner production, eco-efficiency and waste minimisation in both OECD and non-OECD countries. It is striking that despite their potential to promote "win-win" economic and environmental benefits, uptake has been less than might be expected. Barriers inhibiting uptake include inappropriate or contradictory government policy signals, weak support for information dissemination strategies, lack of company senior management interest in, or commitment to, cleaner production concepts, and limited availability of finance for cleaner production investments. There is, however, practical experience in both OECD and non-OECD countries which illustrates some of the steps that can be taken within companies and in their external environment to promote the integration of environmental management into "standard" management practice and thereby maximise economic and environmental benefits.

It was within this context that the OECD organised a Workshop on Cleaner Production and Waste Minimisation in November 1995. The workshop was held under the framework of the OECD's Policy Dialogue with the Dynamic Non-Member Economies programme and brought together government officials, business persons and academics, attending in their personal capacity, from OECD Member countries and ten dynamic non-Member economies in Asia and Latin America. Mr. Jan Suurland of the Ministry of Housing, Spatial Planning and the Environment, the Netherlands chaired the workshop. Selected papers from the workshop are presented in this volume. The views expressed are those of the respective authors and do not necessarily reflect the views of the OECD, its Member countries or of the institutions to which the authors are affiliated. The volume is published on the authority of the Secretary-General of the OECD.

This volume is dedicated to the memory of Harvey Yakowitz, Principal Administrator, OECD Environment Directorate. He contributed enormously to the issues presented in this volume, both within OECD and in other national and international forums.

TABLE OF CONTENTS

Introduction
Chris Chung and Brendan Gillespie, Environment Directorate, OECD 7

Part I: Policy Approaches to Promote Cleaner Production and Waste Minimisation

Policy Approaches for Promoting Cleaner Production and Waste Minimisation
in OECD Member Countries
Rebecca Hanmer, Environment Directorate, OECD..17

Australian and Regional Co-operation Initiatives to Promote Cleaner Production
and Waste Minimisation
Annie Gabriel, Environment Protection Agency, Australia..33

Cleaner Production and Waste Minimisation: Hong Kong's Experience
Planning, Environment and Lands Branch, Hong Kong 41

Cleaner Production and Waste Minimisation: Experience from Malaysia
Khalid Abdul Rahim, Universiti Putra Malaysia , Malaysia...51

The Metro Manila Clean Technology Initiative
Annice Brown, Asia Technical Department, The World Bank..61

Applying Cleaner Production in Thailand
Chaiyod Bunyagidj, Thailand Environment Institute, Thailand.......................................77

China's Cleaner Production Policy Goals
Wang Dehui, National Environmental Protection Agency, China.....................................83

Policy Approaches to Promote Cleaner Production in Argentina, Brazil and Chile
Joachim von Amsberg, Latin America and the Caribbean Department, The World Bank.................87

Cleaner Production and Waste Minimisation: Experience from Mexico
*Luis Guadarrama, Ministry of Environment, Natural Resources and
Fisheries, Mexico*... 109

(continued on next page)

5

Part II: Cleaner Production and the Private Sector

Implementing Waste Minimisation and Eco-efficiency in the Private Sector
Joel Hirschhorn, Hirschhorn and Associates, USA 125

Cleaner Production in Small and Medium-sized Enterprises: The Role of Cleaner
Production Programmes
C.M. Lin, Hong Kong Productivity Council, Hong Kong 135

The Environmental Goods and Services Industry in OECD and Dynamic Non-Member Economies
Graham Vickery and Maria Iarrera, Directorate
for Science, Technology and Industry, OECD 143

Part III: Assessing the Cost-effectiveness of Cleaner Production

Assessing the Cost-effectiveness of Cleaner Production
Harvey Yakowitz, Environment Directorate, OECD 163

Improving Cleaner Production in China
Ning Duan, Environmental Management Institute, Chinese Academy of
Environmental Sciences, and China National Cleaner Production Centre, China 179

The Cost-effectiveness of Cleaner Production: Experience From Central
and Eastern Europe
Olav Nedenes, World Cleaner Production Society, Norway 195

Part IV: The International Dimension

Management of Hazardous Wastes and Control of their Transfrontier Movements
Pierre Lieben, Environmental Consultant, France 211

Control Measures Concerning the Import of Hazardous Wastes into China
Youfu Xia, China Institute of Trade and Environment, and University of International
Business and Economics, China 239

The ISO 14000 Series of Environmental Management Standards
Philippe Bergeron, Regional Institute of Environmental Technology, Singapore 253

INTRODUCTION

Chris Chung and Brendan Gillespie
Environment Directorate, OECD

As governments face up to the challenge of implementing sustainable development strategies, increased attention is being focused on the roles of cleaner production, eco-efficiency and waste minimisation in re-orienting production and consumption patterns. Definitions of these and related terms overlap but in its 1996 publication "Sustainable Production and Consumption: Cleaner Production" UNEP defined cleaner production as "... the continuous application of an integrated preventive environmental strategy applied in processes, products, and services to increase eco-efficiency and reduce risks to humans and the environment. Cleaner production requires changing attitudes, responsible environmental management and evaluating technology options."

To better understand the challenges and opportunities of cleaner production and waste minimisation, the OECD organised a workshop on this subject in Paris in November 1995. Selected papers from the workshop are presented in this volume. The workshop was held within the framework of the OECD's Policy Dialogue with the Dynamic Non-Member Economies (DNMEs: Argentina, Brazil, Chile, Hong Kong, Korea[1], Malaysia, Singapore, Chinese Taipei, Thailand), and brought together, in their personal capacity, over 80 government officials, academics and business persons from OECD Member countries, the DNMEs and China. It followed a previous workshop held in 1993 on the use of economic instruments in environmental policies[2].

The objectives of the workshop were three-fold:

- to review recent trends in policies and policy instruments to promote cleaner production in the OECD area, the DNMEs and China;

- to examine opportunities for, and barriers to, private sector investment in cleaner technologies and the role of the environmental goods and services industry; and

---

[1] Since 1996, an OECD Member country.

[2] Proceedings published as OECD, 1994: *Applying Economic Instruments to Environmental Policies in OECD and Dynamic Non-Member Economies*. OECD. Paris.

- to examine the role of international instruments and environmental management standards, with reference to the management and control of transfrontier movements of hazardous wastes and ISO 14000.

Part I of the volume focuses on policy approaches to promote cleaner production in OECD countries and the DNMEs. Rebecca Hanmer begins by reviewing the range of approaches being implemented in OECD Member countries. In her paper, *"Policy Approaches for Promoting Cleaner Production and Waste Minimisation in OECD Member Countries"*, she notes that there is no single approach but rather that a mix of policy tools is usually deployed. Different government's have placed emphasis on different policy tools, including support for cleaner technology research and development, increased attention to product-related strategies, increased efforts to raise public awareness and education and greater use of voluntary agreements between industry and government. Common elements which support cleaner production efforts in OECD countries are also identified, such as the role of a robust and well enforced regulatory framework and the wider application of market-based instruments. Opportunities and challenges to co-operation between OECD and other countries in the diffusion of cleaner technologies are also discussed, recognising that this is an issue of mutual interest.

Annie Gabriel's paper on *"Australian and Regional Co-operation Initiatives to Promote Cleaner Production and Waste Minimisation"* describes the range of activities undertaken to reach out to stakeholders. They include the provision of training and educational materials, such as handbooks, information kits and case study pamphlets. The federal and state governments, business and research institutes have also contributed in refining tools such as environmental auditing, life cycle analysis and environmental management systems. Moreover, Australia is providing practical assistance to developing countries in the Asia-Pacific region to support their environmental management, including cleaner production, programmes. With over 950,000 small businesses in Australia, disseminating the concept of cleaner production to this sector is considered an especially important task for local government.

In *"Cleaner Production and Waste Minimisation: Hong Kong's Experience"*, the 1989 White Paper on Pollution is noted as the genesis of a comprehensive package of waste management programmes. The 1993 review of this White Paper resulted in a government commitment to examine how waste reduction and waste minimisation could be further promoted in Hong Kong, recognising that cleaner production is a particularly useful approach. The areas of material/product substitution and process/equipment modification were considered especially fruitful in applying cleaner production. A number of mutually supportive policy measures have been introduced to deepen the implementation of cleaner production, including wide dissemination of information and technical advice to SMEs, targeted support funding for technology and sector-specific database development, progressive tightening of legislation and the introduction of economic incentives such as charging for disposal of chemical waste and discharge of trade effluents. Local NGOs have played an important role in promoting cleaner production through the provision of information and technical assistance/training, supporting pilot projects and undertaking in-plant environmental audits.

Industrialisation and export-led growth have underpinned Malaysia's rapid economic development. The goal of achieving developed country status by 2020 is reinforcing the industrialisation process, particularly in higher technology products and services. Khalid Abdul Rahim in his paper *"Cleaner Production and Waste Minimisation: Experience from Malaysia"* describes some of the achievements to date and further challenges in applying cleaner production as Malaysia further industrialises. The potential to implement cleaner production is high in the manufacturing sector, especially in electronics in which a wide range of consumer and industrial components is produced. Successful examples in the rubber, palm oil and electroplating industries have demonstrated the cost-effectiveness of cleaner production in these sectors. A particular challenge concerns SMEs. It is estimated that there are more than 16,000 SMEs in Malaysia but this figure does not include the un-registered plants operating in areas and premises where industrial activities are a permitted use. The paper notes that the largest environmental problem created by the SMEs is disposal of hazardous and toxic wastes. The delay in completing the central toxic waste treatment facility is exacerbating problems of waste storage for both SMEs and some larger companies. A recent amendment to the Environmental Quality Act, Malaysia's principal environmental statute, has extended the provisions for the Department of Environment to monitor the environmental performance of SMEs.

Annice Brown's paper *"The Metro Manila Clean Technology Initiative"* describes a programme developed to promote cleaner technology and waste minimisation efforts in Metro Manila, the Philippines. The programme comprised the implementation of environmental audits in 25 plants spread among six industrial sectors (food processing, dairy, beverages, electroplating, chemicals and tannery); six technology matching missions, one for each sector, in which industry representatives and regulators from the Philippines undertook study visits to the USA; and follow-up eco-seminars in Manila in which study visit participants shared their experiences and findings with local industrial associations and other interested parties. A notable feature of Brown's paper is the summary of the practical approaches to cleaner production adopted by the companies visited by the technology matching missions.

In his paper *"Applying Cleaner Production in Thailand"*, Chaiyod Bunyagidj notes that industrial development in Thailand has assisted overall development of the economy but it has also had adverse effects on natural resources and environmental quality. The Bangkok Metropolitan Region, which has particularly high densities of population and industrial facilities, has borne a heavy share of air and water pollution; approximately 40% of industry in the Region is SMEs while less than 1% is large scale industry. Recognising that past efforts to control industrial pollution by regulatory instruments have been insufficient to achieve desired results, greater emphasis is now being given to pollution prevention by cleaner production. Research into cleaner technologies and demonstration projects have been particular targets for collaborative work between Thai and foreign partners, including in the pulp and paper, chemicals, textiles, electroplating, food and leather tanning industries. Although these projects have demonstrated the economic and environmental benefits attainable by cleaner production, the author notes that they have nonetheless been small in scale and partial in focus. The next step is to implement cleaner production on a wide scale throughout Thai industry. While the challenge is considered more easily met by large companies, fundamental barriers of information transfer, limited understanding of environmental management practices and its impact on the bottom line, and short-term outlook impede uptake of cleaner production in SMEs. To address these barriers the author suggests implementation of a range of mutually supportive measures covering sector-specific technical assistance to SMEs, the establishment of a regional cleaner production technologies centre, an information database on cleaner technologies applicable in the Thai industrial context, environmental education of SME managers, "seed" finance for demonstration projects and development of networks among SMEs, among NGOs, academics and SMEs and between government pollution control agencies and SMEs.

China's industrial structure is undergoing modernisation as its domestic economic reforms and a closer integration into the world economy catalyse change. Wider implementation of cleaner production and waste minimisation has been identified by the Chinese government as one of the principal overarching policy goals associated with industrial modernisation. The paper on *"China's Cleaner Production Policy Goals"* prepared by Wang Dehui lists the principal policy goals that guide action. These goals range from integrating cleaner production measures into production plan development to the wider use of regulatory and economic instruments to promote cleaner production and the enhancement of international co-operation in information exchange, policy dialogue and clean technology transfer.

The last two papers in this Part of the volume concern experiences from Argentina, Brazil, Chile and Mexico. In his *paper "Policy Approaches to Promote Cleaner Production in Argentina, Brazil and Chile"*, Joachim von Amsberg discusses the experience in each of these countries and presents some preliminary lessons which have emerged. His analysis highlights the complementarity of a troika comprising stable macro-economic policies, robust environmental policies and legislation that set targets for environmental quality and which supports a longer-term "vision" of sustainable development, and focused approaches to cleaner production according to the needs of different types of industry and industrial sectors.

Luis Guadarrama's *paper "Cleaner Production and Waste Minimisation: Experience from Mexico"* notes that manufacturing accounted for 73% of industrial production and 24% of GDP in Mexico in 1993. Greater efforts are being made by government and business to promote cleaner production to improve the competitiveness of Mexican industrial products in world markets and to enhance environmental performance. An environmental protection and industrial competitiveness programme which, *inter alia*, promotes waste prevention by focusing on efficiency and total quality control in industrial processes is one tangible result. He suggests, however, that further efforts are needed to strengthen uptake of cleaner technologies and pollution prevention strategies. An innovative approach which is being considered is a pollution prevention guarantee scheme. Based on the polluter-pays-principle and on deposit refund systems, the scheme requires that at the beginning of a specified time period (e.g. a year, a six-monthly interval) a company deposits with the regulatory agency a sum of money as a financial guarantee of compliance; the amount is calculated as a percentage of the estimated volume of hazardous waste the company is likely to generate and its treatment cost. At the end of the period, the guarantee is returned to the company if it can demonstrate that it has reduced its waste volume or managed the waste in compliance with all relevant legislation. If this condition is not met, deductions in proportion to the cost of managing the waste and/or ensuring regulatory compliance are made. The author acknowledges that there are a number of challenges to implementing this scheme, but it nonetheless should provide firms with an incentive to reduce waste generation by the most cost-effective means available and encourage innovation.

Part II of the volume concerns challenges to, and opportunities for, the private sector in implementing cleaner production and eco-efficiency. It is striking that despite many companies recognising that sound environmental management, including the adoption of cleaner production and eco-efficiency, can contribute to raising profits and reducing exposure to environmental risks and liabilities, the rate of uptake is less than might be expected.

Joel Hirschhorn in his paper *"Implementing Waste Minimisation and Eco-efficiency in the Private Sector"* identifies a number of "push" economic incentives and rewards internal to a firm that encourage companies to consider adopting eco-efficiency approaches: reducing the direct costs of production by decreasing input usage; increasing the productivity of an existing plant; increasing the quality of existing products or creating new products; and increasing the economic value of the company to owners, shareholders and society by reducing actual and potential liabilities from poor environmental performance. He also notes a range of external "pull" factors that can contribute to the growth of eco-efficient companies and industrial sectors: government policies, legislation and programmes; education and outreach to the public and specific stakeholder groups; and the influence of financial institutions and the news media. Hirschhorn then describes six opportunities for accelerating eco-efficiency in industry. These include enhanced technology and information transfer, adopting a life cycle approach with more emphasis on raw materials and product design, coherent government policy and global sunsetting of highly toxic or harmful chemicals used in industrial operations. A major challenge, however, is to develop quantitative 'benchmarks' of the performance of eco-efficiency within industrial sectors and countries to spur higher levels of application and targets.

Environmental management is a particular challenge to small and medium-sized enterprises. Based upon his experience in working with SMEs in Hong Kong, C.M. Lin's paper on *"Cleaner Production in Small and Medium-sized Enterprises: The Role of Cleaner Production Programmes"* describes some of the principal barriers to uptake of cleaner production and strategies for overcoming them. In developing cleaner production programmes targeted on SMEs the key elements are considered to be the development and diffusion of cleaner technologies, the provision of comprehensive advisory services and pro-active marketing of the cleaner production concept. Strategically, governments should establish the policy framework but leave the detailed implementation and technical assistance to groups such as cleaner production centres or national productivity organisations.

A major opportunity associated with cleaner production lies in the environmental goods and services industry. Graham Vickery and Maria Iarrera's paper on *"The Environmental Goods and Services Industry in OECD and Dynamic Non-Member Economies"* reviews the situation and prospects in the OECD area and in each DNME. They estimate the global market for the environmental goods and services industry to be of the order of US$250 billion and growing at about 5% per year. Growth of the industry is highly dependent on public and corporate awareness of environmental protection and environmental regulations, and robust enforcement of environmental legislation. The authors suggest that geographical differentiation's in the characteristics of the environmental goods and services industry could emerge. In the OECD area, the trend is away from stand-alone and end-of-pipe equipment towards providing integrated solutions. In addition, developments in the non-OECD area such as deeper trade and investment liberalisation and privatisation of utilities, further tightening of environmental standards and the opening of new markets for new technologies are stimulating the emergence of a more internationally focused and export-oriented environmental goods and services industry. In the Asian DNMEs, the authors suggest that the environmental goods and services industry will probably emphasise cleaner production and waste minimisation since high rates of investment and rapid economic development favour technological innovation. The market demand for end-of-pipe technology will remain strong, however. The environmental goods and services industry in the Latin American DNMEs of Argentina, Brazil and Chile is likely to concentrate on end-of-pipe equipment but joint ventures and technology co-operation with foreign companies will support technology innovation and new market opportunities.

Approaches to <u>assessing the cost-effectiveness of cleaner production</u> is the theme of <u>Part III</u> of the volume. Harvey Yakowitz's paper on *"Assessing the Cost-effectiveness of Cleaner Production"* focuses on the role of developing a managerial accounting system which enables firms to isolate and quantify environmental costs. He notes that good housekeeping measures by industry can help reduce variable costs but do not greatly affect fixed costs, the latter attributable for the majority of environmental costs. Beginning with an in-plant audit of processes and emissions, a numerical accounting system can be developed which identifies current and future fixed and variable environmental costs. These results can then be used to identify cost reducing good housekeeping measures in the short-term and options for longer-term investment in cleaner technologies. Opportunities to adopt a managerial accounting system in both large firms and SMEs are presented, together with evidence from practical application of such systems. The paper concludes with a discussion of the role which governments can play to promote cleaner technologies and cleaner production.

In his paper *"Improving Cleaner Production in China"*, Ning Duan describes the objectives, implementation and emerging results of a co-operative project involving China's National Environmental Protection Agency, the World Bank and the UN Environment Programme. Industrial emissions from both state-owned enterprises and the burgeoning township and village enterprise sector have contributed to serious air and water pollution and waste management problems. Cleaner production is considered by the Chinese authorities as a strategic tool for raising the economic and environmental performance of industry. Accordingly, a project specific to China's situation and needs was developed based upon four pillars: project preparation through translation into Mandarin of selected manuals on cleaner production methodologies and training a pool of cleaner production trainers; demonstration projects in several provinces involving environmental audits in 27 enterprises spanning a range of industrial sectors; policy analysis to determine barriers to and opportunities for implementing cleaner production in China culminating in a number of policy recommendations; and wide dissemination of the cleaner production concept. An economic analysis of no/low cost technologies indicated benefits of almost 31,000 yuan/year per 1000 yuan investment with a payback period of almost 4 months. In the case of equipment update technologies the analysis showed benefits of just over 1000 yuan/year per 1000 yuan investment and a payback period of just over 31 months. No/low cost technologies also outperformed equipment update technologies in reducing chemical oxygen demand, adopted in the study as a representative pollutant. Given the economic situation of many industries in China, a sequenced approach starting with no/low cost technologies is considered realistic. The most important point is to "start from my plant and start from today."

The transition to a market economy in Central and Eastern Europe has had a profound effect on the region's industry. Macro-economic reforms such as privatisation and more realistic pricing of energy and raw materials as well as structural change in the industrial sector is underpinning the emergence of more efficient and productive industries. Cleaner production has also played a role in this on-going reform. Using empirical evidence Olav Nedenes reviews some of the results emerging from the region in his paper *"The Cost-effectiveness of Cleaner Production: Experience from Central and Eastern Europe"*. He suggests that the single most important initiative to promote cleaner production in industry is for the government to offer subsidised participation in programmes which combine plant assessments, demonstration projects and training of trainers. Where established, national and local cleaner production centres have demonstrated their strong capacity to implement such programmes. Experience in the region has shown that the costs of running such programmes are between US$ 2000-3000 per company. Results from no/low cost cleaner production measures (less than US$40,000) in 150 Polish companies indicate a 40% reduction in emissions. Nonetheless, important obstacles inside and outside the firm remain, including financing of cleaner production investments once good housekeeping measures have been exhausted, low motivation of senior managers in firms to learn about or apply cleaner production techniques and inappropriate incentives or poor enforcement of legislation.

Part IV of the volume concerns the international dimension. The *"Management of Hazardous Wastes and Control of their Transfrontier Movements"* is the subject of the paper by Pierre Lieben. It describes the evolution and range of the systems applied in the OECD area, noting for example that a 1986 OECD instrument established a precedent by requiring OECD Member countries to apply no less strict controls on transfrontier movements of hazardous wastes involving non-Member countries than would be applied on movements involving only Member countries. Reference is also made to the relationship between some of the OECD systems and provisions contained in the Basel Convention and relevant European Community legislation. The paper concludes with a section on the provisions and operation of the OECD control system for transfrontier movements of wastes destined for recovery operations within the OECD area.

Youfu Xia's paper discusses *"Control Measures Concerning the Import of Hazardous Wastes into China"*. He notes that the incidence of illegal import of hazardous wastes intercepted by China's customs authorities has increased substantially in recent years. Both exporters and importers play a role; the former by not following the specifications set out in the Basel Convention and the latter by providing incorrect information on the type of material imported. Environmental effects which have been linked to the illegal import of hazardous wastes to China include skin disorders, air and water pollution through burning or leakage of wastes, and contamination of land used for cultivation. China has undertaken a number of initiatives to address the problem. These include active participation in the meetings of parties to the Basel Convention and enactment of more than 20 domestic laws and regulations to prevent and control the illegal import of hazardous wastes. Nonetheless, the problem remains urgent and serious. The paper make several recommendations, including the need to increase the environmental awareness of business persons involved in foreign trade with China, strengthening China's institutional and policy capacity in environmental and hazardous waste management, improving enforcement of waste import controls and deepening international co-operation within the framework of the Basel Convention and other arrangements.

The final paper is by Philippe Bergeron. In *"The ISO 14000 Series of Environmental Management Standards"*, he begins by setting out the process under which the ISO 14000 suite of standards has been developed. The environmental management system standard is the core of ISO 14000 and requires organisations to commit to a continual process of environmental improvement by regularly updating objectives and targets, or as Bergeron puts it to implement an "upward spiral of continuous improvement." He considers that ISO 14000 is complementary to cleaner production in that it promotes a gradual move away from an end-of-pipe pollution treatment focus towards cleaner technologies and improved process and product designs that use resources more efficiently. ISO 14000 accreditation is also considered by the author to offer good potential to help companies improve the market access of their products and services. In addition, ISO 14000 can assist the SME sector improve its environmental performance, especially in areas such as recycling, energy saving and waste management. Finally, Bergeron notes that a major challenge in implementing the environmental management standards will the availability of appropriately trained personnel both in certification bodies and within companies.

PART I:

POLICY APPROACHES TO PROMOTE CLEANER PRODUCTION AND WASTE MINIMISATION

POLICY APPROACHES FOR PROMOTING CLEANER PRODUCTION AND WASTE MINIMISATION IN OECD MEMBER COUNTRIES

Rebecca Hanmer
Environment Directorate, OECD

1.0 Introduction: Cleaner Production and Waste Minimisation for Sustainable Development

OECD governments have concluded that sustainable development is impossible without the development and use of "cleaner" technologies[1] which fundamentally alter current pollution, waste generation and resource consumption patterns. Technology innovations in energy and resource conservation, reduction of toxic components, and waste reduction have led to considerable progress in reducing the pollution burden. However, the sheer growth of OECD country economies continues to outpace improvements in technology and other environmental protection measures. Thus, new emphasis is being placed on ways to *prevent* pollution occurring along the full life cycle of products and services. OECD governments are experimenting with a wide range of new, prevention-oriented policies and mechanisms to encourage greater emphasis on cleaner, less natural resource-intensive production systems, as well as energy efficiency and waste minimisation at all stages in the life cycle. Figure 1 indicates generally how environmental policy in OECD countries has evolved over the past 20 years.

To achieve a technological transformation, three broad plans of action are likely to be needed:

- First, to identify, deploy and implement the many *existing* cleaner technologies. To date, most actions in this field have fallen under the rubric of "good housekeeping". Certainly, exploiting low-cost or virtually cost-free practices for pollution, waste and energy reduction is extremely valuable. However, there are feasible cleaner production technologies and products which can achieve even more measurable pollution prevention results. These are available today, but their market penetration is slight. Even low-cost

---

[1] Throughout this paper references to "cleaner technologies" should be read in a broad sense, incorporating technologies for pollutant and waste minimization, as well as energy and natural resource efficiency, applicable to various stages in the production, use, and disposal/reuse of products and to the provision of services. Technologies include both hardware and management practices.

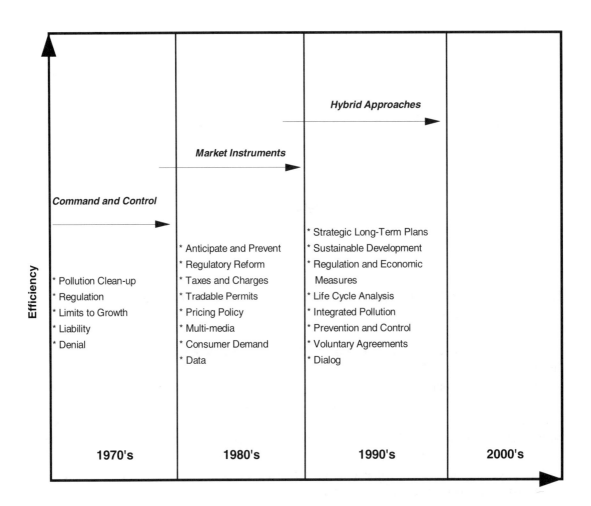

process improvements are often neglected because of such factors as lack of information and management inertia.

- Second, to proceed with investments and other actions leading to the "next generation" of cleaner technologies. Here it is crucial to see the challenge in the broadest sense, involving production systems and hardware, products, and social and organisational mechanisms for improving the efficiency of resource use and reuse.

- Third, to act to ensure that cleaner technologies play their appropriate role in global economic development in the long term, especially within the context of more environmentally sustainable consumption and production systems.

Acting to accelerate and deepen the transformation to cleaner production technologies and products is a major concern for OECD countries. The key point of focus is the private sector – the creator of most technologies. In recent years, costs associated with energy and materials, waste treatment, disposal, environmental liability, worker concern for safe working conditions, and consumer preference for more environmentally sound products have all put pressure on the private sector to modify its production systems and products. The private sector responded by cutting use of energy, materials, pollutants and waste per unit of production in many cases and producing "greener" goods. This encouraging trend needs to be maintained and amplified.

Responding to the demands for better environmental performance has also given rise to a new generation of business leaders who have notably higher environmental awareness and concern. The challenge is to spread this awareness generally among enterprises, especially among small and medium-sized enterprises. Governments can play a strong role in promoting cleaner technologies and must seek to assure that environmental and economic policies reward good environmental performance.

2.0   Policy Approaches in OECD Member Countries

OECD governments are using many policies and tools to stimulate a wider and faster diffusion of existing cleaner technologies, and to spur the development of a new generation of prevention-oriented production systems and products. In fact, experience has shown that successful pollution prevention entails the use of a mix of tools – there is no single approach. Although not an exhaustive list, some examples are noted below.

2.1   Government Support for Cleaner Technology Research and Development

Technology Development

Where governments want to foster the development of cleaner technologies, OECD analysis has shown that part of the strategy is to provide incentives for private sector firms to invest their retained earnings in R&D. One way for governments to accelerate such research is through joint arrangements of limited duration under which different firms, which may normally compete with one another, share laboratories, research personnel and costs. The government provides some cash and tax relief.

This general approach was pioneered in the UK in the 1920s and implemented in a number of other Member countries through the decades. Today, the Japanese government is using this approach to develop technologies to slow global warming: Japan's New Sunshine Project will include all existing energy and environment projects under the New Earth 21 approach, because "energy and environment problems represent two sides of the same coin." New Sunshine co-operative R&D projects include studies on:

- steps to commercialise high-efficiency power generation technologies such as ceramic/gas turbines and superconducting power generation;

- reducing costs of practical photovoltaic arrays and fuel cells; and

- fuel cell power generation and solar applications suitable in developing countries, and advanced and efficient ways to reuse "waste" heat.

Because the "corporate culture" of many different firms and economic sectors is represented in these co-operative ventures, the blending of technical breakthroughs in several different sectors is likely to occur (*"technology fusion"* is the jargon). Entirely new technologies may be born as a result.

Technology Demonstration and Diffusion

Information from eight Member countries shows that around US$350 million is being channelled directly into financial assistance programmes to promote cleaner technologies, and estimates for the OECD region exceed US$1.5 billion of investment. Most funds are used to offset costs and risks associated with the development/demonstration phase. This phase is where costs and risks are more significant, chances for technical failure are much higher, and private venture capital is often not available. Funds are also being used to support the practical implementation phase.

The objective of these investments is to develop and implement cleaner technologies which prevent pollution and wastes at the source and reduce the environmental burden, while at the same time contributing to economic goals. A key question facing governments is how to attain this objective as efficiently as possible. Government financial support thus seeks to invest limited funds to obtain a good return on the investment, i.e. rapid deployment of cleaner technologies which contribute to sustainable development and which would not have been implemented as quickly or effectively in the absence of government support. Table 1 shows examples of the types of financial support mechanisms used.

Germany has several programmes which direct financial assistance to the research, development and demonstration of technologies. The German Environmental Protection Agency administers an investment programme to promote large-scale technical demonstration projects. These projects should demonstrate how existing plants can be upgraded to advanced levels of pollution avoidance, how innovative processes can avoid and reduce pollution, or how cleaner products and substitutes can be produced and applied. Up to 50 per cent of the investment costs can be reimbursed through programme grants.

Experience in Canada has shown that incentive programmes need to be reviewed and evaluated systematically to ensure that they do not degenerate into subsidies for the implementation of standard technologies. In order to qualify for support from an incentive programme in Canada, the technology to be developed or demonstrated must have a significant technical risk. Canada has also pointed out that the normal large profit margin is frequently missing with the development of a cleaner technology; this is where governments' underwriting of part of that risk is particularly warranted. Other forms of financial support, such as tax relief in the form of accelerated tax depreciation, have been in use in Canada, the Netherlands, and other OECD countries to spur the diffusion and implementation of demonstrated cleaner technologies.

OECD governments are thus supporting the increased *supply* of cleaner technologies. The next logical step would seem to be to develop complementary proposals and policy options to create a stronger *demand* to implement them. Some demand-creating policies are discussed below.

Table 1: Financial Support Instruments for Promoting Cleaner Technologies

	Project grants	Favour-able interest loans	Secured loans	Royalty grant or loan	Tax relief
Australia	X	X			
Austria	X				
Canada	X	X			X
Denmark	X				
Finland	X	X			
Germany	X	X			X
Greece	X	X			
Italy	X	X			
Japan	X	X			X
Netherlands	X				X
New Zealand	X				
Norway	X		X		
Sweden	X	X	X	X	
Switzerland	X				
United Kingdom	X				
United States	X				
European Union	X				

Source: OECD, 1994: *Supply Side Policies to Augment Government Support for Promoting Cleaner Technologies.* OCDE/GD(94)31. Paris.

Studies conducted during OECD's Programme on Technology and Environment[2] confirmed the importance in OECD countries of having a supportive framework of environmental regulations to create a strong demand for development and diffusion of cleaner technologies. During interviews with businesses which had installed cleaner production equipment or taken other pollution prevention actions, the most frequent rationale was "we were forced to do something about our pollution and waste". Conversely, businesses lack motivation to install even the most cost-effective pollution and waste reduction technologies if there is no societal demand (generally expressed in environmental standards and regulation of polluting sources) for pollution prevention and control. Also, while there may be cost savings in terms of energy and materials, businesses which expend substantial capital on pollution prevention may be placed at an economic disadvantage (at least in the short run) vis-à-vis competitors which don't have to meet environmental requirements. There is thus industry demand for a "level playing field".

During the Programme, a review was also made of experience with cleaner technology transfer (based on seven technology case studies). The work was initiated because of questions about the role of patents and intellectual property rights in environmental technology transfer. An OECD report was issued in 1992 based on extensive interviews with both exporting and importing firms as well as trade associations, research institutions and other organisations.[1] The report noted the somewhat surprising finding that trade policies were not a major barrier to cleaner technology trade in any of the seven technology areas. Rather, along with lack of access to financing, lack of demand was the major impediment. Where environmental standards were not sufficient (or were not enforced) to create a demand for cleaner technologies, trade in those technologies was significantly hindered.

OECD countries generally have well-developed systems for regulating sources of pollution (especially "point" sources) and managing wastes. However, these systems have tended to encourage end-of-pipe pollution control and waste management rather than pollution prevention. Using regulations to address non-point sources (such as environmental problems resulting from agriculture, transportation use, and product consumption) has proven difficult, resource-intensive and often not politically feasible. Thus, many OECD governments have evaluated and made changes to their regulatory programmes, or are considering them, to increase their effectiveness in pollution prevention and their overall efficiency.

Three considerations are paramount if countries' regulatory systems are to be effective in accelerating pollution prevention and cleaner technologies:

- Countries need to establish a long-term "environmental blueprint" for sustainability, which includes environmental quality targets (or standards) which are specific, monitorable, enforceable and verifiable. The blueprint provides a stable set of objectives for technology and product design. To do this, governments must have an accepted means to measure the state of the environment, identify sources of degradation, and monitor the effectiveness of efforts to attain the environmental targets;

---

[2]   The findings of the Programme were published as OECD, 1995: *Technologies for Cleaner Production and Products. Towards Technological Transformation for Sustainable Development*. Paris.

[1]   See OECD, 1992: *Trade Issues in the Transfer of Clean Technologies*. OCDE/GD(92)93. Paris.

- Regulatory systems must become "innovation-friendly", i.e. there must be flexibility for regulated sources (industry and service providers) to assess and choose specific technical measures to meet environmental targets. Enforcement must not stifle risk-taking to find better technology approaches;

- Continuing attention must be paid to effects of regulations across the full life cycle, in order to assure that emphasis is being correctly placed.

The Netherlands has established a notable environmental blueprint through its National Environmental Policy Plan (and subsequent updates). The Plan built upon a comprehensive examination of the country's environmental status and projections of future environmental degradation, incorporated a long-term set of goals, and set clear targets for reduction of important pollutants. Sweden has also delineated specific goals for sustainability, with action plans to achieve these goals which reflect in-depth analysis of sources of environmental degradation and specific targets and timetables to meet them. Such blueprints provide a clear framework for designing and evaluating regulatory programmes and other instruments, and for deciding upon the proper mix of instruments.

In 1991, based on a proposal of the OECD Environment Ministers' meeting, the OECD Council issued a Recommendation encouraging OECD governments to practise "integrated pollution prevention and control" (IPPC), taking into account "the effects of activities and substances on the environment as a whole" and the "whole commercial and environmental life cycles of substances and products" (OECD Council Recommendation C(90)164/FINAL). A priority area of concern was to promote multi-media regulation of polluting sources, so that all environmental pollution and waste requirements for a particular source were assessed at the same time and the best overall environmental option selected. The Recommendation specifically emphasised pollution prevention, to assure that government regulations provided an incentive for sources to install cleaner technologies.

2.3   Increased Attention to Product-related Strategies

Reviewing the progress over the years in pollution reduction in OECD countries, it is especially striking to note that wastes in particular have not been reduced overall; they are still growing with gross domestic product. For many sources of waste, as for energy efficiency and reduction of risks from toxic substances, attention to product-related strategies is essential.

Early in 1994, the OECD Waste Management Policy Group (WMPG) held an international workshop on waste minimisation.[2] Workshop participants reviewed the results of a range of policies through case studies on priority waste streams, and also considered cross-cutting issues such as priority-setting and measurement, conditions which favour or discourage waste minimisation, and waste minimisation instruments. Special attention was paid to recently established programmes for "Extended Producer Responsibility" (EPR) in Germany and elsewhere, and one result of the workshop was that the WMPG supported producer responsibility both as a basic principle and as an overarching strategy for waste minimisation (noting that this responsibility needs to be shared with other actors in the product chain for some products). In particular, countries are seeking through EPR to encourage pollution

---

[2]   See OECD, 1995: *Washington Waste Minimization Workshop. Volume II: Which Policies, Which Tools?* Paris; and OECD, 1996: *Washington Waste Minimization Workshop. Volume I: Five Waste Streams to Reduce.* Paris.

prevention/source reduction, by increasing the degree to which manufacturers are responsible for waste management costs, and to internalise these costs in product prices.

Most experience to date has been with EPR for packaging wastes. The most common approach is to require manufacturers to take back and recycle, reuse or dispose of these wastes or sponsor an organisation to perform these tasks on behalf of the manufacturers. An OECD paper has reviewed implementation of EPR programmes and suggested a framework for evaluating what kind of programme should be established in a particular country.[3]

Many OECD countries have established eco-labelling programmes with the express purpose of identifying and promoting products whose producers have taken the most action to incorporate environmental objectives in the product and in the production process. These programmes have generally been initiated by governments, but are operated by quasi-private bodies.   OECD   reviewed the status, rationale and criteria for labelling programmes in a 1991 publication[4] and updated the information more recently in a working paper. There is some question about how effective such programmes have been to date in promoting cleaner production and products overall, given their limited coverage. However, mechanisms which give consumers access to environmental information about products (and stimulate producers to assess and produce such information) are fundamental for any successful programme to promote cleaner technologies.

The Netherlands performed a comprehensive review of possible approaches for improving the environmental quality of products and concluded, among other things, that:

> It is crucial to the attainment of policy objectives that everyone concerned has access
> to good, reliable information regarding product-related environmental impact. The
> government will therefore, in tandem with the market actors, develop systems for the
> reliable determination of such impact and the clear and objective communication of
> the information thus obtained (*Policy Document on Products and the Environment*,
> Ministry of Housing, Spatial Planning and the Environment, The Hague, 1994).

The Dutch document is a good overall summary of product-related issues and practical considerations for government action.

Finally, a programme on risk management being carried out under the OECD's Environmental Health and Safety Programme is concerned with ways to manage products' use so that society can take advantage of their benefits while any risks are minimised. As part of this work, detailed studies have been carried out on particular chemicals or groups of chemicals – most recently lead, mercury, cadmium, brominated flame retardants and methylene chloride (dichloromethane). These published studies, which contain information provided by Member countries and by other international organisations, address the commercial and environmental life cycles, including sources of environmental

---

[3]   See OECD, 1996: *Extended Producer Responsibility in the OECD Area. Phase I Report: Legal and Administrative Approaches in Member Countries and Policy Options for EPR Programmes.* OCDE/GD(96)48. Paris.

[4]   See OECD, 1991: *Environmental Labelling in OECD Countries.* Paris.

releases, pathways, and estimations of exposure; risk reduction and control measures; and international and national positions on perceived risks.[5]

2.4   Public Awareness and Education

The importance of public awareness has already been noted in connection with product information. Another aspect of public awareness is "the right to know" about releases of contaminants to air, water and land by sources of pollution and waste. The United States pioneered public reporting of pollutant releases, and in particular has reported that its Toxics Release Inventory (TRI) has been responsible not only for better awareness but also for stimulating polluting industries to engage in voluntary pollution prevention and reduction.

The OECD, as part of its UNCED follow-up efforts, has co-operated with several UN agencies to develop guidelines for national governments which may wish to implement toxics release inventories (called "Pollutant Release and Transfer Registers" in the OECD parlance) so as to provide for accountability of sources of releases; promote public awareness of pollution problems, sources and opportunities; and help set priorities for cleaner technology initiatives and pollution reduction goals. The OECD released a PRTR guidance manual for governments in 1996.[6]

Pollution control and waste management, it is argued, have basically been spheres for action by major polluting sources and government authorities at national, regional and local levels. Pollution prevention and sustainable development, however, will require actions by everyone in society. The OECD's 1995 publication on *Technologies for Cleaner Production and Products*[7] stressed the importance of appropriate educational approaches at all levels related to the full variety of pollution prevention/waste minimisation actions. There are many ways in which governments can foster such education – such as through informational materials, curriculum requirements, and support for special programmes by both schools and non-governmental organisations.

2.5   Voluntary Approaches Gaining in Popularity

Voluntary agreements can be a very effective means of promoting cleaner technologies (including product improvements) and pollution prevention in general. They often work faster and with more flexibility than regulatory programmes, and so help to promote innovative and cost-effective approaches to cutting pollution and wastes. Voluntary approaches also serve a very important function in building trust and credibility among the private sector, governments and the public. As practised in a number of OECD countries, a voluntary agreement is a contract between the authorities and the private sector (as represented by a trade association or by individual firms). Under the contract, the private sector representatives act to attain specified environmental objectives. Government is not involved except for an informal commitment not to alter regulations relating to the area covered by the agreement while it remains in force. So far about half the OECD countries, including Australia, Austria, Canada,

---

[5]   For information about the OECD's Environmental Health and Safety Programme, and for the full texts of many of the EHS Programme's publications including the "Risk Reduction Monographs" published on these chemicals in 1993-94, consult *http://www.oecd.org/ehs/*.

[6]   See OECD, 1996: *Pollutant Release and Transfer Registers (PRTRs). A Tool for Environmental Policy and Sustainable Development. Guidance Manual for Governments.* OCDE/GD(96)32. Paris.

[7]   See footnote 2 above.

Finland, France, Germany, Italy, Japan, the Netherlands, Switzerland, the United Kingdom and the United States, have concluded voluntary agreements.

In addition to the advantages of flexibility and cost-effectiveness, voluntary agreements can help governments to co-ordinate national actions with regional and local regulations and needs. For any voluntary agreement, a key issue is to decide how well the agreement is being implemented by parties to it. In practice, many existing voluntary agreements involve well-organised business sectors and/or large firms; there are some questions about how such agreements would apply to small firms, and if they might pose any competitive or trade problems.

An example of a voluntary approach which specifically aims at pollution reduction through cleaner production is the U.S. EPA's "33/50 Program", which seeks to reduce releases and transfers of 17 priority toxic chemicals identified from the EPA's Toxics Release Inventory. A 33 per cent reduction by 1992 as compared with the 1988 baseline, and at least a 50 per cent reduction by 1995, has been the programme's goal – hence its name. Companies are encouraged to develop less toxic substitutes, reformulate products, and redesign production processes in order to reduce pollution at source. Over 1,200 companies have participated in the programme. The goal for 1992 was exceeded: levels of target chemicals were reduced by more than 40 per cent. According to projections by participants, the 1995 target is likely to be attained.[8] Reductions in other pollutants and wastes may also occur through the technology improvements made.

Examination of the U.S. programme shows that those most likely to participate are the companies with the largest releases. This suggests that governments interested in applying voluntary approaches might encourage substantial shifts towards cleaner technologies by targeting companies with the greatest pollution reduction potential. The potential for voluntary efforts to succeed increases when progress can be tracked by means of information that is readily available to and understandable by the public. Indeed, greater public awareness of private sector participation in such approaches is crucial to their success.

2.6   Economic Instruments as a Driving Force

The purpose of economic instruments used in the environmental field is to influence decision-making and behaviour by firms and individuals. As compared to direct regulations, economic instruments allow actors the freedom to respond to the stimulus in ways they themselves decide are most beneficial. Moreover, if a certain environmental goal is to be attained, economic instruments will, at least in theory, promote the most cost-effective behaviour.

Most OECD countries apply economic instruments; several hundred specific types (for example, emission and effluent fees, deposit-refund systems, taxes on inputs such as fertiliser and energy) are in effect at present. The findings of an extensive review of recent developments in the application of economic instruments to environmental policies in OECD Member countries were published in 1994.[9]

---

[8]   Emission levels reported for 1995 were 55.6 per cent lower than those reported for 1988.

[9]   See OECD, 1994: *Managing the Environment: The Role of Economic Instruments*. Paris.

Limited information is available on the specific role economic instruments have played to date in pollution prevention and the promotion of cleaner technologies, and on what instruments have been most effective. In the Netherlands and Norway, water pollution charges – coupled with governmental efforts to provide in-depth information about technological options – have led to significant changes in technologies used by potential polluters. The amount of the charges is a key factor in whether they provide an incentive for significant technology improvements. In the U.S., increased waste disposal charges (and stringent liability rules applied to hazardous waste disposal) were estimated to be responsible for well over 75 per cent of technology changes leading to solid waste reductions from 1978 through 1989.

In the Netherlands, water pollution charges provided national authorities with funds to subsidise the expansion of sewage treatment plants. Several elements of the Dutch example are noteworthy: first, subsidies were offered only when possible in-plant measures had also been applied, and those measures were eligible for a 25 per cent subsidy from a scheme financed by a general government programme for cleaner technologies. Secondly, an essential role was played by research institutes and consulting firms in communicating information on technology options to firms.

The Dutch and U.S. examples show that economic-environmental relationships can indeed affect technology pathways. Moreover, these examples also underline a central finding of OECD work concerning technology and the environment: economic instruments appear to operate best in combination with, and/or in support of, other instruments such as properly enforced regulations.

In the larger sense, sustainable development and sustained pollution prevention require that economic policies – both general and for specific economic sectors – send "the right signals" over time which reward good environmental performance. Just as environmental policies have to be assessed in terms of their cost-effectiveness, governments need to continue to evaluate how their economic policies affect the environment and to make adjustments where necessary. Current priority is being given in OECD to the evaluation of government subsidies in the energy, agriculture and transport sectors and how reduction or removal of these subsidies might affect incentives within these sectors to protect the environment. An area which has received particular attention by OECD governments is agriculture subsidies, which tend to encourage overuse of inputs such as chemicals, fertiliser and water.

An economic instrument of a different type is purchasing power. The market for environmentally preferable goods and services will be stimulated by the purchasing behaviour of governments and other large institutions. In the U.S., an Executive Order requires government agencies to purchase "environmentally preferable" products. The Japanese government recently issued its "Action Plan for Greening Government Operations", which includes several provisions for selecting goods and raw materials that have minimal environmental impact at the production stage and in use. Examples are using recycled paper and other recycled products, introducing energy-efficient office automation equipment and water-saving washing machines, and purchasing low-emission vehicles. OECD is conducting a survey of purchasing initiatives in Member countries to promote cleaner technologies, and will evaluate options for such programmes.

2.7   The Role of Workers in Transforming to Cleaner Production

The impact of clean technology on workers is an area that has received relatively little attention from either international organisations or research institutions. In the past, labour unionists feared that stringent environmental regulations would inevitably lead to industrial restructuring and, with it, job losses. Experience has shown that these fears have been unwarranted. Jobs associated with meeting stricter environmental requirements increased by 4 million in the U.S. in 1992. Still, introducing cleaner technology is the same as introducing any new technology. Workers may worry about job losses, possible reductions in safety, and the need to master new skills. They may prefer to prolong the use of machinery that embodies the familiar rhythm and style of work.

Such worries have prompted unions in the OECD area to demand advance notification of technological changes. Managers have had to bargain over necessary workforce skills, training, and other adjustments. Such bargaining may bring benefits, as workers often have ideas to improve manufacturing processes. There seems to be an increasing awareness that if labour and management co-operate in the introduction of cleaner technology, the result may be to enhance worker skills, avert job dislocations, and improve the competitiveness of the firm.

In order to evaluate the probable impacts of greater use of cleaner technologies on labour, a joint meeting was held by the Business and Industry and Trade Union Advisory Committees to the OECD (BIAC and TUAC, respectively). This meeting concluded that the economic effects of implementing cleaner production practices and technologies are generally benign (at least for large enterprises). The labour consequences are essentially indistinguishable from the consequences of implementing any new technologies (for example, the need for worker training, the need for multi-skilled labour). Many specific examples can be found where cleaner technologies (especially the reduction of toxic chemicals) reduce risks to workers.

These outcomes may point out certain capacity-building needs when cleaner production technologies are implemented. Workers dealing with these technologies are likely to need to be able to:

- anticipate and act to prevent problems, such as spills, leaks and mixing of incompatible wastes; and, if these do occur, know how to react and cure the problem rapidly and with minimal worker risk;

- understand and use information concerning materials safety, for example Material Safety Data Sheets; and

- be prepared to search for and evaluate possibilities for cutting the use of energy, materials, hazardous chemicals, and possibilities for pollutant releases, and communicate this information to management.

2.8   Small and Medium-sized Enterprises (SMEs) and Cleaner Production/ Waste Minimisation

The majority of business ventures are SMEs; for example, over 68 per cent of German firms are so classified. These firms play an important role in the economic fabric of all OECD countries. Often, SMEs lack information and resources (money and people) to invest in cleaner technologies. Lack of demand by purchasers – often large firms – for products made using cleaner technologies also hinders their introduction. SMEs lack access to finance, technological, and/or managerial know-how, or to outlets for their products. For many, it is difficult enough to ensure that marketable goods are available for sale on a daily basis and that there is sufficient cash flow.

On the positive side, low-cost (or no-cost) pollution prevention measures can often be found through relatively inexpensive waste minimisation audits. While taking these measures may only produce limited environmental benefits, they are a place to start. A number of large firms are setting environmental specifications for their suppliers: for instance, demanding the reduction or elimination of certain potentially hazardous components. Some firms are helping their SME suppliers to choose cleaner production technologies when investments in new technology are to be made. Trade associations are also helping to provide environmental advice to SMEs; for example, by pointing out that costs of compliance with current environmental rules must be fully factored into determining the target cost of every item offered for sale.

In some cases, large firms which supply SMEs with feedstock have agreed to provide what is referred to as "product stewardship". The large firm produces and sells a product which, if improperly disposed, might be an environmental hazard. The costs of proper disposal to the SME customer might be prohibitive, as would the cost of insurance. The supplier firm therefore collects and disposes the potentially hazardous material from its SME customer.

Public authorities in virtually every OECD country are seeking – as part of general industrial policy objectives – to remove obstacles to SME investment in technologies to improve their competitiveness, particularly cleaner production technologies. Current policies concerning SMEs in OECD countries include improving the provision of training, information, counselling and technical aid, as well as access to finance.

Many government officials in OECD countries believe that the most effective means to inform SMEs about waste minimisation opportunities and cleaner technologies is through consultants who can work directly with the businesses and often in them. A number of countries have programmes to provide funding and personnel for this purpose: Canada's National Research Council does this, Denmark has two institutes devoted to such efforts, the U.S. has established six regional Manufacturing Technology Centres to work with SMEs to improve their productivity, and the Netherlands has set up 18 centres whose work will be directed towards technology innovation and SMEs. The German Foundation for the Environment (funded with interest payments on the proceeds of selling off state-owned enterprises) is charged with promoting cleaner technologies especially among SMEs.

Where SME operators in OECD countries are finding that they must anticipate and budget for tightened environmental controls, cleaner production technologies will very often be attractive if the SME capital allocation process is made aware of them and the firm can afford them. The development and transfer of life cycle costing analysis methods to SMEs is likely to be a crucial factor in motivating SMEs to select cleaner technologies.

2.9 International Co-operation

Direct Efforts to Develop Technologies for a Specific Goal

Implementing cleaner technologies to combat global environmental problems has attracted very high-level attention. The 1993 Tokyo G-7 summit meeting called for international co-operation to develop and deploy technologies to respond to global climate change concerns. This responsibility was given to the OECD and the International Energy Agency, which together prepared a scoping study on energy and environmental technologies to respond to global climate change concerns. The study identified areas where international co-operation could enhance the development and eventual implementation of longer-term energy and environmental technology options.

Based in large part on the results of this study, 23 OECD Member countries and the European Union agreed in March 1995 to establish the Climate Technology Initiative (CTI).[10] Among other things, this Initiative promotes international research collaboration on greenhouse gas reduction technologies. Specific projects are now being identified to implement the CTI.

Technology Co-operation and Outreach from the OECD Area

In OECD countries, changes in technological systems are likely to be evolutionary. Elsewhere, many countries will have opportunities to "leap-frog" the "dirty stages" in technological development. Governments in the OECD area can do much to make cleaner technologies available in other parts of the world. Indeed, it is more important that such technologies should be rapidly adopted outside the OECD area than within it, given that the fastest growth in population and economic activity in the years ahead is likely to come from the non-OECD area. The UN Industrial Development Organisation (UNIDO) predicts that manufacturing value-added will triple in developing countries by 2010.

In many non-OECD countries, electricity capacity and energy demand are doubling every twelve years; demand for transport – especially private mobility – is also very strong. These facts pose challenges for sustainability in the 21st century. OECD governments see that it will be necessary to promote diffusion of technologies for cleaner production and to train people to use them.

In the case of official development assistance (ODA) for environmental purposes, governments have all too often favoured end-of-pipe devices rather than cleaner technologies. This approach can help reduce the pollution burden in recipient countries, but does little to encourage capacity-building. A strong signal from governments that cleaner technologies will be favoured for their ODA programmes would create demand for them. In pursuit of this goal, OECD, UNEP, and UNIDO, with strong financial support from OECD Member governments, organised a workshop on development assistance and technology co-operation for cleaner industrial production in developing countries.[11] This workshop was targeted towards developing approaches for increasing the quantity of cleaner technologies in low- to medium-income countries, and over 30 persons from these countries participated (representing government and private sector organisations). From the OECD area, representatives of environment, aid and other ministries were present. Also present were representatives of non-governmental organisations, international bodies, and academia.

A key objective was that OECD donors should become fully aware of the value of promoting cleaner technology transfer and co-operation. Special attempts were made to identify the specific roles and issues associated with SME acquisition and the use of cleaner technologies. Attention was also given to the role of the private sector. Policy frameworks, information transfer, and financial issues were addressed. The main findings of the workshop were that cleaner technologies and waste minimisation offer overall *the most cost-effective approach* to environmental pollution control for developing countries. Although financing is available for such investments, access to available financing is a problem which must be addressed in each country. Mechanisms ("cleaner technology centres") must be established and maintained – initially through public financing – for appropriate technology

---

[10] The Republic of Korea, which at the time this paper was written had not yet become an OECD Member country, also announced its support for the CTI.

[11] A summary of the workshop discussions and selected presentations were published in OECD, 1995: *Promoting Cleaner Production in Developing Countries. The Role of Development Co-operation*. OECD Document Series. Paris.

evaluation, training, technical assistance, and brokering of individual cleaner technology projects. Such centres are now being supported in several developing countries through ODA and a joint UNEP-UNIDO programme.

Technological capacity-building is at least as important, if not more so, than the transfer of machines. Recipients must be able to adapt imported technologies to local needs.

Japan, Norway, and other countries are actively pursuing this approach, which broadly speaking consists of:

- having a team of technology and environment experts live and work in a country for some period of time in order to learn about capacity, infrastructure, and cultural settings for technological implementation;

- helping to develop appropriate capacity and infrastructure to use various types of technology efficiently and in an environmentally sound manner;

- supporting a cleaner technology centre within the country (as noted above), staffed by nationals of that country, to transfer information about environmental protection, environmental risks, efficient energy and resource use, and so on; this approach can suggest ways for the host country to develop and enforce its own environmental laws and regulations in an appropriate fashion;

- providing advice (including assistance in identifying financing options) and follow-up on the transfer and implementation of appropriate cleaner technologies.

Export Promotion

Governments are increasingly interested in promoting the export of environmental technologies because of the trade benefits to be derived by OECD countries and the environmental benefits to be reaped by non-OECD countries. Focus has been placed on facilitating commercial trade, where by far the largest majority of transfers take place.

Government support for export credits has been the most common form of export promotion in OECD countries. Most OECD export credit agencies do not keep data on the amount of support given specifically to environmental technologies. However, some OECD governments are now starting to conduct environmental review and assessments of their export credit programmes to determine the amount of funding devoted to environmental technologies, as well as the environmental content or impact of the goods and projects which are being funded. A few governments are targeting a percentage of export credits for transferring environmental technologies to developing countries.

Governments are also increasingly using a variety of general export promotion activities to encourage the export of environmental technologies and services. Currently, the majority of environmental technologies supported through export promotion are for pollution control ("end-of-pipe") equipment; there is room, therefore, for OECD countries to increase their efforts to promote the international diffusion of pollution prevention and cleaner technologies.

3.0   Conclusions

Pollution prevention, adoption throughout society of cleaner production technologies, waste minimisation, and preference for environmentally friendly products are all essential for sustainable development. All are viable in terms of emerging policies and practices. They may well prove to be more economically beneficial than past practices. However, they require a significant shift in the way goods and services are produced, used, and disposed of and require action by millions of different actors. Thus, such approaches are fragile and require concerted action by governments for attainment.

Environmental sustainability cannot be attained in OECD countries without addressing the present and future environmental issues of non-member countries. Cleaner production and waste minimisation technologies and practices can offer developing countries a significant opportunity to increase production without creating the proportionate level of environmental burden associated with traditional technologies. OECD countries should support the diffusion of cleaner technologies and associated capacity-building.

This paper has surveyed briefly a variety of policies and instruments which OECD governments are using or are in the process of designing. Because many of the approaches are new, they require experimentation, evaluation and fine-tuning, posing major challenges for governments! However, there are many mechanisms available and if the political will is there, ways will be found to resolve problems and find the most cost-effective solutions. Public awareness and support are essential to building the political will.

Effective government policy does not lie in one area only. Pollution prevention has many dimensions, and evaluation of opportunities over the life cycle of products and services could reveal that a variety of interventions are necessary to achieve the desired environmental objectives. Thus, governments must take a systematic approach, using a mix of instruments. The best mix of economic, regulatory and information policies will have to be determined by each country, although attention must be paid to the international effects (for example, in relation to trade issues) of national policies, especially when they concern products. Countries must have mechanisms to assess the results that are being achieved.

These tasks can be facilitated by international information-sharing about the results of national policies and programmes. One of OECD's main goals for the future is to continue to provide a forum in which information about pollution prevention approaches can be shared and evaluated.

AUSTRALIAN AND REGIONAL CO-OPERATION INITIATIVES TO PROMOTE CLEANER PRODUCTION AND WASTE MINIMISATION

Annie Gabriel
Environment Protection Agency, Australia

1.0   Introduction

Australian governments, industry and other stakeholders are taking up cleaner production and waste minimisation strategies. Emphasis is being placed on developing techniques for cleaner production and cleaner technologies and products designed for environmental performance. The federal and state governments, working in co-operation with industry, have implemented a wide variety of training, educational and demonstration projects, and grant, loan and award schemes, to strengthen awareness and uptake. Industry has begun to implement cleaner production practices and has been co-operative in providing information for a national database to document these initiatives. Other stakeholders, such as trade unions, environmental consultants and financial institutions, are also participating in implementing cleaner production. In addition, Australian expertise in cleaner production and products and services is being disseminated to developing countries in the Asia-Pacific region.

In the past year, the concept of cleaner production (CP) has been understood and adopted more widely throughout Australia, with more of the six state and many local governments and industries taking practical measures for its implementation. The states of South Australia and Victoria have specific programmes to promote CP and provide grants to small and medium-sized enterprises (SMEs). The New South Wales State Environment Protection Authority incorporates CP concepts throughout its programme activities. Queensland has introduced an award scheme for companies that aspire to the highest level. The other two states, Western Australia and Tasmania, have expressed an interest in undertaking CP activities following a recent round of national workshops organised in co-operation with the federal Environment Protection Agency (EPA).

The federal CP programme has expanded in the past year to respond to industries' specific demand for evidence of demonstrated benefits from adopting CP measures and the need to provide general and industry-specific information on how to implement CP practices. The concept is also being incorporated in broader federal programmes designed to assist primary industries, energy production and distribution industries, urban and regional planning, science and technology development and transfer, and general industry assistance.

In the area of waste minimisation, in 1992 the federal government released a National Waste Minimisation and Recycling Strategy which set a national target of a 50 per cent reduction in the volume of waste destined for landfills by the year 2000, based on 1990 weight per capita levels. The Strategy includes a preferred hierarchy of waste minimisation actions which are, in descending order of preference: waste avoidance, reduction, reuse, recycling, treatment and, lastly, disposal.

2.0   Education, Training and Working Methods

A principal contributor to strengthening implementation of CP is education and training of all stakeholders. There are now a variety of workshop programmes, printed materials and videos, and a national database, available within Australia. More supporting materials are under development.

The federal Environment Protection Agency recently held a series of national workshops to raise awareness of CP, approaches to its implementation, and potential benefits to be realised. Further workshops are planned in specific industrial sectors in conjunction with the publication of CP handbooks for particular industries. A number of conferences on CP, initiated by industry and industry consultants as well as the EPA , will also be convened around Australia over the next one to two years.

Printed materials on CP include handbooks, information kits, newsletters and industry-specific literature. The handbooks include a series of state-specific guides for SMEs on how to implement CP measures, a handbook for local governments on how to assist local industries in implementing CP and how to apply it to municipal services, and a guide to CP in hospitals and health-care institutions. The federal EPA has been working with the mining industry and environmental organisations to produce a series of modules which document best practice environmental management in Australian mining. These publications were launched in Durban, South Africa, in June 1995 and have been well-received by national and international mining industry and associated professionals.

A general CP case study handbook will shortly be published. Case study pamphlets are planned for several specific industries, initially focusing on the tanning, dairy processing, dairy shed, wool scouring, winemaking and piggery industries. The pamphlets will complement guidelines on effluent quality being developed for the same industries, and will assist individual businesses to meet or better the environmental targets set out in these guidelines.

With the increasing popularity and expanded use of the Internet, the EPA has developed a database on CP, accessible on *http://kaos.erin.gov.au/human-env*. The National Cleaner Production Database contains case studies of CP projects, which range from simple "good housekeeping" measures to those involving the installation of highly technical or complex innovations. The database also contains EPA publications on CP and other relevant information. Information is also available on hard copy, through a telephone request line, for people who do not have access to Internet.

Other initiatives in education and training are also being implemented. The New South Wales State Government has funded the Australian Centre for Cleaner Production to develop a training package for State Government environment officers. Moreover, in a major inter-departmental initiative, the Australian federal government has funded a Green Jobs programme to train long-term unemployed people in environmental management and cleaner production. These people are then placed in industry and local government, where they use their new skills to broaden industry awareness of environmental management issues. For example, eight trained people are now working in a supervised team with the

Brisbane City Council to provide an advisory service. The local focus of this project is particularly important in reaching out to SMEs.

Disseminating information on the economic benefits of CP is important, but it must be backed up by methodologies or tools which support the realisation of the potential benefits. Environmental auditing, life cycle analysis, and environmental management systems are some of the practical tools available. Australian governments, companies and research institutes have been contributing to refinements in the application of these tools. The New South Wales EPA, for example, funded the development of a software programme for auditing a company's production processes in support of introducing CP. The software development was undertaken by the CRC for Waste Management and Pollution Control, which is also developing a life cycle analysis methodology applicable to Australian conditions. In addition, the Royal Melbourne Institute of Technology is conducting research in this area, as is one of Australia's leading companies, Broken Hill Proprietary (BHP).

3.0 Environmental Management Systems

Australia considers that Environmental Management Systems (EMS), including ISO 14001, could be key elements in expanding implementation of cleaner production. The federal and state governments are concerned, however, that the implementation of ISO 14001 might be so focused on its system elements that continuous environmental improvement may not be realised. There is further concern that the complexity and cost of obtaining third party certification against ISO 14001 might work against the adoption of environmental management systems by SMEs.

The "vision" established by environmental objectives in an EMS will greatly influence how effectively it contributes to moving an organisation in the direction of cleaner production. The environmental capability of the people defining an organisation's environmental policy will most likely be the key factor governing the degree to which the EMS promotes environmental protection. Engaging an environmentally competent auditing team will help ensure that the environmental policy is based on the broadest possible assessment of the organisation's environmental situation. In addition, credible monitoring of the effectiveness of an EMS requires the definition and selection of measurable environmental performance indicators.

Australian governments at national and state levels have acknowledged the importance of environmental auditing to the success of EMS. The Australian and New Zealand Environment and Conservation Council (ANZECC) established a Task Force report on the environmental implications of the ISO 14000 standards. The Task Force recommended that ANZECC should take a leading role in the accreditation of third party certifiers, including environmental auditors, to safeguard the environmental integrity of EMS certification. ANZECC now has two representatives on the Technical Committee charged with developing criteria which will be used for accrediting Australian and New Zealand certification bodies.

In 1995, the federal EPA together with the New South Wales Environment Protection Authority funded a scoping study to assess the national acceptance of an environmental auditor certification and registration scheme proposed by an ad hoc group of interested professionals. The study was recently concluded, and a proposed option is being reviewed by relevant stakeholders.

Another group is developing criteria to be used with the certification and registration scheme, with due consideration being given to the relevant ISO 14000 series of international standards.

4.0   Industry Awareness

Australian industry is increasingly environmentally aware. The case studies on the national CP database show that some companies are voluntarily introducing CP practices into their operations. Although the sample of business contained in the database is small, representing those companies which are willing to share their innovations with competitors, as knowledge of the database extends into the community more companies are coming forward each week to contribute case studies.

The concept of industrial ecology is beginning to be reflected in the planning and operation of industrial business zones. For example, the Noarlunga City Council in South Australia and several other state and local governments are investigating waste exchange systems to encourage the use of wastes as positive by-products by industries in their local area.

5.0   Sustainable Products and Technologies

The Royal Melbourne Institute of Technology, with a major grant from the federal EPA, is working with five companies to redesign products for better environmental performance. The project aims to reduce the environmental impacts of a product from its inception through manufacture to disposal using "cradle to grave" life cycle analysis. This includes designing a durable product which can be easily disassembled into its component parts for repair and recycling. Products being redesigned include an office vending machine, packaging, a shower head, office furniture, a dishwasher, and another household good. Promotion of the concept of designing products for environmental performance is part of the project, with regular newsletters being published on Australian and international activities in this area.

A number of voluntary material-specific recycling targets, mainly for packaging materials, have also been agreed to by relevant industry groups. Despite the voluntary nature of the agreements, industry's participation has facilitated good progress in meeting the targets.

Australia is providing assistance to developing countries in the Asian region to encourage their adoption of CP. AusAid, the federal government agency with responsibility for the administration of Australia's official aid programme, manages several programmes to assist developing countries to achieve ecologically sustainable development. Some of these projects have CP components. Under the federal Environment Protection Agency's "Environmental Co-operation with Asia Programme" (ECAP), a grant was given to conduct a waste audit and waste minimisation study at a major hotel in Indonesia and to provide the report to other Indonesian hotels. Other projects have introduced cleaner technologies such as methods for reducing pesticide use and for treating wastewater. In October 1993, ECAP funded a CP workshop in Jakarta run by Australia's Environment Institute. In early 1996, the federal EPA is to hold CP workshops in Indonesia, China, and possibly one other country in the region.

6.0   Government's Role: Regulations, Economic Instruments, Knowledge Transfer and Demonstration

As with other stakeholders in the environmental and economic welfare of Australia, the three levels of government in Australia (federal, state, local) have important roles to play in encouraging the uptake of CP and ecologically sustainable development. As policy-makers, legislators and regulators, governments can use a range of approaches to encourage and accelerate the uptake of CP in industry.

In general, Australian governments have not opted to legislate for CP, but have been achieving their objectives through implementing discharge licensing schemes, establishing agreements with industry, offering awards and providing economic incentive schemes, and funding education programmes and demonstration projects.

State and territorial governments and some local councils are responsible for any environmental discharge or operation licensing in their jurisdiction. The Victorian, New South Wales and South Australian governments have extensive licensing schemes which incorporate agreements with companies on environmental management plans and target levels to be met within certain time frames. In Queensland, the State Government has recently introduced a three-tier licensing scheme for companies (red, amber and green). The licences allow companies to increase self-regulation and decrease regulatory costs as their environmental performance improves. Companies with levels of pollution in excess of the current target are issued with a strictly controlled red licence which includes a negotiated environmental management programme to bring the company into compliance. Green licences are issued to companies which meet and continue to achieve better than compliance levels. All the environmental agencies in these states encourage use of CP to fulfil environmental targets in preference to more expensive end-of-pipe measures.

In 1995, the national material recycling targets expired. ANZECC has agreed to develop new industry waste reduction initiatives. It has agreed to go beyond setting recycling targets and also to include waste reduction and other measures to encourage waste minimisation across the product life cycle. While a primary focus of waste minimisation efforts to date has been the packaging industry, ANZECC recognises that other waste streams, often of greater volume, also require attention. Thus, in addition to proposing new directions for handling packaging wastes, ANZECC is likely to focus on construction and demolition waste, commercial packaging waste, and organic waste.

Industry agreements are being negotiated at the state and national government levels with industry associations. The industry associations are responsible for ensuring conformity by their members with the agreed goals, reducing the legislative and enforcement burden on government. In New South Wales, for example, the Drycleaners Institute of Australia took responsibility for registering and training CFC-113 users during the phase-out period leading up to the ban on the use of this chemical on 1 January 1996. At the national level, a voluntary waste reduction agreement with the construction and demolition industry is being negotiated. Also, as part of Australia's national greenhouse gas reduction programme, co-operative agreements are being developed with industry to reduce energy use and/or emissions of carbon dioxide and other greenhouse gases.

Economic incentive schemes to encourage cleaner production in Australia include an energy card, a study of innovative financing options for greenhouse gas reductions, and grant schemes. The energy card, administered by the federal Department of Primary Industries and Energy, allows loans at a lower rate of interest for purchase of environmentally preferred technology such as solar panels and solar hot water heaters. This programme is under review. The potential of several forms of innovative financing schemes to encourage organisations to preferentially purchase energy-efficient equipment is being investigated as part of the federal government programme to reduce greenhouse gases.

Economic instruments have been applied in limited cases to waste minimisation in Australia. One example is the application by most state governments of a waste disposal levy on waste disposed in metropolitan landfills, the proceeds of which are used to fund recycling programmes established by local governments. The South Australian Government has container deposit legislation for beverage bottles.

Other federal government initiatives include a national scheme to provide grants to organisations to use a business diagnostic kit to audit all aspects of their company's performance. The environmental element of this general business assistance programme has been developed using cleaner production principles and is based on the ISO 14001 standards.

The Victoria State Government provides grants to small and medium-sized businesses to implement cleaner production practices. A similar grants programme operates in South Australia under the joint federal and South Australian Government Cleaner Industries Demonstration Scheme. Companies participating in this scheme can obtain grants for the purpose of consultancy or low-interest loans to implement cleaner production technology or practices. In return, the companies must document and allow public dissemination of their costs and benefits from the implementation of the technology or practices. Information on the South Australia and Victoria projects is included in the National Cleaner Production Database.

A national Demonstration Programme is also underway through the federal EPA. Under this programme, ten companies receive free cleaner production audits and recommendations on ways to improve performance from an environmental consultant. In return, they must implement one or more of the recommended cleaner production practices which has significant demonstrative value and document the costs and benefits. A public relations consultant is disseminating the information in newspapers, journals, and other forms of media, with a focus on reaching small to medium-sized businesses.

7.0   Governments, Small Businesses and Cleaner Production

Taking the cleaner production message to small and medium-sized businesses is an important step towards ecologically sustainable development. Worldwide, there is growing recognition that a special focus is needed on this particular stakeholder group since the cumulative environmental impact of their operations is significant.

There are estimated to be over 950,000 small businesses in Australia. Of these, approximately 67,000 are in manufacturing; 145,000 are in construction; and 2000 in mining industries. These businesses often face difficulties in employing expertise or taking time out to attend educative forums to gain environmental knowledge. There is also a continuous training need, as there is a high turnover of businesses and staff. A third of small businesses are less than five years old. Reaching out to this group is also hindered by their wide geographical location across Australia.

Local government is best placed to reach the small and medium-sized businesses within their area. With the appropriate resources, local government is able to engage these industries on a more individual basis. The two projects described below provide an example of this.

The Brisbane City Council in Queensland has established an industry cleaner production advisory service. Brisbane City Council covers a relatively large urban area with approximately 2500 industrial premises. Noarlunga City Council in South Australia prepares a regular newsletter and holds seminars on chemicals management and cleaner production. Noarlunga City has a major industrial estate, located in a river catchment feeding into an environmentally sensitive estuarine area that also supports valuable fishing and tourism industries. Both Brisbane and Noarlunga City Councils have direct contact with the local businesses in their areas and visit industry sites on request to give advice on methods for implementing cleaner production.

Other local councils have undertaken to survey all business premises in their area and to evaluate the environmental impact of each. While conducting the survey of each premises, council staff provide the business with information on cleaner production and, if inappropriate practices below compliance levels are observed, a fair warning for the practice to be stopped will be issued.

The federal government has funded the employment of Environment Resource Officers in the Local Government Associations of each state to provide advice to local governments on waste minimisation and other environmental issues. This recognises the "front-line" importance of local government in implementing environmental management programmes in co-operation with industry.

8.0   The Roles of Other Stakeholders

In addition to government and industry, there are a range of other important stakeholders with a role to play in implementing cleaner production. In recognition of this, the federal EPA has sponsored a project with one of the larger trade unions to encourage understanding of, and motivation for, cleaner production from employees on the shop floor and inclusion of environmental policies in trade union agenda.

Environmental consultants are also a key to disseminating knowledge of cleaner production. Workshops, information packs, and case study database information are particular resources valued by consultants. The government also calls for consultant studies on cleaner production, which stimulates interest in researching and applying state-of-the art concepts and increases the pool of expertise with experience in this field.

Australia has also established the Australia Centre for Cleaner Production, with support from state and federal governments and leading manufacturing companies. The Centre provides cleaner production advice to organisations, undertakes consultancies for government and industry, and develops training modules for government, industry, business and professional groups, and academic institutions. In addition, the Centre is working closely with the China Centre for Cleaner Production to develop programmes throughout the Asia region.

Finally, insurance and financing institutions are closely examining cleaner production concepts in terms of reducing their financial risk and environmental damage liability. One such company is co-operating with the mining industry and the federal EPA to prepare a module on cleaner production best practice in the mining sector.

CLEANER PRODUCTION AND WASTE MINIMISATION: HONG KONG'S EXPERIENCE

Planning, Environment and Lands Branch, Hong Kong

1.0   Introduction

Hong Kong has sustained steady economic growth during the past few decades. A by-product of its economic success and rapid growth in urbanisation has been accelerated waste generation. Between 1979 and 1994, municipal solid waste from domestic, commercial and industrial sources increased from 4,000 to 8,500 tonnes per day; construction waste disposed of at landfills increased from 1,000 to 15,500 tonnes per day. Sewage and industrial wastewater increased from 1.8 million to 2 million tonnes per day between 1988 and 1995.

To prevent this large volume of waste from becoming an environmental problem, in 1989 the Hong Kong Government proposed a comprehensive package of waste management programmes in its White Paper on Pollution. The objectives of the programmes include:

- the closure of old, environmentally unacceptable waste disposal facilities;

- the provision of new facilities for the disposal of all types of waste in a cost-effective and environmentally satisfactory manner; and

- the introduction and enforcement of a comprehensive legislative framework aimed at safeguarding the health and welfare of the community from any effect associated with the storage, collection, treatment and disposal of all types of wastes.

While most of the waste management programmes included in the 1989 White Paper have been progressed with vigour and success, the Government is aware that prevention is better than cure and that measures to reduce waste generation are essential. Accordingly, in the second review of the 1989 White Paper, undertaken in 1993, the Government made a commitment to examine how waste reduction and minimisation can be further promoted in Hong Kong.

This commitment recognises that cleaner production is a major approach to minimising the generation of waste at source in the industrial sector. In 1993, the Industry Department of the Hong Kong Government commissioned a consultancy study on "Support to Industry on Environmental Matters". The empirical studies conducted by the consultants showed that cleaner production could simultaneously save costs and increase process productivity in the textile bleaching and dyeing, electroplating, printed circuit board manufacturing, and plastics industries.

The consultants found that the main scope for cleaner production in the electroplating sector lay in chemical substitution and water conservation. Solutions for the textile bleaching and dyeing sector involved greater changes to the production processes in terms of chemicals and equipment used, but efforts should be directed at using lower temperature processes or heat recovery and neutralisation. Many of the cleaner production techniques developed elsewhere could be relevant to the Hong Kong situation, but adaptation in view of the constraints of space and floor loadings in local multi-storey factories would be necessary.

The development of clean technology as a tool for achieving cleaner production was also considered by the consultants. The consultants found that there were a few isolated research projects on clean technology in Hong Kong. They also found that there was scope to improve both the range and relevance of research and targeted programmes to develop knowledge in clean technology and waste minimisation. It was recommended that technology dissemination should be targeted at priority problems facing key manufacturing sectors. One such problem was the development of clean technology for the textile bleachers and dyers who experienced problems of compliance with temperature and pH standards.

2.0   Local Application of Cleaner Production

In general, cleaner production involves measures such as good housekeeping, sound process control, optimising plant layout, material/product substitution, and process/equipment modification. Good housekeeping and sound process control rationalise the day-to-day operation of the plant through improvement in working procedures. They are regarded as the simplest, yet effective, measures to reduce waste generation and wastage of raw materials, leading to improvement of productivity and product competitiveness. Cleaner production through better housekeeping and improved process control can usually be implemented without additional capital investment. They are therefore considered the most favourable measures to start with. Since Hong Kong's manufacturing industry relies heavily on imported raw materials, better housekeeping and improved process control can offer immediate substantial savings.

For the other measures, there are local implementation constraints. As land is at a premium in Hong Kong and most of the manufacturing premises in Hong Kong are housed in multi-storeyed buildings, the plant layout design is constrained by the lack of space. Hence, it may not always be possible to choose the optimum layout in terms of promoting cleaner production.

Hong Kong's industrial sector comprises mainly small to medium-sized establishments which have relatively small investment in product research and development. These companies have to rely heavily on professional service organisations to develop feasible material/product substitution and process/equipment modification techniques for each specific industrial application.

In light of these implementation constraints and the limited exposure to the concept of cleaner production, application in local industry has been low. Nevertheless, the scope for such application exists, especially for material/product substitution and process/equipment modification, and there are successful cases of such application. Some examples of clean technology application in Hong Kong are presented in Annex 1. In order to further promote cleaner production and the application of clean technology, the Hong Kong Government has adopted various policy instruments such as providing support infrastructure, tightening up legislative controls, and introducing economic incentives. Apart from the manufacturing industry, such instruments have also been applied to the livestock industry.

3.0   Support Infrastructure

The Hong Kong Government's Industry Department encourages cleaner production through supporting greater use of clean technology by industry and helps provide a support infrastructure to industry for the improvement of its environmental performance. These support measures can be grouped under the headings of information dissemination, technical advice, technology development, and business support.

In the area of information dissemination, the Industry Department publishes an annual "Guide to Pollution Control Legislation Affecting Manufacturing Industries". This Guide provides information to manufacturers on environmental legislation affecting industry, and indicates where technical advice may be obtained. The publication has been distributed free of charge to 7,000 manufacturers and industrial organisations. In addition, three handy reference books for pollution prevention and control in specific industrial sectors have been distributed to offer advice on pollution control and prevention and improving efficiency in production.

To enhance information dissemination to manufacturers, the Industry Department has published a directory on pollution control and pollution prevention equipment and services available in Hong Kong. The Industry Department established an environmental hotline in September 1994. The hotline provides manufacturers with information on local environmental legislation, standards, controls and charges. The Industry Department is also planning to launch a large-scale publicity campaign to increase factory operators' and workers' awareness of environmental controls and what can be done to comply with them.

Concerning technical advice, a technical outreach programme has been implemented by the Industry Department. This consists of a series of seminars and workshops to disseminate information to members of specific industrial sectors on environmental issues affecting their sectors. To provide direct support, a factory visits programme has also been implemented. Factories are visited by experts and advice provided on measures that could be taken to comply with environmental standards. Conducted in parallel with the factory visits is the sampling of effluent to identify the extent of the problems faced by individual factories in complying with environmental standards.

According to the UN Environment Programme (UNEP), accurate information about the origins and sources of environmental releases is a prerequisite for effective reduction of industrial emissions and wastes. This can be done through an eco-audit which assesses where, how, and how much waste is generated in an industrial process. An eco-audit is also the first step and one of the key elements in the application of clean technology in an industrial process. Since most of the small to medium-sized industrial establishments in Hong Kong do not possess the necessary technical expertise and management skill to conduct an effective eco-audit, the Industry Department has produced an eco-audit manual and accompanying video. This helps factory operators to audit their production processes and identify whether they are complying with environmental standards, and to identify where further improvements might be made. In addition, three design manuals have been published for specific industrial sectors to advise manufacturers on production processes. The advice includes how to design production processes in a more environmentally acceptable way.

The Industry Department also operates the Hong Kong Laboratory Accreditation Scheme, which grants accreditation to local testing laboratories. The prime objectives of the scheme are to upgrade the standard of testing and management of local laboratories and to promote the acceptance of their test results both locally and overseas.

To support technology development, the Hong Kong Government has set up an Industrial Support Fund (ISF) with the objective of funding industrial support projects for the wider benefit of the industrial sector, for example development of the application of a specific technology, development of a database, etc. These projects will usually provide very specific technical support and include a number of environmentally related projects, including projects to develop cleaner technology. A number of ISF projects include demonstration elements to enable new environmental control technology to be demonstrated to industrialists.

Business support is also given under a number of ISF projects. For example, a database on clean processes and products in the textiles and clothing industry is under development to provide information on the latest cleaner production methods. Another project is the development of a "green label" certification programme which is recognised internationally and accepted locally.

Good environmental practice is also encouraged in other ways. The Hong Kong Awards for Industry programme, organised annually by the Industry Department, has included an Environmental Performance category since 1992. The aim is to promote a wider appreciation of the importance of environmental protection amongst Hong Kong's manufacturers and encourage them to incorporate practices in their manufacturing processes which recognise the importance of the environment.

There is also support for Hong Kong companies to train their staff in new technology, including environmental technology, under the Government's New Technology Training Scheme. The support is given in the form of a matching grant for local and overseas training.

With regard to the livestock industry, the Government provides a free livestock waste collection service through contractors. At present, livestock farmers send their livestock waste to fixed collection points for eventual transport to the composting plants at Sha Ling and Ngau Tam Mei. The livestock waste is turned into marketable compost at these plants. In future, the Government plans to change this free service to a door-to-door service so as to better meet the needs of the livestock farmers.

4.0   Legislative Control

Since the publication of the 1989 White Paper on Pollution, the Hong Kong Government has tightened up various pollution control legislation. Legislative control over the production, collection and disposal of chemical waste was introduced in May 1993, and all waste producers are now required to register with the Environmental Protection Department. They are also required to employ licensed waste collectors and dispose of their chemical waste at licensed disposal facilities.

Control over water pollution has also been tightened with the progressive declaration of water control zones to cover the whole territory in phases. Within water control zones, commercial and industrial establishments cannot make discharges unless these are in accordance with the conditions stipulated in the discharge licence.

In order to comply with these new legislative controls, manufacturers have to find ways to improve their production process. This is a much more cost-effective means to comply with legislation than end-of-pipe solutions. The latter require additional capital investment and operating cost. Upgrading the production process to cleaner production, however, will enable industry to achieve a win-win solution, with less waste generation and pollution on the one hand and increased productivity on the other.

As from 1994, a Livestock Keeping Licence (LKL) is required for the purpose of livestock keeping in specified areas in Hong Kong. Livestock farmers have to adopt various methods such as dry-muck-out, wet-muck-out, soakaway systems, litter bedding, etc. to reduce the amount of livestock waste which used to be disposed of by flushing into local streams and rivers. Since 1994, Hong Kong livestock farmers have begun to modify their methods towards cleaner production, and waste pollution caused by livestock waste has been reduced by about 70 per cent. Further reduction is envisaged as the livestock control scheme expands to cover more areas.

5.0   Economic Incentives

The Hong Kong Government recognises that there is inadequate economic incentive to stimulate local industry to adopt cleaner production. Until recently, almost all waste disposal facilities in Hong Kong were funded entirely by the Government from general revenue and users were not required to pay any direct waste disposal charges. Free disposal is at variance with the "Polluter Pays Principle" and offers no incentive to industry to consider clean technology to minimise waste generation. It also encourages indiscriminate use of scarce disposal facilities. As a first step to reverse this situation, and shift the attitude of users towards greater consideration for the environment, the Government has introduced charges for the disposal of chemical waste and discharge of trade effluents. Details of these schemes are provided in Annex 2. Plans are also underway to introduce landfill disposal charges for commercial and industrial waste handled by private collectors.

To alleviate the physical constraint posed by the lack of space, the Government is liaising with certain industrial sectors regarding their plans to develop multi-tenanted industrial complexes with communal wastewater treatment facilities in Hong Kong's industrial estates. It is hoped that if such purpose-built industrial complexes are developed, the manufacturing industry can better cope with the space constraint and improve both their environmental and economic performance.

For the livestock industry, an economic incentive to adopt cleaner production is also available in the form of a capital grant (CG). This is available to farmers who wish to continue in business in livestock waste control areas. The Environmental Protection Department provides technical advice and processes the CG application for the installation of any necessary livestock waste treatment facilities. An ex gratia allowance (EGA) is also available to those who choose to cease business completely.

6.0   The Role of Non-Governmental Organisations

Apart from Government-led initiatives, non-governmental organisations (NGOs) also play an important role in encouraging industry to apply the concept of cleaner production. In this context one of the major local NGOs is the Hong Kong Productivity Council (HKPC), which is an independent professional services organisation supported by the Hong Kong Government. The Council's Environmental Management Division provides a wide range of consultancy services to assist industrialists in identifying areas in which clean technology is applicable and develops effective solutions jointly with them. On the research and development side, the HKPC has proposed several study projects on clean technology for local application in the next several years, including clean technology for the textile bleaching and dyeing industry. These projects have been given funding support from the Industrial Support Fund. At present, ongoing development projects on clean technology managed by the HKPC focus mainly on sourcing of information, technology transfer through training, and promotion of application through demonstration and pilot programmes.

The Centre of Environmental Technology is another non-profitmaking NGO assisting industry to meet its obligations under environmental legislation. The Centre organises referral services to put industries in touch with experts in the fields of pollution, technology and training. It also carries out environmental audits and, in co-operation with educational institutions, green groups, industry and government, offers services in environmental impact assessment, treatment processes, and other environmental projects.

7.0   International Developments

As an export-led economy, Hong Kong's manufacturing industry will have to respond to external developments in the environmental policy and practice of its major trading partners and in relevant international standards. Hong Kong manufacturers also have to face increasing demands from overseas buyers to produce goods in an environmentally friendly manner. To stay competitive, organisations of all kinds are facing increasing pressure to give high priority to the environment in their business operations and strive to improve their environmental performance.

One example is the ISO 14000 series of standards. These standards are intended to be the worldwide recognised benchmark on Environmental Management Systems. Even though they are voluntary in nature, the world's major trading nations are involved in their preparation. If the governments of these countries take a role in supporting the adoption of the standards within their own jurisdictions as the various standards are finalised, this can indirectly affect overseas buyers' decisions to source from those suppliers who can meet the international standards.

Another example concerns the Basel Convention on Transboundary Movement of Hazardous Waste, which aims to minimise the generation of hazardous and other waste and the impact of its movement across countries. Hong Kong is planning to introduce measures to tighten control of the import and export of waste. With increased controls on movement of waste across countries for treatment or disposal purposes, manufacturers who have been relying on this means to dispose of their waste will have to find alternative means of treatment. The most effective alternative is to eliminate waste at source through cleaner production.

8.0   Conclusion

Hong Kong recognises the important role of cleaner production in achieving the objective of waste minimisation. In order to promote cleaner production, the Government has introduced various policy instruments – provision of support infrastructure, tightening of environmental legislation, and introduction of economic incentives. Local NGOs have also supported the Government's initiatives. It is expected that local manufacturers will become more aware of opportunities for upgrading to cleaner production and will be more willing to adjust their production processes as a result of the mutually supporting government and NGO programmes, as well as in response to international standards such as ISO 14000.

Annex I: Examples of Clean Technology Applications by Local Industries in Hong Kong

Type of industry	Clean technology applied	Remarks
Printed circuit board manufacturing	Recovery of spent etching solution for reuse Counter-current rinsing techniques to reduce water consumption and effluent discharge	Production of pure copper sulphate for sale
Electroplating of nickel, copper, silver and gold	Installation of a nickel recovery system	Recovery of nickel as nickel sulphate solution which can be reused for nickel plating
Film production	Replacing toxic cyanide by a non-toxic proprietary chemical	Elimination of about 1 kg/day of cyanide discharge to the nearby watercourse
Paper recycling	Fibre recovery and wastewater recycling	Water production output ratio is maintained at about 9.5 to 11 cubic metres/tonne of paper produced
Plastic manufacturing	DOP (di-octyl-phthalate) recovery system	Elimination of white plasticizer mist and unpleasant odour Recovery of the costly DOP for reuse

(1)   Charges for chemical waste disposal at the Chemical Waste Treatment Centre

Introduction

Industrial and manufacturing plants in Hong Kong generate approximately 100,000 tonnes of chemical wastes annually. Prior to the implementation of the chemical waste control scheme in 1993, the majority of these wastes were disposed of indiscriminately down drains and sewers, causing serious environmental problems and damaging the sewage system. Given the small size and operating conditions of local industries, it is often difficult and costly for them to install their own chemical waste treatment facilities. The Chemical Waste Treatment Centre (CWTC) was therefore developed by the Government to provide a chemical waste collection and treatment service to waste producers. An average of 1.6 tonnes/day of heavy metals such as copper and nickel have been recovered from the sewer and drainage system, substantially reducing the discharge of metals and other toxic materials into the coastal waters off Hong Kong.

Basis of Cost Recovery

The Hong Kong Government aims to recover the variable operating cost (VOC) of the CWTC, but bears the capital cost and the fixed operating cost of the facility. The VOC represents costs relating to the processing of waste and constitutes about two-thirds of the total operating cost. The remaining third of the operating cost comprises fixed recurrent overhead cost.

Charging Mechanism

The Government has adopted a phased direct charging scheme. Charging is in line with the Polluter-Pays Principle, whereas the phasing arrangement allows waste producers time to adjust to the new concept of waste management and minimisation, to factor the cost of waste treatment into production cost, and to make other necessary adjustments in their operation. The charging scheme came into force in March 1995 and has the following key features:

- Chemical waste producers are charged directly for using the services provided by the CWTC and are billed on a monthly basis;

- The initial charges are set such that 20 per cent of the VOC is recovered, except for a small number of special waste types for which full VOC recovery applies from the outset. These wastes are of a special nature or are generated under special circumstances, for example waste containing PCBs, expired or off-specification chemical substances, damaged chemicals, or chemical wastes arising from chemical emergencies due to spillage, leakage or accident; and

- The charging levels will be increased gradually with the aim of achieving 100 per cent VOC by 2003-4 at the latest. Waste producers will be informed in advance of the actual increases.

(2)   The Sewage Charging Scheme

Introduction

In the past, Hong Kong's investment in its sewage system and sewage treatment facilities was not commensurate with its economic growth. This has resulted in serious water pollution problems. With the publication of the White Paper "Pollution in Hong Kong – A Time to Act" in 1989, the Territory embarked on a Sewage Strategy which consists of constructing the necessary infrastructure for sewage disposal and introducing a sewage charging scheme based on the Polluter-Pays Principle to cover the operation and maintenance costs of the sewage services provided, as well as to create an incentive for reducing pollution.

A Strategic Sewage Disposal Scheme (SSDS) is being constructed as part of the Territory's infrastructural building programme. Stage I consists of deep transfer tunnels and construction of a sewage treatment plant on Stonecutters Island. A series of sewage collection system improvements developed on the basis of local sewage master plans will convey the sewage from homes and factories into the SSDS system. Ultimately, both sides of Hong Kong's Victoria Harbour will be served by the SSDS system. The total investment cost for the infrastructure programme is approximately HK$20 billion (in August 1993 prices).

The Sewage Charging Scheme

The Sewage Charging Scheme is based on the Polluter-Pays Principle. The scheme was introduced in April 1995 after the Legislative Council passed the Sewage Services Ordinance and its two subsidiary regulations, the Sewage Services (Sewage Charge) Regulation and the Sewage Services (Trade Effluent Surcharge) Regulation.

The scheme has two components. The first is a general sewage charge paid by all who discharge sewage. The second is a trade effluent surcharge payable by trades and industries that discharge effluent higher in strength than domestic sewage (as measured by chemical oxygen demand: COD). The charges are collected by the Drainage Authority and paid into the Sewage Services Trading Fund.

Charging Mechanism: The General Sewage Charge

This charge is paid by all who discharge sewage into the public sewage system. Those installations with on-site treatment facilities are exempted. The charge for domestic users is based on the amount of water used (i.e. based on water meter readings). Except for large water users, who are billed every month, the charge is billed together with the water charge on a four-month billing cycle. For specified trades and industries which discharge less sewage than the amount of water consumed because of production processes (for example, restaurants), a discount of 30 per cent is provided. At present, the charge is a flat rate charge of HK$1.20 per cubic metre.

Charging Mechanism: The Trade Effluent Surcharge

This surcharge is payable by specified trades and industries that discharge sewage more polluting than that from domestic households. The "strength" of each specified trade's sewage is measured by a generic COD value obtained from sampling surveys or other analyses. Those charged pay for the higher unit cost of treatment required for the more polluting discharge. The rates charged depend on the amount by which the generic COD value is higher than domestic sewage (measured at 500 mg/l COD). A charging matrix has been developed to determine the charging rate at particular COD values. A discount of 20 per cent is provided for specified trades. The legislation allows for appeals on both the COD value and the discount applied, recognising that industry may upgrade its production processes to reduce the surcharge payable. The surcharge bills are issued separately by the Drainage Authority; the periodicity is every four months for most account holders and monthly for large accounts.

CLEANER PRODUCTION AND WASTE MINIMISATION: EXPERIENCE FROM MALAYSIA

Khalid Abdul Rahim
Universiti Putra Malaysia, Malaysia

1.0   Introduction

Technology has brought considerable improvements in living standards and has, to varying degrees, lessened the damage that rapid economic development can have on the environment. The current concern about damage to the environment is not only that pollution is harmful in itself, but also that we are making unsustainable use of natural resources. The goal then is to devise manufacturing processes which are sustainable, involving low waste production, low materials and energy usage per unit of production, and the use of renewable raw materials and renewable energy sources. In short, cleaner production.

The concept of cleaner production is not new, but it has received increasing attention from both developed and developing countries. According to UNEP, some of the following terms used today are synonymous with cleaner production: clean technology, pollution prevention, waste reduction, waste prevention, eco-efficiency and waste minimisation. However, cleaner production encompasses all these terms.

2.0   Policy Measures for Promoting Cleaner Production in Malaysia

The Malaysian Government has depended very much on the existing legal and institutional arrangements for the implementation of its environmental policy objectives and strategies. Malaysia has had more than 35 pieces of environment-related legislation since the early 1920s, when various water enactments were passed. These pieces of legislation contain provisions or references that are related to environmental control. The Water Enactment, 1920, for example, prohibits the disruption of rivers such as by interfering with the flow of water as well as discharging specific substances detrimental to its beneficial uses. Similarly, the Mining Enactments, 1929, control discharges from mining activities into water courses; the Forest Enactment, 1934, provides for the establishment of forest reserves as well as the control of logging practices; the Land Conservation Act, 1960, helps to control soil erosion and siltation; and the National Land Code, 1965, which divides land use into three categories, viz. agriculture, building and industry, enables environmental factors to be taken into consideration in land use planning. The Factories and Machinery Act, 1967, deals with the working environment.

These pieces of legislation were found to be limited in scope and insufficient to handle more complex emerging environmental problems. Comprehensive legislation and the establishment of an agency to control pollution and enhance the environment came into being with the Environmental Quality Act, 1974 (EQA). The EQA and its subsidiary legislation, and the establishment of the Department of Environment (DOE), were conscious efforts by the Government to manage the environment in the wake of economic development.

2.1 The 1974 Environmental Quality Act

The 1974 Environmental Quality Act (EQA) is a comprehensive piece of legislation in the effort to improve the quality of life of the people and "to [prevent, abate, and control] pollution and [enhance] the environment, and for purposes connected therewith".[1] It provides a common legal basis for co-ordinating all environmental control activities throughout the country, giving the DOE the mandate and means to accomplish national environmental protection goals. The DOE, which administers the EQA, is empowered to gazette regulations and orders, and to issue licenses to regulate the discharge of wastes. A study of the provisions in the EQA shows that the Malaysian approach to environmental management is wide-ranging in scope and is not concerned with pollution *per se*, but with pollution that affects the beneficial use of the environment or is hazardous to its general use. Beneficial use involves "a use of the environment or any element or segment of the environment that is conducive to public health, welfare or safety and which requires protection from the effects of wastes, discharges, emissions and deposits".[2] The EQA further declares that pollution consists of "any direct or indirect alteration of the physical, thermal, chemical, biological or radioactive properties of any part of the environment by discharging, emitting or depositing wastes so as to affect any beneficial use adversely, to cause [a] condition which is hazardous or potentially hazardous to public health, safety, or welfare, or to animals, birds, wildlife, fish or aquatic life, or to plants or to cause a contravention of any condition, limitation or restriction to which a license under this Act is subject."

In relation to the preservation of the environment, the EQA leans more towards controlling pollution. This "control" of pollution is done through the mechanism of licenses issued by the DOE. The mode of control is to prescribe, by means of a ministerial regulation, that licenses are required for:

- the use and occupation of prescribed premises;
- discharging or emitting wastes exceeding acceptable conditions into the atmosphere, noise pollution, polluting or causing to pollute any soil or surface of any land;
- emitting, discharging or depositing any wastes or oil into inland waters or Malaysian waters exceeding acceptable conditions.

The EQA authorises the Minister to prescribe the level of "acceptable conditions", and it is only pollution over and above this permitted level that attracts liability. The installation of pollution abatement equipment, as required by the EQA, is subject to the best practicable means and to the expenses that would be borne by the polluters. Polluters are granted licenses to contravene "acceptable conditions" where there are no known practicable means of control to ensure compliance with the regulations.

Criminal sanctions are provided for in several sections of the EQA. A maximum fine of RM10,000 or two years' imprisonment or both is imposed for offences related to emitting or discharging any waste into the atmosphere, polluting or causing or permitting to be polluted any soil or surface of any land, and emitting, discharging or depositing any wastes into any inland waters in contravention of acceptable conditions. A

---

[1]   Preamble to the EQA.

[2]   Section 2 of the EQA.

further maximum penalty of RM1,000 per day is imposed for every day the offence is continued, after a notice from the Director General is served on the offender requiring him to cease the act.

An offender is liable to a maximum fine of RM5,000 or one year's imprisonment, and a maximum fine of RM500 a day for every day the offence is continued, for offences related to emitting or causing or permitting to be emitted any noise whose volume, intensity or quality is in contravention of the acceptable conditions.

A maximum fine of RM10,000 or two years' imprisonment or both is also imposed on persons discharging wastes (whether liquid, solid, gaseous or radioactive) into Malaysian waters in such volume, composition or manner as to cause an alteration of the environment. An offender is liable to a maximum fine of RM25,000 or two years' imprisonment for offences relating to the discharge or spill of any oil or mixture containing oil into any part of the sea outside the territorial waters of Malaysia if such discharge or spill will result in oil or a mixture containing oil being carried, spread or washed into Malaysian waters.

Amendments to the EQA were passed by Parliament in 1996. The amendments call for, *inter alia*, stiffer penalties against polluters, including vessels. The Ministry of Science, Technology and the Environment sought to increase the maximum fine from RM25,000 to RM500,000 for vessels caught desludging or dumping oil waste into the sea. Furthermore, the amendments make it compulsory for companies to use recycled materials and practise environmental labelling in keeping with the international coding system.

Major changes to the EQA have been approved, paving the way for stricter regulations and stiffer penalties for environment-related offences. The amendments include an increase in maximum fines related to agro-based waste discharge from RM10,000 to 50,000 or two years' imprisonment or both, and a maximum fine of RM100,000 instead of RM10,000 for contravening a prohibition order under the Act. The Ministry had also sought to increase the daily fine imposed on those who continue to pollute from RM1,000 to 5,000.

Among the new provisions are the power to close down factories to protect public health and the environment, and mandatory compensation by the polluter to the victims as a result of environmental damage. Other new provisions and amendments to the act include:

- the definitions of inland waters, sludge, and environmentally hazardous substance;
- the prohibition of import, export, production, storage, transportation, and use of hazardous chemicals;
- the establishment of a fund to promote research in clean technology;
- the establishment of a fund to control and prevent oil spills;
- the mandatory use of eco-labelling; and
- the mandatory environmental auditing of companies to ensure compliance.

The control of air and water pollution continues to play a significant role in environmental management, and more recently the management of scheduled wastes has received much attention. The regulation sets out the requirements for storage, collection, packaging, labelling, treatment and disposal of scheduled wastes.

2.2   Environmental Impact Assessment

The drive for economic growth in both developed and developing countries can be witnessed in the current upsurge of interest in the financing, planning and implementation of a wide range of development projects. In many cases, there have been harmful consequences for human health and environmental quality as a result of both the scale and nature of resource-based and industrial developments. At the same time, many established industrial areas now face major pollution problems. To minimise potential adverse impacts of development and maximise benefits, the Environmental Impact Assessment (EIA) is required. It aims to provide decision-makers with an appraisal of the environmental, health and social implications of alternative courses of action.

The mandatory system of EIA was introduced through a piece of legislation, Environmental Quality (Prescribed Activities) (Environmental Impact Assessment) Order, 1987. The EIA Order, 1987, which was made under powers conferred by section 34A of the Environmental Quality (Amendment) Act, 1985, specifies those activities that are subject to EIA. Nineteen categories of activities are prescribed, related to agriculture, airports, drainage and irrigation, fisheries, forestry, housing, industry, infrastructure, land reclamation, mining, petroleum, ports, power generation, quarries, railways, resort and recreational development, transportation, waste treatment and disposal, and water supply. Many of the activities related to these 19 categories are defined in terms of project size (as area) or capacity, while others are not defined by any unit of measure.

2.3   Vision 2020

Vision 2020 was introduced in a paper presented by Prime Minister Matahir at the inaugural meeting of the Malaysian Business Council in February 1991. Its goal is that Malaysia should attain developed country status by 2020 not only in the economic sense, but also in other dimensions such as the political, social, spiritual, psychological and cultural. It is an economic blueprint for Malaysia, based on certain key economic policies, such as:

- reaffirming the role of the private sector as the primary engine of economic growth;
- continuing deregulation and a lesser government role in business and economic production;
- accelerating privatisation and industrialisation;
- expanding the manufacturing base away from the current heavy reliance on electronics;
- assisting small and medium-scale enterprises (SMEs);
- supporting export-led growth as a way to rapid growth;
- maximising the benefits from inflow of foreign investment;
- promoting the development of indigenous technologies;
- according high priority to human resources development;
- developing a pool of skilled manpower to handle emerging technologies; and
- developing a positive culture based on integrity, discipline and diligence.

Vision 2020 envisages all of the above to be realised within an economic development framework where environmental conservation and protection are assured. It warns against "growth fixation", the danger of pushing for growth figures oblivious to the need to ensure sustainability and to improve the quality of life, among others. Within this framework, there are opportunities for sustainable development which will see a shift towards:

- the sustainable use of natural resources;

- the prevention of environmental harm or damage;
- the remediation of past environmental damages; and
- the development of replacement strategies for non-renewable resources.

All of these will require state-of-the-art technologies, backed by ecosystem-based scientific knowledge, in order to set and achieve sustainability targets across all sectors of the economy. The emergence of telecommunications and global communications based upon information technologies is changing the way business is performed.

3.0   The Private Sector's Contribution to Cleaner Production

In the 1990s, the present Administration has been actively pursuing its aim to fully realise cost-efficiency and deregulation, largely through "self-regulation". The purpose is not only to enhance the effectiveness of managing public services, but also to increase the role of the private sector in the delivery of public goods, including environmental protection and services. The recent initiatives introduced by the Government, with forthcoming responses from the private sector, include the promotion of private investments in the handling of toxic and hazardous waste and the privatisation of the sewage system, sewage treatment works, and both air and water quality monitoring systems. Other initiatives being pursued include the privatisation of garbage collection, recovery, treatment and disposal; maritime surveillance; and prior evaluation on pre-siting of projects.

3.1   Industrial Structure

Since independence in 1957, the Malaysian economy has diversified. The share of agriculture in the Gross Domestic Product (GDP) has decreased from 38 per cent in 1960 to about 16 per cent in 1993, whereas manufacturing has grown from a mere 9 per cent to nearly 30 per cent of GDP during the same period. The electronics industry dominates the manufacturing sector, contributing the largest macroeconomic benefits in terms of output, export earnings and employment. The electronics industry took off in the early 1970s, when the Government shifted its emphasis from an import substitution to an export-oriented strategy in order to promote the country's industrial development. This was at a time when major structural changes were taking place in the electronics production sector in the United States, Western Europe and Japan. Industries in those countries needed to adjust very quickly to the intensely competitive international market and, inevitably, to locate some operations in lower-cost production centres overseas. Malaysia, then on the threshold of its new export-led industrial programme, offered an ideal location. The attractive investment climate, including a ten-year pioneer status incentive for the electronics industry, the huge reservoir of trainable labour at low cost, and the establishment of Free Trade Zones (FTZs) and Licensed Manufacturing Warehouse facilities (LMWs), was one which many multi-national electrical and electronics companies found difficult to resist in their quest for greater competitive advantage.

The electrical and electronics (E&E) industry is one trade-driven activity favoured for the "value-added" edge of its manufactured products over primary commodities. Indeed, current statistics have shown the electronics industry to be the country's major revenue earner next to crude petroleum. The down side is its pollution impact, which has to be adequately addressed in order to maintain the environmental soundness and competitiveness of this important economic activity. Pollution from the electronics industry is addressed by retrofitting and by in-plant approaches, dealing respectively with wastes and the use of ozone-depleting substances.

With the Government taking the lead in local electronics research and development, the industry has been transformed from the assembly and testing of semiconductors using imported technology and materials in the 1960s into three broad sectors:

- electronic components, comprising integrated circuits, discrete active components such as transistors, diodes, optoelectronic devices, and discrete passive components such as capacitors, resistors, relays, inductors;

- consumer electronics, covering home entertainment products such as radios, TV receivers, video cassette recorders, and electronic household goods such as microwave ovens, telephone receivers; and

- industrial electronics, including computers and peripherals, office electronic equipment, and process control.

Indeed, the electronics industry is now a major component in Malaysia's manufacturing sector due to government efforts to encourage multinationals from the United States, Japan, Europe, Chinese Taipei, Singapore, Korea and Hong Kong to set up export-oriented plants in the country.

3.2   Central Toxic Waste Treatment Facility

The implementation of a RM353 million (US$144 million) central toxic waste treatment plant in Bukit Nenas, Negri Sembilan, has been delayed. The Economic Planning Unit (EPU) is reviewing the contract awarded to the consortium Kualiti Alam Sdn. Bhd. (The consortium comprises United Engineers (M) Bhd (50 per cent stake), Arab-Malaysian Development Bhd (20 per cent), and three Danish companies (I Kruger, Enviroplan and Chemcontrol.) This follows concern over a further delay by the consortium in completing the project. The consortium had indicated that it would only be able to receive toxic waste from August 1996, instead of September 1995 as scheduled. The project was initially set for completion by the end of 1997. A temporary site for nation-wide collection of toxic waste was to be built by May 1995, but was delayed. Following discussions, the consortium was directed to complete the construction of the storage facility within six months. However, it was obvious that the consortium could not meet the deadline.

As a result of the delays, the consortium has been criticised by both the Government and industries. Industries facing space constraints have to accommodate their own toxic wastes until the storage facility is ready. One of the reasons cited for the delay was that the consortium wanted a soft loan from the Government because there were no financial backers after they had projected that the volume of toxic waste generated would be much lower than the actual amount, putting in doubt the commercial viablility of the facility. Having now withdrawn their request for a soft loan, the consortium is now demanding new conditions in order to get the project started. The entire plant, consisting of a waste storage facility, incinerator and landfill, is scheduled to be fully operational in 1998.

3.3   Corporate Environmental Policy

Many electronics firms have drawn up major environmental policies to control pollution, particularly in nearby rivers. The policies have stressed sound environmental management of resources and sustainable growth. Companies are continuously improving their environmental performance by opting for environmentally friendly technology. Under these policies, the companies have pledged to stringently enforce environmental standards and employ energy-saving and waste-recovery controls for manufacturing processes.

Several Malaysian companies are monitoring, and managing, the impact of their manufacturing processes on the environment and are gearing their activities in order to adopt a proactive approach. This is in line with their aim of doing the utmost to protect the environment for future generations. Towards this end, they are training their workers to be more aware of environmental issues. Companies also provide information on environmental conservation activities to the public, including schoolchildren, in line with their responsibility to the community.

Many companies have adopted annual environmental auditing procedures, to ensure that they comply with environmental standards. The audit focuses on management systems, standard operating procedures, and environmental conservation. For example, one of the biggest electronics firms in Johor has engaged consultants from Plant Ecology (Eco) Audit, which has consultants worldwide. Among the steps taken by the company to improve its environmental record, water discharged from the plant is now being treated and recycled in the deionised water plant. Previously, the toxic water was released to drain. Similarly, wastewater which was previously released to drain is now collected in a tank, stabilised and reused. Projected water recovery using this process is 183.6 cubic metres per day, which translates into RM293.76 in savings a day. The company's new general waste segregation system had also resulted in better management of industrial wastes. The plant's air emission and noise control measures have also been improved.

3.4   SMEs: Technology, Investment and Environmental Awareness

Small and medium-sized enterprises (SMEs) play an important role in Malaysia's industrialisation policies. SMEs, a recent phenomenon in Malaysia, emerged over the past two decades as a result of its industrialisation policies. They presently employ more than 45 per cent of the total labour workforce in the country. A majority of these SMEs are "family type" businesses, undercapitalised, with low technology utilisation and insufficient human resource development. It is estimated that there are in excess of 16,000 SMEs in Malaysia. Many more are unregistered or "illegal", conducting operations on premises not gazetted for industrial use.

SMEs are preoccupied with daily operations – securing orders and raw materials, delegating work, delivering goods, looking for financial and credit facilities, and training human resources. They are consistently "mobile" and widely dispersed, and no national organisation adequately represents their interests. It is therefore extremely difficult for the authorities to educate SME manufacturers on pollution control measures and the adoption of environmentally friendly methods.

The problems faced by SMEs are manifold, the biggest being the disposal of hazardous and toxic wastes. Currently, factories have to store wastes generated from manufacturing operations on their premises. The delay in the completion of the Bukit Nenas integrated hazardous waste management facility has created storage problems not only for SMEs, but also for some larger companies facing space constraints in building pollution treatment facilities. Given the circumstances, factories continue to apply for contravention licenses to discharge wastes. While large companies are taking the lead in complying with the regulations and are keeping abreast of new developments, SMEs are placing environmental considerations at low priority levels due to the relatively low level of awareness of regulatory requirements under the EQA. The SMEs are the greatest worry in terms of pollution threats, due to their failure to comply with environmental regulations. The recent amendments to the EQA extend provisions for the Department of Environment (DOE) to monitor the environmental performance of SMEs.

4.0 The Cost-effectiveness of Cleaner Production

Cleaner production approaches vary with the industries that adopt them. Many case studies have demonstrated the tangible and intangible benefits of cleaner production and waste minimisation. Besides the resulting reductions in waste load and volume, waste minimisation efforts have brought about significant cost savings. Three cases concerning waste minimisation efforts in Malaysia are presented below.

4.1 Case 1: Electroplating Plant

Electroplating plants serve various industries, including automobiles production, shipbuilding and ship repair, and furniture making. The metal finishing process involves activities ranging from pickling, anodising, galvanising, painting and engraving to combinations of these and electroplating with nickel, chromium, copper, zinc, brass, gold and tin. High water consumption is associated with flow rinsing, which flushes dissolved salts and particulates from the plated article. The types of pollutants found in the wastewater are determined by the raw materials used.

Waste minimisation alternatives involve reduction in the volume of wastewater, as well as the concentration of pollutants. Modification and rearrangement of the processes, whole plant arrangement, use of mechanical instead of chemical cleaning methods, prevention of spillage, and good housekeeping practices all contribute to the effective implementation of waste minimisation objectives. Wastewater production was reduced by about 50 per cent at one small metal finishing plant in Kuala Lumpur (Rakmi et al., 1991). The cost savings resulting from reduced water consumption were estimated to be about RM230 per day or RM69,000 per year (based on 300 operating days/year). The cost of modifications and installations (including for wastewater treatment) could be recovered in about two years.

4.2 Case 2: Rubber Products Plant

In the rubber products plant the major sources of waste are washing of reactors, acid coagulation of rubber, and rinsing of rubber products. The three waste streams are quite different in composition. Washing the reactors generates wastewater high in latex; acid coagulation generates residual acid and sludge; and product rinsing generates wastewater containing acid. Waste segregation has been found to be most effective for optimal treatment.

Waste minimisation in one of the rubber products plants in Kuala Lumpur (involving water savings in various washing processes, water and energy savings at the rinse tanks, reuse of acids, and recovery of waste latex) was found to be effective in reducing the volume of wastewater as well as lowering BOD and COD concentrations in the wastewater. The savings due to reduced water consumption and treatment costs are estimated to be more than RM1.5 million per year.

4.3 Case 3: Palm Oil Mill

Pollution from palm oil mills alone accounted for about 63 per cent of Malaysia's water pollution load in 1982. However, they have substantially reduced their pollution load and today contribute only 1.13 per cent.

This impressive success story offers several lessons in relation to environmental policy issues such as trade and environment, internalisation of externalities, and the use of economic instruments. With the passing of the Environmental Quality (Prescribed Premises) (Crude Palm Oil) Regulation in 1977, palm oil mills were required to treat their effluents prior to discharging them into streams and rivers and to comply with the standards established by the DOE. Research was also intensified with local expertise, as the waste is unique to the region where the palm oil mills operate. Various efficient treatment technologies for palm oil mill effluents (POME) were developed and adopted by the mills. These treatment systems were able to reduce most of the pollution parameters to acceptable standards. As regulation becomes more stringent, research and development have found beneficial uses for treated POME.

POME has tremendous potential for conversion into useful by-products such as animal feed, as well as being a source of energy. Research has also established that POME in both raw and various treated forms contains very high levels of plant nutrients. It has been estimated that the POME generated in Malaysia could have a fertiliser value amounting to about 40 per cent of the fertiliser expenditure in the oil palm estates in Peninsular Malaysia (Khalid and Wan Mustafa, 1992). Besides liquid POME, the palm oil milling process also generates a large amount of solid by-products, chiefly in the form of mesocarp fibres, empty fruit bunches (EFBs), and shell. Solid by-products can be utilised as sources of energy. Fibres and shells (instead of being disposed as wastes) are currently the main sources of energy in palm oil mills. They can produce more than sufficient energy to meet the mill's demand. EFBs (instead of being burnt for ash, which was used as fertiliser) are now used as mulch on local estates. They can also be easily composted for use as fertiliser. In efforts to minimise wastes during processing, substantial cost savings and revenue have been generated by utilising the POME and the by-products from palm oil mills.

5.0   Conclusion

Industrialisation has contributed much to Malaysia's economic success and will continue to do so. In a situation of rapid industrialisation, the cost-effectiveness of policies that emphasise pollution prevention rather than paying for pollution clean-up offers important "win-win" economic and environmental benefits. In Malaysia efforts to combat pollution have intensified since the early 1970s. Many stakeholders have participated in a number of ways. The Government has imposed emission regulations, non-governmental organisations have kept up their campaigns for a clean environment, and industries have incorporated environmental concerns into their management goals. Both the Government and industry have promoted research and development on cleaner production technologies. The focus is now on low- or non-waste technologies replacing "end-of-the-pipe" technologies. The economic value of cleaner production is increasingly recognised by Malaysian industry. Several industries have demonstrated the usefulness of cleaner production and waste minimisation technologies and practices, while deriving tangible economic benefits from adopting them.

Attitudes to environmental management, coupled with public policy constraints and incentives, have been the driving forces behind industries' interest in cleaner production and waste minimisation. The Government is encouraging industries to use environmentally friendly materials for the manufacture of products and to minimise waste generation at source through various incentives such as the promotion and commercialisation of new and renewable energy resources, differential pricing of fuels, privatisation of waste management, imposition of fees for wastewater discharge, etc. To cope with increasing demands for environmental services, existing institutions are being redefined: many agencies, whether at the Federal or State levels, are involved in environmental management with overlapping functions and unclear jurisdiction. Existing environmental measures, vis-à-vis laws, rules, regulations, standards and guidelines, are being reviewed with the purpose of improving their effectiveness.

REFERENCES

Department of Environment, Malaysia: *Environmental Quality Report*. Various years.

Institute of Strategic and International Studies, Malaysia, 1995: *Trade and Environment Linkages: A Malaysian Case Study. Final Report of a Study of Trade and Environment Linkages for Selected Malaysian Industries Prepared for UNCTAD*, May 1995.

Khalid. A.R. and Wan Mustafa W.A., 1992: "External Benefits of Environmental Regulation: Resource Recovery and the Utilisation of Effluents," *The Environmentalist* 12(4): pp 277-285.

Rakmi, A.R., Hassan B., Salmijah S. and Abu Bakar, M., 1991: *Waste Reduction at Source for Small and Medium Scale Electroplating Plants*. Department of Environment, Kuala Lumpur.

United Nations Environment Programme, Industry and Environment Programme Activity Centre, 1993: *Cleaner Production Worldwide*. Paris.

THE METRO MANILA CLEAN TECHNOLOGY INITIATIVE

Annice Brown[1]
Asia Technical Department, The World Bank

1.0   Introduction

Under a US$586,000 grant from the United States Trade and Development Agency (USTDA), the World Bank and the Metropolitan Environmental Improvement Program (MEIP) developed a programme to promote waste minimisation/clean technology efforts in Metro Manila, the Philippines. The primary objective was to assess the potential of clean technology to prevent and control industrial pollution, and the opportunity for private sector involvement. The grant was administered and executed by the World Bank through the MEIP office, and its intent was to link this initiative to the proposed Industrial Efficiency Pollution Control Project (IEPC). That project is no longer under preparation due to other lines of credit already available through other sources, such as a World Bank industrial sector loan, and other donors (for example, Japan). Philippine businesses are also able to get financing from private financial institutions. The Government of the Philippines (GOP) therefore decided not to seek new funding for the IEPC project, but still believes there is a strong need for downstream IEPC investment through studies and USTDA activities, such as public awareness programmes, feasibility studies for common effluent treatment plants (CETPs), and other demonstration projects by interested donors.

Just as the industrialised countries are coming to recognise the inefficiency of end-of-pipe (EOP) approaches to pollution abatement, and to shift from pollution control to waste minimisation and prevention, developing countries are also beginning to follow the same practices, especially in more profitable sectors such as chemicals. World Bank guidelines for industrial projects have largely focused on EOP, but they are being revised to include source control and cleaner production. Environmental Action Plans are also beginning to incorporate cleaner production. Some World Bank projects that have incorporated clean technology include India Industrial Pollution Control and Industrial Pollution Prevention; Indonesia Industrial Efficiency and Pollution Control; the China Technology Development Project; Beijing Environment Project; and other projects in Brazil, Mexico, Egypt and Sri Lanka.

---

[1]   The findings, interpretations and conclusions of this paper represent the personal views of the author and should not be attributed to the World Bank, its Executive Board of Directors or its member countries.

Originally, the IEPC project in the Philippines consisted of five components:

- review of existing clean technology (CT) experience in developed and developing countries and identification of priority subsections for technical assistance;
- training in Environmental Assessment (EA) to build local capabilities;
- EA in selected industrial sectors;
- clean technology institution-building; and
- assessing the potential of CT applications in specific sectors (Technology Matching).

The six industrial sectors selected for Pollution Management Assessments (PMAs) were chosen based on the gap in the level of support that existed in Manila for these industries. Support for other sectors such as cement and distilleries, etc. was being provided by other donors and the Department of Environment and Natural Resources (DENR). Therefore, it was determined that MEIP and USTDA could have an impact on cleaner production by providing technical assistance to the following six industrial sectors in Metro Manila: (i) food processing (meat, poultry, and pork); (ii) electroplating; (iii) tanning; (iv) chemicals; (v) dairy; and vi) beverage.

2.0   Pollution Management Assessments (PMAs)

Perhaps the most substantive component of the study consisted of the PMAs or environmental audits of 25 plants. The DENR and MEIP-Manila invited applications from industries to participate in the waste minimisation/clean technology initiative. Criteria were established and selection was made based on issues including the company's overall financial viability; commitment by the industry to environmental improvement; willingness to implement PMA findings; and agreement with DENR on the appropriate time frame. Each industry was asked to form a team led by a key technical or management staff member to work with local and foreign consultants, in order to foster collaboration between local plant engineers and external technology transfer experts. The PMAs' emphasis included auditing general plant management and good housekeeping, opportunities for major and minor process changes, and waste reduction. PMA's were conducted by expert consultants, and confidentiality of the results was agreed upon. Once the PMAs were completed, a follow-up workshop was organised to disseminate the findings to the industrial sector and an audit report was produced for each plant.

3.0   The Technology Matching Mission

The concept of the Technology Matching Mission directly responds to Agenda 21's call to promote the "transfer of environmentally sound technology, co-operation and capacity-building," taking into consideration the introduction of hard technologies (equipment), soft technologies (management practices) and clean production (prevention, minimisation and integration). Assessment of "clean technology" and Technology Matching potential was an important project component.

3.1   Design and Management

The clean technology team at the World Bank and MEIP designed the programme instead of contracting it out, primarily for two reasons. First, both groups believed they could design a good programme and wanted to gain expertise in managing such a programme. Second, designing and managing the programme in-house would save on limited financial resources and allow more participants to come to the United States for the Technology Matching Mission. It was decided that each group would be accompanied by a World Bank manager and, in some cases, an expert consultant from that particular industrial sector. Each of the six groups comprised three to four industry representatives who participated in the PMAs and were strong advocates of cleaner production within his or her industrial sector, and one or two regulators from the DENR Environmental Management Bureau or a local agency. The regulators participated in the Technology Matching Mission not only to learn about the U.S. regulatory system, but also to strengthen their relationship with their industrial colleagues while learning about voluntary pollution prevention practices and enforcement issues in the United States. The Technology Matching Mission provided regulators the opportunity to meet with U.S. regulators to learn about policies and economic incentives used to promote cleaner production.

The six missions took place between March and August 1995. Each mission was led by myself or a colleague from our clean technology team, and/or a consultant experienced in the appropriate industrial sector. The choice of companies and enforcement agencies to visit was based on several factors:

- companies should have good environmental management practices and state-of-the-art technology and be willing to receive the Filipino group (usually dependent on the consultant's or the team's contacts);

- there should be access to as many companies as possible in one geographical area (to save on travel time and costs);

- there should be the possibility of meeting with industrial associations (when applicable); and

- there should be willingness by state, local or federal regulators to meet with the groups.

4.0   Summary of the Technology Matching Mission by Industrial Sector

4.1   Food Processing (Beef, Poultry and Pork) Industry

The consultant for this sector was a leading Food Sciences professor from North Carolina State University, who is regarded by the U.S. Environmental Protection Agency (EPA) and Department of Agriculture (USDA) as a pioneer in this field. Because North Carolina was a leader in pollution prevention in the United States, and EPA had used it as a model for the federal programme, the group focused its visit on that area. In addition to meeting with a leading industry expert, the group was able to see how a university group acted as consultants to industry. Many industries regarded university consultants as "honest" partners between industry and the regulators. This view was expressed not only by industry representatives themselves, but also by EPA and USDA.

Water use is the biggest problem in the food processing industry, as large volumes are used in animal processing. Large waste loads generate serious environmental problems, including regional water shortages, increasing the costs of suitable water and of wastewater treatment and disposal. Reducing water consumption, and recycling and reusing water, are desirable both economically and environmentally. Two solutions for controlling water use in food processing plants are available: in-plant water reduction, and process wastewater reuse after treatment. Technologies contributing to these methods are of particular interest to this industry. The Technology Matching Mission focused on observing these technologies. While many of the companies had similar technologies, one plant, Hatfield Quality Meats, was the most innovative company as they were the first (and to date the only) plant to design and operate a water reuse system. They explained to the group how it took them ten years to get a permit from USDA to reuse recycled water in their processing plant. USDA hoped to work with other plants to promote this activity. Another plant, Carolina Hogs, demonstrated how they used biogas for heating, which saved the firm US$30,000 in heating bills every month.

Other technologies observed during plant visits were:

- DAFs – aerated lagoons – land application;
- Anaerobic pond – activated sludge UV disinfection – direct discharge;
- DAFs – activated sludge – indirect discharge;
- DAFs – anaerobic lagoon – oxidation ditch – activated sludge – chlorination direct discharge; and
- DAFs – activated sludge (SBR – sequence batch reactor) – land application.

Land application was deemed inappropriate for the Philippines due to scarcity of land and heavy rainfall. The Schrieber System (second bullet above) appeared the most promising to the group due to its low labour, operating and maintenance costs.

Some issues discussed with the companies revolved around the different regulations from the various agencies, including EPA, USDA, and the Occupational Safety and Health Administration (OSHA). The U.S. industries shared useful tips with the group, which they claimed were essential to them in order to meet compliance and maintain a high level of good housekeeping:

- data collection must be consistent;
- staff training is critical for determining and analysing data;
- testing and monitoring must be maintained, and followed closely in the lab;
- monitoring and control should be automated;
- think of wastewater as product recovery;
- work in collaboration with EPA and other agencies;
- select treatment technologies to minimise both capital and operating costs while assuring desirable levels of treatment; and
- pollution prevention and water conservation can result in 40–50 per cent reductions in water use in this sector and are cost-effective. Thus, these strategies should be promoted before spending additional money on treatment facilities.

A visit to the American Meat Institute demonstrated to the group how a large institute can directly influence both industry and government. Information was shared on the Institute's partnership with industry to foster and promote pollution prevention practices, in order to demonstrate lower costs and other benefits. This partnership included the industry, growers, and the state regulators. Also being promoted were new legislation regarding "self-audits" in five states. EPA was being pushed to develop a national policy.

4.2   Electroplating Industry

The Philippine delegation consisted of five participants, three from the private sector (members of the Philippine Electroplaters' Association) and two regulators from the Environmental Management Bureau. The group's visit, hosted by the Illinois State EPA, was based on a good working relationship between the agency and the World Bank. As a result of that relationship, no consultant was needed. There were talks and site visits with Chicago area electroplaters during one week. In addition to the Chicago industrial sites, the group visited a municipal wastewater reclamation centre and met with the National Association of Metal Finishers in Washington, D.C. They also visited the Metal Finishing Lab at Goddard Space Center (NASA) for a look at state-of-the-art metal finishing technology R&D, as well as visiting high-tech industries in and around California's Silicon Valley.

In Chicago the group met with state and local EPA regulators and several area electroplaters, who shared their experiences with waste minimisation and with participating in pollution prevention programmes sponsored by the Illinois EPA. Industry was very clear about the cost-saving benefits to their companies, and were very supportive of the state's efforts. The Philippine group benefited greatly by having the state EPA as their facilitator, as they were able to experience first-hand how local regulators work with industry to help them reach compliance and pursue a win-win strategy for all involved. The local regulators also proved a great resource to the group, as they are frequently in the field and understand industry's problems. The Illinois EPA provided a valuable forum for the group to learn about the institutional relationship between regulators and the regulated.

One programme sponsored by the Illinois EPA which was of special interest to the group was the Industrial Internship Program, in which students had the possibility of joining a company for three months to study some of the environmental bottlenecks companies face. Participation in the programme was voluntary for industry, which benefited from the time saved in having students review their permits. Two hundred companies were participating in the programme, and a pilot project had been set up to make it applicable to small businesses.

Visits to plants and discussion with plant managers/environmental directors provided insights. Navistar, a large company with 14,000 employees and five plants nation-wide, built engines for trucks and school buses. Since 1989, the company had had an aggressive environmental management plan focusing on waste minimisation and pollution prevention. It had incorporated many management changes, including the use of non-hazardous substitutes, the reuse of coolants, trash reduction, and working directly with suppliers to obtain environmentally acceptable raw materials. A plant source reduction committee was examining further changes. The company was already in compliance with ISO 14000 standards and was trying to anticipate what it would have to do next to stay in compliance, especially with the new Clean Air Act.

In addition to environmental changes, which had been documented from a cost-benefit perspective, Navistar had made energy conservation an important goal. It had built its own co-generation power plant to reduce electricity costs (approximately US$36 million in 1995). The cost of the plant was around US$8 million, and it would save US$2 million in energy, making the payback period four years. Excess electricity would be sold to neighbouring companies, which showed that high energy prices did not guarantee a decrease in energy use by industry. Navistar had an impressive community outreach programme. The home telephone number of the plant's environmental director had been given to the company's neighbours, to use as needed. The corporation's Environmental Director was a Philippine engineer, who was pleased to receive this group and offered future assistance to the electroplaters. Navistar was an excellent example of a proactive company. It was working closely with the Illinois EPA and the community to better manage its resources, while going beyond EPA's mandated compliance.

A visit to Caterpillar, a major firm manufacturing cylinders, hydraulics, and suspension components for trucks, was centred around the electroplating and chrome finishing shop. The group focused on techniques for chrome recovery and reuse. The plant engineers shared with the group their hard chromium plating process and their system for treating chrome, which they had been developing since 1980 when regulations were imposed. Like Navistar, Caterpillar maintained excellent relations with regulators and depended on their understanding of the problem to resolve compliance issues.

Another visit, to API Industries, was particularly interesting for the group. This job shop with 150 employees operated 24 hours per day, seven days per week, with 75 per cent of its business coming from the automotive industry. It plated 275,000 parts per day and had the capacity to process 400,000. The shop was investigating ways to reduce hazardous waste, and ultimately the cost of handling it. There was only one place to send hazardous waste, and the costs were high. The shop's biggest problem was cyanide, as it used a zinc/cyanide mix. It was working on ways to convert to a less hazardous zinc/copper mix, as well as looking at ways to reduce cadmium use and experimenting with a zinc/cobalt mix which it hoped would be acceptable to the auto industry. With a consultant, it was working on reducing water use. This company explained it could not afford to be shut down for lack of compliance because customers in the U.S. auto industry relied on it and trusted it to meet all the regulations. It could not afford to lose its strong customer base.

The National Metal Finishers Association took a very proactive approach to helping its members meet U.S. EPA regulations. The association wrote the definitive work on environmental guidelines for the industry, based on a survey of over 320 electroplaters. The results were published in a book which several members of the group purchased. As a follow-up to the book, the association planned to establish an Internet-accessible environmental clearinghouse, developed with EPA and the National Institute of Standards and Technology (NIST). The clearinghouse was to be accessible at a fee-for-service. The association offered its members a competent in-house technical programme that promoted pollution prevention/cleaner production. It was working closely with small and medium-sized enterprises (SMEs), in collaboration with the nation-wide Manufacturing Extension Centres sponsored by NIST. The Association was emphasising pollution prevention as a cost-effective environmental management system, rather than the use of new technologies, and claimed that 97 per cent of the industry complied now.

The Director of Legislative Affairs felt it would be a good idea for the group to visit traditional Chicago region platers since Illinois did not have a water problem, as did California. According to him, California provided the worst example of unrealistic regulations. He claimed that, between regulations and competition, it was next to impossible for metal finishers to operate there. It seemed that the industry was not expanding, but moving overseas due to strict regulations. The group also discussed the idea of a common effluent treatment plant and the U.S. experience. This approach was too costly for companies in the U.S., as transport costs were very high. It was cheaper for a company to purchase equipment and treat the effluent on-site. Minnesota had a centralised ion exchange unit facility using mobile hauling units. In Philadelphia, where 90 per cent of members were small firms, a CETP might work. But each plant produced about 5000 gallons per day, requiring enormous co-operation from the platers. Some of the questions raised were: who would ensure the safety of the system? and who would police it?

The Association insisted that the regulations being enforced by EPA had not changed since 1984 and were not scientifically sound. It had challenged EPA on its science and had recently won a major lawsuit because EPA was not using accurate scientific data. The Association believed that standards should be locally driven, as opposed to the "one-size-fits-all" approach it believed was currently mandated by EPA.

For most industries in the electroplating sector, the rationale for considering cleaner production appeared to be:

- external pressures (regulators, potential financial liabilities, environmental groups, and neighbourhood communities);

- cost-control and cost-saving possibilities;

- increasing landfill prices;

- having a designated person responsible for environmental affairs. The larger companies had their own environmental division of three to eight people, depending on plant size.

In addition,

- regarding revenue margins for electroplaters, U.S. rates were low (between 2.5 and 3 per cent), and the price was about 30 per cent higher with environment-related investments.

- some electroplaters had educated their clients, and others had switched to cleaner production as a result of customer demand.

- funding problems always arose when a new concept was introduced and operationalised. An effective way to communicate the cleaner production concept was through financial intermediaries. The experience of American consultants showed that when a thorough business plan was developed, and cleaner production measures were incorporated, banks would fund cleaner production.

Among the lessons learned from the visits and discussions were the following:

- Institutional development/enforcement. There were strong benefits to having the regulators (Illinois EPA) and the regulated (electroplaters) at the same table to discuss pollution prevention policies, programmes and compliance. Likewise, the Philippine group of regulators and industry representatives believed co-operation would enable them to foster a better working relationship on their return. U.S. regulators' attitudes had shifted over the last ten years; they realised they could no longer act as "policemen", but should be facilitators with industry if they were to achieve their common goals.

- Training. Industry, especially small and medium-sized enterprises (SMEs), required training on new techniques and technologies if it was to meet regulations. Technical assistance was important for businesses that wanted to comply but found it technically and financially difficult to do so.

- Dissemination of information. The Illinois EPA carried out extensive outreach to companies (often through trade associations) to educate them on new technologies, new programmes, new regulations, standardisation of chemical processes, and other innovations.

- Funding of treatment plants, technologies. In the past, U.S. firms had received a 35 per cent tax break for R&D for environmental investments. This was no longer the case, and small firms felt the crunch as they must bear the cost and be competitive at the same time. It could be very difficult for a small firm to withstand the pay-back period on large investments.

It was recommended that the World Bank remain an active partner in facilitating future clean technology opportunities in the Philippines. The electroplaters suffered from lack of cleaner production knowledge and experience, and this prevented them from implementing urgently needed environmental management plans such as a better wastewater management system. The group felt that World Bank support could be in the form of assisting them with writing proposals to donors, selecting consultants, knowledge acquisition (for example, know-how), technical assistance, etc.

4.3   Tanning Industry

The Philippine delegation consisted of six participants, two from the DENR regulatory branch and four industry executives (members of the Tannery Association). The group's visit was facilitated by the Wisconsin/Milwaukee Department of Natural Resources (DNR) and a U.S. tannery expert.

In Milwaukee, the group spent the afternoon with the Wisconsin DNR for informal discussions with local regulators, the manager of the Milwaukee Metropolitan Sewage District (where more than ten tanneries are located) and the tannery expert, discussing their shared experiences of waste minimisation and the pollution prevention programmes sponsored by the Wisconsin DNR. Documents handed out to the group included a guide to managing hazardous waste, a guide to pollution prevention programme implementation, and effluent guidelines and standards. The Wisconsin DNR provided valuable information on the institutional relationship between the regulators and the regulated.

The Wisconsin DNR also provided a brief history of tannery regulations in the United States, which became fairly severe in the 1980s, causing many small tanneries to close. Prior to the 1980s, Milwaukee had approximately 17 tanneries; presently there are five full tanners and five finishers in operation.

Visits to the following companies were made.

Pfister and Vogel (which owned several manufacturing operations in the United States) was one of the oldest and largest tanneries in the country, dating back to 1848. Waste treatment was scattered all over the plant, unlike in more modern plants that had a single treatment facility. The tannery discharged waste directly into the Milwaukee sewer system. The requirements were: chromium: < 8 mg/l; sulphides: < 24 mg/l; pH: 6–10.

The tannery, which processed over 2,900 hides per day, operated seven days a week, 50 weeks a year. It manufactured upper premium leather for shoes and garments. There was complete recycling of the spent chrome tanning solutions, involving segregation, screening grease removal, precipitation with lime, filtration, and redissolving in acid. No hexavalent chromium was used in the tannery. The wastes containing sulphides were segregated and the sulphide destroyed by air oxidation.

The spent solutions from all other processes were mixed with the treated sulphide-free and chromium-free solutions, coagulated with polymers and lime, clarified, and pH adjusted by adding carbon dioxide.

The company, together with the local leather industry, had been instrumental in suing the local Department of Natural Resources (DNR) over chromium limitations. The industry challenged the DNR on its science and won the case, proving to the EPA that the tanning industry did not produce a hazardous waste. EPA published a summary document on the toxicity of chromium (EPA 430/976013, *Chromium*) which concluded that chromium 3 (as used in the leather industry) is stable, non-toxic, and essentially insoluble in soil under normal soil conditions. Thus, land applications of sludges or leather waste products containing tannery chromium 3 (as fertiliser) or sending them to landfill is no longer prohibited. An anticipated local waiver option could save the plant US$20,000 in CO_2 used to lower the pH.

Cornell St. Facility, a new facility owned by Pfister and Vogel, was essentially a pilot plant that collected the leather shavings from the main plant. With an initial grant of US$100,000 from the local DNR, Pfister and Vogel established this facility, which produced hydrolysed fertiliser. The process combined the cooked leather shavings, which at this stage contain 2-3 per cent chromium, 2-3 per cent fat, 40-50 per cent protein, and the rest water. The new process involved heating the ground leather in water and lime. The cooking liquefied the protein and precipitated the chromium. The fat and chromium solids were removed by flotation and filtration. The solids were sent to the tannery for chromium recovery. The protein was recovered by vacuum evaporation, and could be spray-dried. The product had potential value in animal feed, glue feedstock, and as a foaming agent. It was being used as an organic fertiliser. Further market possibilities were being explored, and the plant was interested in licensing out this technology.

Gebhardt Tanning Co. was 65 years old and was also owned by Pfister and Vogel. Its newer treatment facility was located in a single area. Gebhardt leather was used for wallets, billfolds and softball leather, requiring more oil and grease than in the Pfister and Vogel process. This facility produced wet blue, crust and finished side leather from cattle hides. The spent chrome tanning solutions were treated with lime and coagulants, filtered, and sent to the main plant for chrome recovery. The sulphide-bearing wastes were separated, air-oxidised, and mixed with the balance of the processing wastes. The mixed-solution solids were removed by air flotation, filtered, and disposed of as solid waste.

Law Tanning produced a variety of split leathers from chrome-tanned splits purchased from other tanneries. The wastes are primarily from the colouring and fat-liquoring processes. The operations run two and one-half shifts, and 120,000 gallons of wastes is processed. The solutions are equalised, screened and precipitated with lime and polymers. Polymer addition and pH control are automated. The solids are removed by air flotation and de-watered by a filter press. The solids are 30-40 per cent moisture. The treated wastewater is discharged to the municipal sewer system, and the sludge goes to landfill. The plant has no problem meeting the pH levels of 6 to 8.

Wolverine Leathers, which made Rockford and Hush Puppy shoes, produced approximately 17 million square feet of pigskin per year, with a capacity of 23 million. The tannery was not a direct discharger. It sent its wastes to the city of Grand Rapids, Michigan, 26 miles away. Wolverine maintained two shoe factories in Michigan, with facilities in Puerto Rico and the Dominican Republic for stitching and sewing and facilities in New York, Arkansas, Mexico and Costa Rica for selling.

The raw material was scalded domestic pigskins, purchased in the salted condition. The skins had to be limed with sulphide to remove the hair. Tannage was in drums in a modern tannery. Chrome tannage fixed a large percentage of the chrome tanning material, so the spent solutions were not recycled. All the wastes were combined in a large open-topped tank, where the solution was aerated to oxidise the sulphides. The solids were settled and de-watered, then filtered in a filter press and disposed of in a landfill. The final wastewater had BOD 400–500 mg/l, chromium <1 mg/l, and sulphides <5 mg/l.

Cudahy Tanning Co. is owned by Law Tanning and produces a wide variety of leathers from cattle hides (mostly sides), resulting in about 400,00 gallons of effluent per day. Cudahy dates back to the early 1900s. Its business peaked during the war years, as it made shoes for the military. In 1946 the Law family bought it and manufactured baseball leather for gloves. Today it manufactured diversified leather for shoes, gloves and handbags. In the 1980s the company was going out of business due in large part to its lack of investment in quality equipment needed to stay competitive. It was able to downsize and make the necessary investments to turn the business around, and was doing very well due to the procurement of quality equipment from Italy and France. The firm bought all the hides from the packers pre-fleshed, like most other tanneries. This way they did not have to deal with the fleshings and the subsequent oil and grease problem.

Production was approximately 2,000 sides per day. Wastewaters was treated and discharged into the municipal sewer system. There was no chrome recycling. The tannery was limited in available space that could be used for treating wastes. In the very near future, the plant wanted to add manufacturing space and use some of the additional space for separating waste streams and for recovering chromium. The entire waste stream was combined and coagulated, and the pH was adjusted with lime. The mixed wastes were floated to remove the solids, which were then de-watered in a filter press. The solid sludge was disposed in a landfill.

The group was particularly interested in a stretching (Dynovac) machine that yielded a 13 per cent gain in leather. The machine cost approximately US$250,000 and the payback time was one to one and a half years.

The Badger State Tanning plant was a split tannery, colouring and fat-liquoring chrome-tanned splits. All wastewater was collected in a 44,000-gallon tank to allow ten hours of equalisation and pH adjustment to pH 8.5 with lime and polymers. The wastes were separated from the treated water by air flotation. The flotation equipment was shallow, and separation was obtained through small air bubbles and minimum turbulence in the system. The sludge was filtered to about 40 per cent moisture on a moving belt filter press. The system met the standards required by the municipality and was, in the opinion of the vice-president and the consultant, very cost-effective for the company. However, the company was not recovering any chrome. The treatment system, which cost approximately US$1 million, was operated by one person, who also helped the company build the system from used equipment.

The group was very interested in the possibility of a common effluent treatment plant for the tanneries located in Region III (40 kilometres from Manila), where most tanneries were located. This region consisted of approximately 55 members of the Tannery Association, mostly SMEs. The tanners in the group who were not in that region nevertheless fully endorsed the proposal.

The tannery group presented the findings of the Technology Matching Mission to the Tannery Association. Recommendations to their industrial colleagues (based on that mission) included:

- recovery of chrome;
- legal and technical discussions regarding chrome 3;
- separation of waste;

- lower-cost equipment options (for example, sand filters);
- modification of designs;
- upgrading of existing facilities (for those which have treatment facilities);
- protein recovery scheme and making of fertiliser from leather shavings;
- strengthening the Metropolitan Environmental Improvement Programme (MEIP) to provide pollution prevention outreach and technical assistance for better environmental management, for industry and the Department of Environment and Natural Resources (DENR);
- updating industry on the consultative process with labs and engineering firms;
- strengthening DENR to work more closely with industry, for better compliance with regulations;
- more training in self-monitoring;
- revisiting of standards;
- establishing a demonstration plant;
- organising workshops to disseminate information to industry, such as ISO 14000; and
- possibly establishing a cleaner production centre.

4.4 Chemical Industry

The Philippine group consisted of five participants: one from the DENR regulatory branch, the director of MEIP-Manila, and three industry executives (members of the Chemical Association). The group's visit, hosted and facilitated by the University of Tennessee Center for Clean Products and Clean Technologies, included tours of plants and discussions with university researchers, persons involved with state pollution prevention technical assistance programmes, government regulators, environmental consultants, and environmental NGOs.

At the University of Tennessee Center for Clean Products and Clean Technologies, invited experts from within the state participated in a half-day seminar on environmental laws and regulations in the United States and the State of Tennessee and how they apply to the chemical industry, and how government, industry, environmental consultants and universities have responded to the need for waste minimisation and environmental technologies. State regulators and environmental extension service providers (supported by the state and by private fees) also briefed the group on state-wide programmes to help small and medium-sized companies.

Eastman Chemicals, the largest chemical plant in the United States, produces a wide range of products including synthetic fibres, polymers, and industrial organic chemicals. The major products include polyethylene terephthalate, cellulose acetate, and photographic chemicals. As one of the largest sources of chemical releases in the U.S. EPA's Toxics Release Inventory (TRI), Eastman had focused on reducing toxic releases to air, water and soil. It was also a major player in the Chemical Manufacturers Association and in the implementation of the Responsible Care programme, which promotes environmental compliance, pollution prevention, process safety, and product stewardship within the industry.

The group toured the cellulose acetate unit, where the company had recently invested US$25 million to reduce acetone emissions to air by 50 per cent through recycling. It also toured a hazardous waste incinerator and a wastewater treatment facility. Since 1987, the amount of waste sent to the incinerator had been reduced by 46 per cent. The wastewater treatment plant removed organic material from all the wastewater generated in the complex by biological oxidation in large aerated basins above ground.

The group also visited Rohm and Haas, a company which produces paints, coatings chemicals and detergent additives. The plant, located in an urban area, employed waste minimisation and treatment processes to reduce releases of highly odorous monomers such as ethyl acrylate and methyl methacrylate. The group toured the monomer storage area, where conservation vents and a negative pressure vent header for storage tanks prevented chemical losses to the air. The group also saw polymerisation reactors where the vent header was directed to a wet scrubber and a fume incinerator to reduce releases to the atmosphere.

The group then met with representatives of the plant's Community Advisory Council, an advisory body composed of neighbouring residents, city and county officials, and other community leaders who advised Rohm and Haas on environmental compliance, community concerns, and pollution prevention matters. The group was very impressed with the community council, as it demonstrated how responsible care can be practised by a chemical company.

DuPont's White Pigments and Mineral Products Plant, the world's largest producer of titanium dioxide pigments, was carrying out a major process change to eliminate disposal of millions of gallons of acidic wastewater in a deep well. As an alternative, DuPont was going to process the by-products in order to recover sodium chloride as a saleable product. Although its sale would not generate a positive return on investment, there was a commitment to eliminating deep-well disposal to comply with EPA regulations and dramatically reduce toxic chemical releases reportable under the Toxics Release Inventory. DuPont was very forthcoming in sharing experience with the group concerning negotiating with EPA and the procedures for developing a time schedule of arrangements and agreements in order to make this process change operable in the company without major economic losses.

The following is a summary of the lessons learned by the group:

- Pollution prevention in the chemical industry is not just a technological challenge. Industry (through associations), government agencies, universities, and neighbouring communities must work in partnership to achieve the level of awareness and commitment to prevention found in the United States.

- Responsible Care, as promoted by the U.S. Chemical Manufacturers Association, is an important step towards voluntary pollution prevention and process safety programmes.

- An important component which is often under-utilised, but which has had great success in Tennessee, consists of institutional partnerships built up within the university system. As seen in other sectors, universities can play an important intermediary role as the liaison between government and industry while providing valuable resources for training, technical assistance and research.

- Community outreach might be reinforced in the Philippines through increased awareness and the use of a community advisory council such as that established by Rohm and Haas. Given that the companies represented in the mission are all in the Metro Manila area, companies can play a greater role in fostering that awareness in their community.

- Industry might examine the possibility of a centralised hazardous waste treatment facility incorporating incineration. However, such a facility should not result in a disincentive to waste minimisation.

4.5   Dairy Industry

The Philippine group consisted of four participants: one from the DNR regulatory branch and three industry executives. The group's visit was facilitated by the expert consultant we used for the meat processing industry from the Food Sciences Group at the University of North Carolina. Again, his contacts, familiarity with the Philippines, and expertise in the food processing industry proved invaluable. After visiting many plant sites, the group met with environmental experts at the International Dairy Foods Association in Washington, D.C.

Dairy plants can use large volumes of water and generate considerable pollution during the processing of milk and milk products into milk, butter, cheese and ice cream. It is essential that management effectively control water use and wastes in dairy processing. Otherwise, serious regulatory actions may be taken and profits will be lost. The waste load from a dairy processing plant is largely the result of the loss (intentionally or inadvertently) of milk products to the sewer system. In fact, researchers have found that over 90 per cent of the waste load is of product origin (milk or milk products). The reduction of water and waste in a dairy processing plant demands the application of the best technology to reduce product loss, water use, and ingredient loss. Losses are an accepted fact in many dairy plants, and ice cream plants often lose 5–10 per cent of their production from filler losses and product left in tanks and lines to be removed by flushing processes.

There are two proven ways to reduce water use – reduce wastewater discharge, and reduce waste loads and product loss. One method involves operating the plant more efficiently, and the other involves process changes such as reducing waste load, water use or product waste. Improved operating and management practices may effectively reduce water use and waste loads in dairy plants by as much as 50 per cent. When greater reduction is desirable, engineering modifications may be necessary to install cleaner technologies. Stringent standards must be met in dairy plants in the Philippines before wastewater may be discharged, and this requires expensive pre-treatment and treatment systems.

The group noted four reasons why a dairy plant needs a water and waste management programme:

- water conservation and waste reduction are important economic considerations;
- management is often unaware of a problem;
- management has little experience in solving water and waste problems; and
- most excess water use and product loss is due to careless or uninformed employees.

About 2,500 gallons of water containing about 500 pounds of BOD is discharged during the processing of 1,000 gallons of milk into consumer dairy products. Rising costs are forcing the dairy processing industry to initiate water and waste management techniques to reduce water usage and waste. Cost reductions of 50 per cent are not uncommon as a result of an effective water and waste programme. Stemming the average 4 per cent unrecognised product loss may increase profit by 200 per cent.

Water should be considered as a raw material with a real cost, and wastes in the effluent as primarily lost product with a substantial value in addition to savings in waste treatment or surcharge costs. Because pre-treatment alone will not help dairy plants meet regulations, and because it is expensive and not easily available, a solution might be to use the coagulation/flotation process to remove protein and fats from dairy wastewater, as is common in Europe. The advantage of this system is that it can be installed inside most dairy plants, and thus no extra outside space is needed. Also tanks, lines and pumps can be cleaned in place, which helps eliminate pathogenic organisms. Finally, the sanitary recovery of proteins and fats can yield a premium price.

4.6   Beverage Industry

The Philippine group consisted of two participants from the DENR regulatory branches, the director of the Pollution Control Association, and two industry executives belonging to the Beverage Manufacturers Association. The group's visit was facilitated by an expert consultant with numerous contacts in the industry and a strong familiarity with the Philippine situation, who proved invaluable.

Three soft drink bottling plants were visited. The Coca-Cola facility in Cincinnati, one of the most automated bottling plants in the U.S., used PLC (programmable logic controllers) to control the bottling equipment. Water conservation techniques and waste minimisation practically eliminated wastewater discharge. During production, only 22 gallons/minute of wastewater was discharged. The plant also had the only fully automated warehouse operation in the U.S. The second plant, the Pepsi-Cola facility in Dayton, was an older plant in an older industrial section of the city. Finally, the Coca-Cola Fountain plant in Ontario, California, was a highly automated syrup plant where all high-strength waste streams were collected and transported by a waste hauler to an alcohol-producing facility.

5.0   The Eco Seminars

As part of the follow-up to the Technology Matching Mission, each sector presented an Eco Seminar to their respective industrial group, where they briefed their colleagues on what they had learned from their visits. The seminars were designed by the groups and co-ordinated by the MEIP office in Manila. A MIEP representative presented the background and history of the project, and participants in the groups made presentations on various topics such as: compliance and enforcement; good housekeeping practices; innovative technologies; technical description of waste treatment facilities visited; the role of consultants, universities and community groups; and environmental audits. Copies of documents collected in the U.S. were disseminated, and photographs were shown. Videos made at treatment facilities that permitted filming were also shown.

The Eco Seminars provided an excellent forum for the dissemination of information to industrial groups regarding cleaner production. Some of the issues raised at the seminars were:

- the need for more information on available international technology;
- the need for a business centre for information dissemination, technical assistance, training, audits, etc.;
- the need for a common effluent treatment plant, especially in the electroplating and tannery sectors;
- the need for more industrial estates or relocation assistance for some industries;
- the need for more waste exchange programmes to be established.

In addition,

- a demonstration treatment facility would facilitate increased understanding of cleaner production concepts in industry;
- better co-ordination is required between government and industrial associations regarding environmental policies and programmes; and
- industry supports a phased compliance period for specific circumstances.

6.0   Lessons Learned

The Technology Matching Mission allowed the groups to learn first-hand from plant managers and others how cleaner production practices and technologies improve overall environmental management by cutting down on operating costs (in some instances) and energy consumption. It also helped ensure better compliance and a better relationship with local regulators. The "learning by observing" approach was immediately translated into "learning by doing" upon group members' return to Manila as they disseminated the knowledge within their company and incorporated initial no-cost and low-cost options.

There are several advantages to using a university as a resource centre. First, it operates independently and does not have the problem of being viewed as a regulator. Second, it often has the human resources, laboratories and R&D engineering capabilities needed for problem-solving. Third, it can provide technical assistance at a low cost and maintain an "honest partner" status between industry and government.

The main incentives to invest in pollution treatment and waste minimisation in the Philippines are enforcement of regulations, and economic improvement. When there is a strong, active and well-trained field office with management capabilities, such as the MEIP office in Manila, pollution prevention programmes can be promoted without the need for micro-management from headquarters. The Technology Matching Mission programme provided an excellent opportunity for the MEIP office and the Clean Technology Initiative Team at the World Bank to collaboratively design and manage a waste minimisation/cleaner production programme that strengthened not only the institutional capacity within the Philippines but also the World Bank's efforts to promote pollution prevention and cleaner production in Asia.

Similarly to their industry colleagues, the regulators were able to learn different approaches and mechanisms from state and local regulators who accompanied the group on industrial visits. Again this "learning by observing" approach, followed by "learning by doing", offered an invaluable opportunity for regulators to learn from other regulators what works and what does not, and to participate in an open exchange between the regulators and the regulated.

Dissemination of information is critical to the pollution prevention process. Extensive outreach to companies (often through trade associations) is essential to educate industry and regulators about the latest technologies, new programmes, new regulations, standardisation of chemical processes, etc. Management is often unaware of specific environmental problems, and when the problem surfaces, management doesn't have experience in solving them. It was recommended that government and industrial associations develop a better mechanism for disseminating information regarding environmental policies and programmes.

Pollution prevention is not just a technological challenge, but an institutional one. Support of industry through associations, government agencies, universities and neighbouring communities is essential in order to create the partnerships necessary to achieve the level of awareness and commitment to prevention found in the United States and other industrialised countries.

Training is critical for better environmental management, for both industry and the regulatory agencies. As industry is required to have a Pollution Control Officer (PCO) to deal with regulatory procedures, industry felt that more sector-specific training should be coupled with the issuing of those procedures.

The community component, such as a good neighbour policy between industry and the community, might be reinforced in the Philippines through increased awareness and the use of a community advisory council such as that established by Rohm Haas. Given that the companies on the mission were all in the metro Manila area, companies can play a greater role in fostering that awareness in their community.

APPLYING CLEANER PRODUCTION IN THAILAND

Chaiyod Bunyagidj
Thailand Environment Institute, Thailand

1.0   Background

1.1   Economic Profile

Thailand, traditionally an agricultural country, has experienced rapid economic growth, as characterised by consistently high growth in real Gross Domestic Product (GDP) beginning in the early 1960s. In 1993, the growth of real GDP was estimated at 8.3 per cent, the highest of the ASEAN member countries. In 1994, a modest increase in GDP growth to 8.5 per cent was experienced, resulting in a per capita GDP of $US2,348. Continued high growth rates are forecast through the end of the Thai Seventh National Five-Year Plan (1992-1996).

Thailand's economic growth can be characterised by agriculture and natural resource extraction, rapid industrialisation, rapid and concentrated urbanisation, and increased income and consumption. During the period 1970-1992, industry's share of GDP increased from 16 per cent to approximately 37 per cent, while agriculture's share declined to approximately 15 per cent. Industry's share of exports increased from less than 10 per cent to almost 80 per cent over the same period. The Thai Government's support of the agro and food processing, textile and garment, electronics, metalworking, petrochemical, and iron and steel industries is expected to result in international competitive advantage for these strategic industries.

1.2   Industrial Pollution

Industrial development in Thailand has benefited overall economic development, but has also caused rapid deterioration of natural resources and environmental quality. Urban centres, characterised by high population and industrial densities, generate wastes at rates that have both overwhelmed local governments' abilities to cope and overwhelmed the capacities of the natural ecosystems. A 1993 World Bank study indicated that, for the period 1975-1988, pollution intensity in all forms increased by 1,000 per cent in Thailand, significantly higher than the 800 per cent and 400 per cent increases in the Philippines and Indonesia, respectively. Thailand is faced with the dilemma of how to maintain sustainable economic growth and development while managing the effects of deforestation and natural resources depletion, air and water pollution, and solid and hazardous waste generation and disposal

The Bangkok Metropolitan Region (BMR) is the centre of Thai industrial production, accounting for roughly 52 per cent of the total factories. Due to its high density of population and industrial facilities, the BMR suffers from severe pollution, particularly of air and water. The Thai Ministry of Industry (MOI) has reported that less than 1 per cent of the industries located in the BMR are large-scale, while small and medium-sized enterprises (SMEs) account for roughly 40 per cent of the total. While SMEs may not be the major polluters within industrial subsections, the waste per unit of output produced by SMEs is often higher than that of large industries.

The Thai government has enacted several measures to control industrial pollution and conserve natural resources. These measures are mainly built around "command-and-control" (CAC) regulations. However, in the Thai context CAC has not been sufficient to effect significant reductions in industrial pollution and resource utilisation, primarily due to (i) the slow implementation and enforcement of environmental regulations; (ii) cultural resistance to CAC structures; and (iii) an industrial structure heavily biased towards industries that have historically been pollution-intensive.

2.0   Applying Cleaner Technology Principles in Thailand

Recognition of the limitations of CAC structures in inducing industry to reduce its resource consumption and pollution outputs has prompted the development of several cleaner technology research and demonstration projects in Thailand. The majority of these projects have focused on large industries, but a growing emphasis is being placed on the application of cleaner production technologies in SMEs. This broadening of cleaner technology applications to include SMEs is in response to an increased understanding of the role SMEs play in natural resource use and waste production, resulting in environmental degradation.

Recent research indicates that the high number of SMEs in Thailand, especially in urban areas, creates special problems for pollution prevention. Reasons identified include:

- SMEs tend to utilise poorly maintained and out-of-date technology, resulting in production inefficiencies and high levels of pollution as compared to new technologies;

- SME manager and employee skills tend to be under-developed, resulting in operating inefficiencies and a lack of understanding of potential efficiency improvements;

- SMEs generally do not benefit from modern pollution control technology, as such controls are designed for economies of scale;

- SMEs generally have limited capital with which to finance equipment "upgrades" that incorporate reduced pollution design, and they often have limited access to outside financial resources; and

- SMEs generally have limited access to information detailing types of pollution, the effects of such pollution, existing pollution prevention and control methods, and emerging pollution prevention and control technologies.

3.0   Cleaner Production Activities in Thailand

The Seventh Economic and Social Development Plan (1992-1996) gave environmental issues, particularly those related to the control of industrial pollution, high priority. Within the framework of the Seventh Five-Year Plan, the government set out guiding principles encouraging pollution control and prevention. While providing some guidance for pollution prevention, the majority of the guidelines focused on strengthening current command-and-control mechanisms as part of the "Polluter-Pays Principle." Guidelines encouraging pollution prevention were generally limited to advocating the use of clean technology, waste recycling, and water reuse. The plan did not provide incentives for pollution prevention other than the aforementioned encouragement. Recently enacted environmental legislation has sought to strengthen CAC mechanisms, while putting little emphasis on pollution prevention. Indeed, the regulations establishing the Environment Fund make no provision for funding cleaner production and other pollution prevention activities.

While the Thai government has not enacted a policy giving pollution prevention priority over end-of-pipe treatment schemes, the opportunities for development and expansion of environmental markets is gaining momentum, in part due to the "greening" of developed countries but also due to a similar movement rapidly developing in Thailand. The Government's Board of Investment (BOI) has declared that, along with the markets for pollution control equipment and services, markets for clean technologies for the power industry, energy-efficient products and services, and specialist engineering and consulting services have the highest investment opportunity. However, current BOI investment promotions favour end-of-pipe pollution control technologies

To date, the majority of cleaner production activities in Thailand have been collaborative efforts between foreign aid agencies and Thai universities, non-governmental organisations, and non-profit industrial organisations. International training activities promoting cleaner production and/or pollution prevention have been organised by UNEP, the Asian Productivity Organisation and UNIDO. Technical assistance and demonstration projects have been introduced by the Deutsche Gesellschaft für Technische Zusammenarbeit (GTZ), the Carl Duisberg Gesselchaft-South East Asia Program (CDG-SEAPO), the US Agency for International Development (USAID), the Japan International Co-operation Agency (JICA), UNEP and UNIDO. With the exception of a CDG-SEAPO project, all other cleaner technology assistance projects thus far conducted in Thailand have targeted large industries rather than SMEs. The bilateral assistance programme recently initiated between the Danish Co-operation on Environment and Development (DANCED) and the Thailand Environment Institute (TEI) is the only current project to specifically target SMEs.

Cleaner production assistance and development projects targeting large Thai industries which have been completed thus far include:

- a Federation of Thai Industries' Industrial Environment programme (IEM), funded by USAID, which assisted several industrial sectors including pulp and paper, chemicals and textiles;

- bilateral assistance provided by Germany's GTZ, in co-operation with the Thai Department of Industrial Works (DIW), targeting agriculture and the leather tanning industry;

- the Industrial Pollution Control Application for Small and Medium-Sized Enterprises (IPCA), a CDG project in co-ordination with the DIW, the Asian Institute of Technology,

Chulalongkorn University and Chiangmai University. The IPCA programme targeted SMEs and provided assistance to the electroplating, textile, food and leather tanning industries.

These cleaner production projects can be characterised as small projects having a narrow focus, usually reviewing one production plant per targeted sector. Furthermore, they have tended to focus on only a portion of the resource utilisation and waste management systems in each industry, rather than using a holistic approach to process reviews and to the application of cleaner production techniques to Thai industry. The overall results from these projects have been encouraging, as each has been successful in reducing resource consumption and waste production while also decreasing production costs. However, the short-term focus of the projects needs to be expanded to include long-term, holistic application of cleaner production techniques if Thailand is to experience significant benefits from this approach to pollution prevention.

4.0   Next Steps: Implementing Cleaner Production on a Wide Scale

With the completion of small-scale cleaner production assistance and development projects, Thailand is ready to move on to the next step necessary to integrate cleaner production into the overall ideology and methodology of Thai industry. For large-scale industries, this next step is not expected to be a difficult transition. Large Thai industries are expected to be capable of making the transition to cleaner production with minimal funding assistance from outside sources, relying instead on training and technological assistance. Their greater capital reserves, more skilled management, and relationships with one another provide Thailand's large industries with the tools to evaluate and adapt their processes to cleaner production, as well as to install end-of-pipe treatment systems.

Unlike the large industries, Thailand's SMEs have not formed the nation-wide horizontal linkages associated with formal trade and industry organisations. This lack of linkage to other SMEs creates fundamental barriers to the transfer of knowledge and understanding. For small-scale cleaner production projects, this barrier is not particularly problematic. However, if significant improvements in resource utilisation efficiency and waste minimisation are to occur, these relationships need to be built.

The typical SME owner and management have little understanding of the environmental impacts of pollutants. They often do not understand the environmental impacts of their particular production operations. Further, they are often not aware of the relationship between their resource consumption, production processes, and waste production.

Similarly, SME owners and staff are usually not versed in current production technologies, or in the production economics driving many of the newest production and waste minimisation innovations within their particular industrial sectors. The typical Thai SME is family-owned. Thus, as long as the profitability of production operations remains reasonably high, the owners have little incentive or need to explore resource and waste minimisation techniques.

Thailand's SMEs could play a major role within the overall context of improving the environment, while also strengthening the Thai economy and its businesses. Indeed, Thai SMEs must play a major role if all three goals are to be achieved. To achieve this, cleaner production technologies must be integrated into SME production practices. The integration of cleaner production technologies will require additional technical and financial assistance to develop the necessary awareness and understanding within individual SME sectors and across sectors. Future cleaner production assistance and development projects will need to be holistic in scope, specifically targeting SMEs and incorporating the following:

- wide-scale assistance focused on an industrial sector, in order to develop linkages to individual SME production processes;

- establishment of a regional Cleaner Production Technologies Center to act as an information clearing house, as well as to co-ordinate and provide training, seminars and workshops related to cleaner production applications and evaluation. Further, the Centre would act as a catalyst to establish contact, dialogue and collaboration between Thai industries, academic institutions, NGOs, and the Thai government;

- development of a cleaner production technologies information database containing information specifically applicable to Thai SMEs that is both accessible and easily understood by SME owners and staff;

- programmes to educate SME owners and staff about types of pollution and their resulting effects;

- financial assistance to develop "seed" cleaner production applications for a number of similar production processes;

- long-term support and evaluation of applied cleaner production technologies, in order to determine individual and overall effectiveness and to instil an awareness of and sense of the value of cleaner production benefits, both environmental and economic, in SME owners and staff; and

- catalysing and co-ordinating networks between SMEs within their industrial sectors and SMEs in other sectors, between NGOs and academic institutions and SMEs, and between government pollution control agencies and SMEs.

With continued technical and financial assistance for the application of cleaner production technologies by development agencies, and active co-operation between Thai industry, particularly SMEs, and academic institutions, NGOs and the Thai government, Thailand can move towards sustainable resource utilisation and environmentally friendly industrial production while maintaining economic development.

REFERENCES

Brandon, C. and Ramankutty, R., 1993: *Towards an Environmental Strategy for Asia*. World Bank Discussion Paper No. 224. Washington, D.C.

Hampel, R., Oberndörfer, R. and Srichai, W.,1994: *Industrial Pollution Control Applications for Small- and Medium-Scale Industries in Thailand (IPCA): An End-term Evaluation of a CDG-SEAPO Project.*

Høgsted, N., 1995: *Clean Technology in Small and Medium Sized Enterprises in Thailand.* Copenhagen Business School.

Joint Public-Private Consultative Committee, 1995: *Thailand Update* No. 35.

Office of the Board of Investments, 1993: *Key Investment Indicators in Thailand* (September).

CHINA'S CLEANER PRODUCTION POLICY GOALS

Wang Dehui
National Environmental Protection Agency, China

1.0   Introduction

Environmental protection is one of China's fundamental national policy goals. In tandem with accelerating its economic development, China has also strengthened the framework for environmental protection and pollution control. In some cities urban environmental quality indicators indicate an improvement, but overall the situation remains almost unchanged; because of rapid economic development and the growth in the country's population, pollution and ecological deterioration are serious problems. In many rural areas, environmental pollution and ecological damage are alarming.

To promote sustainable development in China, the Government prepared an "Environmental Action Plan of China 1991-2000" in which a set of environmental targets to be achieved by the year 2000 were established. These targets reinforce China's commitment to protect its environment and natural resources. For example, one target is to limit the total amount of discharge of waste gas, wastewater and solid waste by strengthening policies, implementing and enforcing new regulations, and increasing environmental investment.

The adoption of cleaner production and waste minimisation is a major tool to support the realisation of established environmental targets. Cleaner production's focus on pollution prevention highlights the potential opportunities for an enterprise to simultaneously improve its economic performance through more efficient raw materials use and production processes, and raise its environmental performance through lowering emissions of wastes and pollutants. In this context, there exist many no- or low-cost measures which Chinese industry might deploy to reap such "win-win" economic and environmental benefits.

2.0   China's Cleaner Production Policy Goals

China is presently developing a comprehensive cleaner production policy. Some elements of the policy already exist, and will be strengthened, but many other elements need to be established. The following provides a summary of the cleaner production policy goals:

- Cleaner production should be promoted as a strategic approach that supports the achievement of national economic and social development goals. In preparing development plans, individual enterprises should also develop an environmental protection action plan that not only ensures compliance with relevant environmental regulations but also identifies opportunities to implement cleaner production measures.

- In order to meet the established environmental targets, attention will be given to restructuring the industry sector, accelerating technological renovation and modernisation, and setting a deadline for compliance by major polluters. Economic incentives, such as giving loan priority to enterprises which undertake technological improvements and cleaner production actions, will also be used. To enforce the deadline for compliance by major polluters, a range of options are available: authority to close enterprises, or to stop production, or to require relocation. During the period 1985-1990, the State set deadlines for pollution control targets for a first group of 160 enterprises; from 1991 to 1995, deadlines were applied to a further 140 enterprises. From 1996 to 2000, deadlines will be established for another 121 enterprises.

- For any construction project, an Environmental Impact Assessment must be prepared. This should encourage enterprises to adopt cleaner production and waste minimisation as an effective cost-saving and regulatory compliance measure. Figures indicate that in 1994 EIAs were prepared for 62.5 per cent of all construction projects.

- Any construction project must implement the system called the "Three Simultaneous Steps". This system specifies that facilities for preventing and controlling pollution must be designed and built, and become operational, simultaneously with the development of the principal project. The objective of the system is to ensure that enterprises install appropriate equipment to control and treat pollution, implement cleaner production, and protect the environment. In 1994, 87.3 per cent of all construction projects met the requirements of this system.

- A preferential tax policy that encourages the adoption of cleaner technologies and more efficient use of natural resources should be implemented. For example, in 1994 the State Administration of Taxation stipulated that "Enterprises using wastewater, waste gas or solid wastes as their main raw materials should pay reduced, or be exempt from, income tax within five years." In 1994, the rate of reuse of industrial solid wastes was 41.8 per cent; the value of products produced using wastewater, waste gas and solid waste as raw materials was 15.73 billion yuan; and the profit from sales of these products was 4.19 billion yuan.

- Priority should be given to approved domestic and foreign investment projects which employ cleaner production and waste minimisation. Enterprises adopting cleaner production have the possibility to apply for domestic or foreign loans.

- Cleaner production demonstration projects should be promoted nation-wide. At present there are 27 enterprises undertaking demonstration projects; these projects are funded by a World Bank loan.

- There should be legislation, policies and management systems which support cleaner production and which reflect international developments in this field.

- A domestic eco-labelling system should be established. The objective is to encourage enterprises to adopt cleaner production techniques in order to produce environmentally friendly products. So far, eleven products have been awarded an "environmental label".

- International information exchange and policy dialogue on cleaner production should be enhanced. This will enable Chinese environmental policy-makers and enterprise managers to learn from the experience of their foreign colleagues and to promote the harmonization of China's CP policy with international trends.

- International co-operation in the transfer of cleaner production technologies should be promoted.

- There should be strict implementation of relevant international environmental agreements to which China is a party, such as the Montreal Protocol and its amendments, the Framework Convention on Climate Change, the Basel Convention, and the Convention on Biological Diversity.

POLICY APPROACHES TO PROMOTE CLEANER PRODUCTION IN ARGENTINA, BRAZIL AND CHILE

Joachim von Amsberg[1]
Latin America and the Caribbean Region Department, The World Bank

1.0   Introduction

In the search for more cost-effective means of achieving tightening environmental objectives, companies and governments all over the world have come to realise that pollution control through end-of-pipe treatment is only one of several options for the reduction of pollution. The terms "cleaner production", "waste minimisation", and "pollution prevention" are being used to describe those options for the reduction of negative environmental effects of production that go beyond the end-of-pipe treatment of waste flows and increase production efficiency, reduce the generation of wastes, apply intrinsically cleaner technologies, or recycle substances that were previously discarded as wastes.

Cleaner production (CP) refers to a very heterogeneous group of pollution reduction approaches. At the one extreme, CP includes many good-housekeeping measures that reduce waste and can often be implemented with no or very little investment. At the other extreme, CP also includes highly capital-intensive innovations in production technology that require the replacement of an entire production line or plant. Moreover, the boundary between pollution prevention and traditional end-of-pipe pollution control is sometimes blurred, for example when end-of-treatment leads to the recovery of substances that have significant value or can be reused in the production process.

CP has recently received much attention because environmental audits in many different companies have shown the existence of ample opportunities to implement measures that, at the same time, reduce waste and generate positive financial returns (win-win solutions). However, it is important to emphasise that not all changes towards CP are financially profitable. Even though many examples show that CP approaches are more cost-effective than traditional approaches to pollution control, this does not need to be true in every sector and every individual case.

CP should be viewed as a welcome addition to the menu of options for pollution reduction, from which the least-cost approach for a specific industry and a specific situation needs to be selected.

---

[1]   The findings, interpretations and conclusions of this paper represent the personal views of the author and should not be attributed to the World Bank, its Executive Board of Directors, its member countries, or any of the institutions which kindly provided information.

A separate focus on CP appears justified since CP approaches have often been neglected in the past, and expensive end-of-pipe treatment solutions have been applied in situations where low-cost CP solutions for pollution prevention would have been available.

This paper discusses the experiences with, and the effects of, government policies in Argentina, Brazil and Chile that influence the adoption of CP. It addresses not only the direct policies that governments have adopted to advance the implementation of CP, but also the indirect effects of environmental and other policies on the environmental technology choices by enterprises. The paper is based on the premise that the objective is the achievement of an agreed environmental objective at the least social cost, and not the adoption of CP for its own sake.

To understand the effects of government action on the choices of polluters, it is important to appreciate the alternative courses of action open to the polluters. Companies in non-compliance with environmental regulations will usually take one or more of the following actions:

- they can adopt good-housekeeping measures and implement changes that require little or no investment. These measures usually involve some operating costs, and they may or may not pay for themselves;

- they can adopt process changes that often require major investments. These investments may or may not pay for themselves, often depending on the remaining economic lifetime of equipment to be replaced;

- they can adopt end-of-pipe treatment technologies that usually have a negative financial return, since they don't have any financial benefits;

- they can decide to do nothing if the risk of enforcement or the level of penalties imposed does not justify the cost of the least-cost pollution reduction measure; and

- finally, they can close their business if none of the available alternative options allows continued profitable operation of the firm.

The choice that polluting firms make between these options will depend on the nature of the business, on available resources, and on government regulations. Relevant factors regarding the nature of the business include profitability and size, position in the industry life cycle, rate of capital renewal, and possible demand from customers for environmentally friendly production. Resources that are critical for company choices include access to and cost of capital for investment, managerial capacity and attention to pollution problems, and the cost and availability of technical know-how. Finally, the nature of government regulations and their enforcement will determine the feasibility and desirability of different options.

In the case of major process changes, timing is an additional critical factor for the adoption of CP. While a change to a cleaner technology may have low costs or even significant benefits if it is introduced at the time old equipment is to be retired, the same technology change would be associated with very large opportunity costs if it were forced on a company after it had just invested in "dirty" equipment with a long remaining lifetime. As a result, CP approaches are more easily adopted in industries with high growth rate and fast capital renewal. Since the age of equipment varies within any industry, regulatory flexibility is a key factor in the promotion of CP. A company that is allowed to wait, or pay for waiting, until its equipment is due for renewal is more likely to opt for a CP approach than a company that is forced to achieve a particular standard at a specified time.

A government that wants to promote the consideration of CP approaches for achieving the most cost-effective path towards an environmental objective can choose from two broad groups of instruments: those for the establishment and enforcement of an appropriate regulatory framework, and those for actively assisting industry in their efforts to reduce pollution. Governments have, among others, the following instruments at their disposal:

- *Pricing policies* for inputs associated with pollution are critical. Water and energy are two obvious examples of inputs whose appropriate pricing can create significant incentives for measures that increase energy and water use efficiency and at the same time reduce the associated pollution. In many cases, environmental taxes or charges applied to these inputs can be an indirect policy instrument that is effective and relatively simple to administer. On the other hand, subsidies on these inputs can seriously distort incentives against CP approaches.

- *Environmental regulation* can hinder or advance the introduction of CP. Flexible instruments that leave polluters freedom to choose between technologies and to choose the time of adoption will give polluters the option to apply CP. Rigid instruments, on the other hand, often bias choices in favour of end-of-pipe control technology. Economic instruments, such as charges or tradable permits, are by design flexible. Command-and-control instruments such as emission standards are by design more rigid, but they can be applied such that they provide some flexibility to polluters.

- *Financing for the costs of pollution reduction* can be offered to overcome limited access to capital markets, especially by smaller firms. If directed credit lines are targeted at the right firms and include the flexibility to finance CP investments, they can be important instruments in an environment of shallow or distorted capital markets. If not properly designed, however, they may bias companies towards capital-intensive options and against more labour-intensive housekeeping solutions.

- *Technical assistance* provided or financed by the government can assist companies through training, pilot projects for technology transfer, studies of life cycle impacts, information dissemination, environmental audits, assistance in obtaining environmental certification, etc.

- *Information policy* is proving to be an increasingly important instrument. Mandatory release of plant-level pollution data can generate market-driven changes in the behaviour of polluting firms. Similarly, the dissemination of information on CP options can build up market pressure on polluting companies.

Looking beyond direct government policies on environment and technology, broader government actions have important effects on the adoption of CP. Macroeconomic policies will determine the framework in which companies make their decisions. Policies that favour investments, for example through deepening of capital markets, will improve access to capital required for CP investments. Similarly, the trade regime will influence the extent of technology transfer and the effect of demand by external markets on domestic environmental performance.

2.0   Country Experiences

Over the last decade, Argentina, Brazil, and Chile have undergone a significant macroeconomic transition that has profound implications for the structure of their industrial sectors, their choices of technologies, and their behaviour towards environmental regulations. Reforms aimed at increasing the role of the private sector, opening the economy to international competition, reducing the burden of government regulation, and fighting inflation have been adopted in all three countries. While Chile adopted these measures in the mid-eighties, Argentina has implemented a radical reform programme only since 1991. Brazil began some reforms in 1990 and implemented more fundamental measures in 1994. In general, these reforms are important since they set the economic framework within which companies make their technology choices. Moreover, macroeconomic stability appears to be a precondition for serious attention by policy-makers to the implementation of environmental policies.

In all three countries, the orientation towards export markets and the degree of foreign participation has increased. Regional free trade agreements are likely to strengthen this trend. Chile is negotiating membership in NAFTA, a process which implies close scrutiny of Chile's environmental record and policies. Argentina, Brazil, Paraguay and Uruguay have joined in a free-trade agreement (MERCOSUR), with which Chile is also negotiating association. Harmonization of environmental policies is a continuing theme in the MERCOSUR discussions.

Some basic indicators for the three countries are shown in Table 1.

The three countries have established more or less comprehensive systems of environmental regulation. However, the effective implementation and enforcement of regulations is slow. Typical common problems include the focus on command-and-control type regulation, underfunding of environmental institutions, lack of basic information, overlap in institutional responsibility, insufficient enforcement and penalties, and contradictions and excessive complexity in environmental regulations.[2] While Brazil and Argentina have highly decentralized public administrations, with resulting differences in the environmental policy of different provinces/states, Chile has a centralised government system with a higher degree of homogeneity within the country.

This section of the paper does not attempt to present a comprehensive survey of environmental policies in the three countries. Rather, some very selective experience with interesting implications for the adoption of CP is presented. For each country, the discussion begins with a broad introduction to the economic situation and the major pollution problems, followed by a review of environmental policies in general and experiences with government initiatives to promote cleaner production in particular. Unfortunately, the specific experience with cleaner production in the surveyed countries is not very extensive and not very well-documented. In particular, reviews of government environmental programmes often do not explicitly distinguish between CP and more traditional pollution control approaches. The analysis of national policies is, thus, necessarily tentative and based on incomplete information.

---

[2]   See Margulis, 1994.

Table 1: Basic Indicators for the Three Countries

	Argentina	Brazil	Chile
1993 per capita GNP			
in market prices	$7,220	$2,930	$3,170
in purchasing power	$8,250	$5,370	$8,400
1980-93 annual growth	-0.5%	0.3%	3.6%
Population			
total (million)	33.8	156.5	13.8
of which urban	87%	71%	84%
Population with access to safe water	64%	96%	86%
Energy efficiency (GDP per kg oil equivalent)	$5.6	$4.9	$3.5
Gross domestic investment as share of GDP	18%	19%	26%
Merchandise exports as share of GNP	5.4%	8.4%	21.3%

Source: World Bank, 1995a

2.1   Argentina[3]

The Macroeconomic Framework

After a period of hyperinflation, macroeconomic instability, and inward-looking economic management, Argentina has since 1991 implemented an economic reform programme that has drastically changed the macroeconomic environment. Inflation has been reduced to less than 4 per cent annually, trade has been liberalised, and output and productivity have increased remarkably. Also,

---

[3]   This section draws from information kindly provided by the Instituto Nacional de Ciencia y Técnicas Hidricas (INCYTH) and from World Bank, 1995: *Argentina: Managing Environmental Pollution – Issues and Options,* Washington, D.C.

recent growth and investment levels have been high. A stagnant, protected, and relatively old industrial sector is now rapidly modernising.

The legislated dollar parity of the national currency eliminates the possibility of promoting exports through devaluation. Thus, increased focus is being placed on increasing the competitiveness of the industrial sector through innovation and cost-savings. At the same time, financial markets are still weak and thin and shaken by the recent financial crisis in Mexico. The weakness of financial markets and the heavy burden of economic adjustment on small and medium-sized enterprises (SMEs) often make it difficult for SMEs to obtain credit for investment from market sources.

Over 60 per cent of Argentina's industrial production is concentrated in Gran Buenos Aires. Argentina's most important industries are agriculture-based. Within these industries, tanning and meat processing are important sectors with significant pollution problems. Among other industrial activities, there are serious pollution problems in manufacturing (for example, in textiles, metal processing and electroplating) and petroleum (oil extraction and refineries).

Major Pollution Problems

As a result of low population density, favourable geographic conditions, and a well-educated population, overall pollution damages in Argentina are only modest. On the other hand, pollution problems are more serious than one would expect in a country of Argentina's upper-middle levels of income and economic development. Industrial activity is concentrated along the Paraná and Plate Rivers, generating pollution problems in Gran Buenos Aires, Rosario and Santa Fe, as well as some other urban centres such as Córdoba, Mendoza and Tucumán.

Industrial discharges are a major source of air, water and solid waste pollution in Argentina. Industrial sources account for nearly half of wastewater discharges which are responsible for the poor quality of rivers and groundwater in Gran Buenos Aires. In a few areas, industrial effluent is reported to be the dominant source of pollution. The Río Santiago in La Plata, Río Salí in Tucumán, and some irrigation channels in Mendoza are seriously contaminated with industrial effluent. In Rosario, industrial effluent from the upstream suburbs on the Paraná River have adversely affected the operation of the main water treatment plant.

The heavy pollution of rivers and creeks, as well as groundwater, in Gran Buenos Aires is particularly serious since it affects about 4 million people, primarily in low-income neighbourhoods, who are not connected to public water supply and receive their drinking water from individual wells. Not much is known about air pollution, but there appears to be no large-scale problem in Buenos Aires. The uncontrolled disposal of hazardous wastes is a potential problem of significant scale.

Environmental Policy

During the last decade, governments were predominantly occupied by macroeconomic concerns and environmental management was not a high priority. Decades of neglect and lack of co-ordination have led to an inconsistent and confusing regulatory and institutional framework for environmental management. The most critical constraint for improving the management of pollution in Argentina is the absence of clear institutional responsibility for environmental management and the lack of effective enforcement. Some of the government institutions charged with administering environmental policies are still weak, their responsibilities are fragmented, and enforcement is inadequate in many areas. The institutional framework for environmental management involves a web of overlapping national, provincial and municipal agencies. The resulting unusually complex system of laws, regulations and authorities has led to unevenness and uncertainty in the enforcement of regulations, and opened many opportunities for polluters to evade compliance with environmental objectives.

In principle, most environmental matters are the responsibility of the provinces unless expressly delegated to the national government. Only under specific circumstances can the national government assume authority for particular environmental issues. At the provincial level, the capacity for the management of environmental problems differs widely. While several of the more industrialised provinces have rather advanced environmental management systems, others lag far behind.

Recently, the national government has taken important steps towards more active national environmental policy. The national organisation of environment policy centres around the Secretaría de Recursos Naturales y Ambiente y Humano (SRNyAH: Secretariat for Natural Resources and the Human Environment), which was created in 1991 and will soon be upgraded into a fully fledged environment ministry. SRNyAH is working on a reorganisation of environmental policy-making in Argentina, but it has not yet had enough time to deliver in many areas. Environmental authority at the national level includes, among others, responsibility for inter-provincial waterways (i.e. the major rivers).

At the level of national-provincial relations, SRNyAH hosts the Consejo Federal de Medio Ambiente (COFEMA), the forum in which all provinces and the national government discuss common themes. In 1993, SRNyAH successfully negotiated an environmental pact ("Pacto Ambiental Federal") with all the provinces. This pact is a political instrument that signals the willingness to co-ordinate provincial and national efforts. After ratification by the provincial congresses, SRNyAH will have to design minimum environmental standards as a result of the latest constitutional changes.

Major federal policies include the passing of the Hazardous Waste Law 24.051 in 1992. This law covers the generation, use, transport, treatment, and final disposal of hazardous wastes and establishes a registry for generators of such wastes. The implementation of the hazardous waste law, however, is constrained by the absence of any approved hazardous waste treatment facility in Gran Buenos Aires. Environmental Impact Assessment is mandated for new projects in several, but not all, provinces. Various emission standards exist at the federal and the provincial levels.

Government attention has focused on projects to clean up some of the worst polluted surface waters in Gran Buenos Aires, which have effectively become open sewers. One of the most polluted local streams, the Río Matanza-Riachuelo, receives discharges from both domestic and industrial sources (some 20,000 plants, of which nearly two-thirds do not have treatment facilities while only 3 per cent of the remaining plants regularly operate them). Another stream, the Río Reconquista, runs through 14 municipalities, receiving direct discharges from 7,500 industrial plants and indirect discharges (through sewers and drainage pipes) from an additional 12,000 plants. Domestic discharges are also an important source of pollution. The government is currently preparing a master plan for the clean-up of the Río Matanza-Riachuelo and is implementing an IDB-supported project for the clean-up of the Río Reconquista.

In 1980, an attempt was made to introduce discharge fees for industrial effluent (Decree 2125/1980: Cuotas de Resarcimiento por Contaminación). In practice, the fees were never applied on a wide basis and the system was modified in 1989 to lower the level of fees and to revise the penalties imposed on enterprises exceeding the maximum allowable discharge. Environmental groups sued the government on the grounds that the Cuota de Resarcimiento amounted to a license to pollute beyond legal limits. The court declared the decree unconstitutional on legal grounds.

The recent privatisation of the water concession for Gran Buenos Aires is likely to significantly change the incentives faced by those polluters discharging into the sewage system. The new private concession ("Aguas Argentinas") has been taking seriously its obligation to monitor the quality of such discharges and to report violations of the sewer discharge regulations. The company also has an incentive to charge prices for water consumption and wastewater discharges by businesses which cover the marginal costs of supply and treatment.

Cleaner Production Developments

The effect that the opening of the economy and the modernisation of industry is having on CP approaches in Argentina is particularly interesting. Among the usual heavily polluting industries, the paper and pulp industry provides an interesting example of the contrast in environmental performance within one sector (see Box 1). The largest pulp mill in Argentina is equipped with modern technology and has been steadily improving its environmental performance in order to expand its position in environmentally sensitive markets. Other pulp mills are older, less oriented to international markets, and have a much worse environmental record. They are coming under increasing pressure to rationalise production and facilities. The result is likely to be the emergence of a m ore efficient, though perhaps smaller, industry with a much higher level of environmental performance. A similar process has been occurring in the steel industry with the additional element of privatisation.

Another major problem area is the oil refining and petrochemical sector. While the recent privatisation of the state petroleum company YPF (Yacimientos Petroliferos Fiscales) did not address the company's environmental problems, there are good reasons to expect that changes in incentives combined with improved access to capital markets following privatisation should bring a gradual improvement in the company's environmental performance. A significant component of the environmental damage caused by refineries and petrochemical plants is the consequence of poor maintenance and management of equipment and operating processes, which represents a loss of valuable feedstocks or products. The economic payback for addressing these problems is large, so that well-managed private firms have a substantial incentive to reduce leaks, recycle water, recover materials, and adopt other changes which will mitigate environmental damage. Initial attention, however, is likely to focus on reducing current levels of emissions rather than on cleaning up the legacy of damage caused by past emissions and waste disposal. In due course a major clean-up effort will be required, but at present there is no satisfactory basis for establishing priorities or for allocating the liability for the costs involved.

With respect to explicit government incentives encouraging choice of cleaner technologies, vehicle fuel pricing represents an interesting example. In 1985, a programme of tax exemptions was introduced to promote the replacement of petroleum fuels by compressed natural gas (CNG). The programme was quickly adopted by mid-sized trucks and taxis. By the end of 1994, 210,000 vehicles in Gran Buenos Aires had been converted to CNG. To date, the CNG programme has led to the substitution of about 12 per cent of diesel use in Gran Buenos Aires, which should correspond to a 6 per cent reduction in particulates emissions.

Box 1: The Case of Argentina's Pulp and Paper Industry

Argentina's pulp and paper industry provides a classic example of the challenge and opportunities associated with the liberalisation of trade. From one perspective it is an industry in deep crisis, with too many inefficient, uncompetitive plants which have an extremely poor environmental record. On the other hand, there are a number of firms which are able to compete successfully on local and world markets and whose environmental performance is exemplary.

The industry's basic problem is that its plants are old and too small. The average capacity of both pulp and paper plants is less than 30 per cent of the equivalent averages for Brazil and Chile. Throughout the 1970s and 1980s the industry enjoyed a protected market, so that few firms invested to adopt modern pulp and paper technologies. The leading firms in 1970 – Celulosa Argentina, Ledesma, Papel Misionera – have been largely displaced by new entrants (Alto Parana, Papel Prensa, and Papel Tucuman). It is these new firms that have been responsible for the substantial growth in production and decline in imports from 1970 to 1990. Subsequent trade liberalisation has put extreme pressure on most of the older plants – especially those producing paper – as a result of competition from Brazilian imports and the depressed state of the world pulp and paper market during the early 1990s. Paper imports increased from 5 per cent of the domestic market in 1990 to 33 per cent in 1993. Only Alto Parana, which only produces kraft pulp and much of whose output is exported, has a plant of sufficient capacity to gain the full benefits of economies of scale and modern technology, though Papel Prensa and Papel Tucuman are reasonably placed, especially as paper producers.

The environmental performance of the older plants is largely deplorable. Many of the older paper plants are based in Gran Buenos Aires and discharge wastewater with only limited treatment. Their reliance upon outdated technology also means that they produce much greater volumes of wastes than do more modern plants. In 1992, the average level of BOD discharges was 24 kg/tonne for paper and 32 kg/tonne for pulp, very similar to the averages for 1975 despite the much better performance of Alto Parana and the other new entrants. The industry association AFCP has agreed a target average of 12-16 kg of BOD per tonne, to be achieved within ten years. This will still be much higher than current standards for new plants in the US and Canada of 5.5-7.5 kg/tonne. By closing down old, uncompetitive, and heavily polluting plants, especially in the paper sector, it should be possible to reduce average emissions of BOD per tonne much more rapidly.

Alto Parana stands out for its environmental performance. At the beginning of the 1990s its emissions were as good or better than those from Scandinavian kraft pulp producers. Since then, it has invested to change its production process to rely more upon chlorine-free bleaching, to reduce its wastewater discharges to match best practice in the industry, and to obtain ISO 14000 certification. The purpose of these changes has been to take advantage of the demand for "environmentally friendly" pulp in Germany and other northern European markets. This is a clear case in which industrial restructuring brought about by trade liberalisation should bring large environmental benefits.

Source: Bercovichand and Chidiak, 1994.

While, under ideal operating conditions, CNG-fuelled vehicles produce less NO_x, CO, hydrocarbons, particulates and lead than gasoline-fuelled vehicles, and less particulates than diesel-fuelled vehicles, there is concern about possibly higher levels of NO_x emissions compared to conventional fuels under real-life operating conditions. On balance, however, based on the scant information, the programme appears to have beneficial effects since there is likely to be a greater health cost attributable to lead and particulate pollution than to NO_x.

Argentina has a complex system of government-run and government-supported science and technology institutions. While a large share of these efforts are directed at basic research, there are also significant efforts in applied technology, of which some are directed at CP approaches. Some of these efforts have been criticised as not sufficiently integrated with applications in the private sector. Projects with important environmental implications have been undertaken by INTI, the national industrial technology institute, and INTA, the agricultural technology agency (for example, concerning less polluting technologies in meat processing). INTI belongs to the Industry Secretariat and provides assistance for product certification, technology transfer, and training. INTI operates sectoral research centres for those industrial sectors that are of most importance for the Argentine economy.

INCYTH, the national institute for water science and technology, is part of the National Environment Secretariat and is engaged in several projects aimed at promoting CP. These initiatives include the optimisation of water use and wastewater reuse in manufacturing, waste minimisation in manufacturing, and non-conventional wastewater treatment. Among the specific projects that have been undertaken are: wastewater reuse in tanneries; reuse and treatment of winery wastewater; and waste minimisation in the metal finishing industry. Together with the Pan-American Center for Health Engineering and Environmental Sciences, INCYTH has recently published handbooks for waste minimisation in hospitals as well as the metal finishing, tanning and textile industries.

The Industry Secretariat of the Economics Ministry offers technical assistance and lines of credit directed at SMEs for investment and technology innovation. In fact, these credit lines constitute one of the few financing sources available to SMEs in Argentina, and the government is currently the major domestic source of term credit for SMEs. While these programmes are primarily directed at the competitiveness and the export orientation of SMEs, some of them are directed specifically at technology transfer and are available for investments in cleaner technologies. The Technological Upgrading Program (FONTAR) makes a total of $80 million available for technology upgrading in the manufacturing sector. Projects being proposed for support under this programme include those for recycling of effluents from the tanneries industry.

2.2   Brazil[4]

The Macroeconomic Framework

Following the debt crisis of the 1980s, Brazil suffered a period of economic stagnation and high inflation. Investment was reduced and per capita output stagnated during the 1985-93 period. Since

---

[4]   This section draws from comprehensive information kindly provided by the Companhia de Tecnologia de Saneamento Ambiental (CETESB), the Federação das Indústrias do Estado de São Paulo (FIESP), the Fundação Estadual de Engenharia do Meio Ambiente (FEEMA), and the Brazilian Federal Ministries of Environment and Foreign Relations.

early 1994, the government has implemented a carefully designed stabilisation programme leading to drastically lower inflation and the first signs of increased economic activity, including higher investment.

Brazil has a large and mature industrial sector that, over a long period, has been promoted through an inward-looking industrialisation policy including protection from external competition and state-led investment. Subsidies for energy and resource-intensive industries (aluminium, steel, pulp and paper, and petrochemicals) contributed to the rapid development of heavy, but also dirty, industries.

As a result of pervasive regulation of business activities, the cost of doing business in Brazil was high and many businesses were not internationally competitive. Since 1990, a programme of deregulation and significant trade liberalisation has been introduced, leading to increasing international integration of the Brazilian economy. Subsidies and other government interventions have been phased out. Together with recent macroeconomic adjustments, these reforms are now rapidly transforming and modernising the Brazilian economy towards more openness and competitiveness.

Major Pollution Problems

Serious industrial pollution problems exist in many Brazilian states. In some areas, contamination levels are serious enough to affect major portions of the population, either through unhealthy air quality, contaminated drinking water, or exposure to hazardous waste. In addition, untreated industrial discharges affect the health and safety of workers (for example, in the mining industry) as well as causing destruction of aquatic and terrestrial habitats. The specific nature of each state's industrial pollution profile varies with the composition of its industry. Overall, the full range of industrial pollution sources are present: from heavy industries, such as steel, petroleum, petrochemicals, fertilisers, and coal mining, to production of intermediate and consumer goods, such as food, textiles, leather and metal finishing.

The highly urbanised south and southeastern regions of Brazil occupy only 19 per cent of the territory, but they contain about 60 per cent of the population. With São Paulo and Rio de Janeiro, Brazil also has two of the world's largest "megacities", with a concentration of serious pollution problems. São Paulo contains the largest industrial aggregation within South America, including a large automotive industry. In São Paulo and other major cities, industrial growth has led to severe air and water pollution levels that, in São Paulo, have required health warnings on most days. Some significant improvements have, however, taken place in recent years. The high income disparity and lack of urban services, such as water supply, sewage collection and sewage treatment, aggravate urban environmental problems and their effects, in particular on the poor population.

Environmental Policy

Comprehensive environmental policy has a longer history in Brazil than in the other surveyed countries, starting in 1973 with the establishment of a National Environment Secretariat in the Ministry of the Interior. In 1981, a federal framework law established the National Environment System (SISNAMA), which includes the agencies and regulations at the national and sub-national level. The Brazilian Institute of the Environment and Renewable Natural Resources (IBAMA) was created in 1989. In 1994, a national Ministry of Environment, Water Resources and the Legal Amazon was established. The national environmental agencies have mostly focused on "green" environmental issues of land use and natural resource protection. Some ambient quality guidelines and emission standards have also been established at the federal level.

During the 1970s, several state environmental agencies were established. Some of them quickly acquired significant capacity and experience, such as CETESB in São Paulo and FEEMA in Rio de Janeiro. Notably, the effectiveness of the state environmental agencies reflects the degree of industrialisation in the various states, and in many states actual capacity is still very limited. Unfortunately, even some of the better state agencies experienced a decline during the macroeconomic crises of the 1980s and early 1990s, as budgets were cut and government attention focused on macroeconomic management. Today, most of the legislation for environmental management and pollution control as well as the day-to-day aspects of environmental policy fall under the responsibility of the states.

The more industrialised states of Brazil have acquired considerable experience in the management of pollution policies. Most policy instruments are based on command-and-control regulation supplemented by a variety of credit lines and tax incentives for pollution control investments. The main instruments of pollution control policies are zoning, emission standards, and a licensing process, which in turn is based on a variety of industry-specific emission standards. Environmental Impact Assessment was introduced at the national level in 1986. Responsibility for the implementation of the Environmental Impact Assessment process is mainly delegated to the states. However, the federal government – through IBAMA – is in charge of licensing and supervising the Environmental Impact Assessment process for particular projects and activities.

More recently, broader discussions on the use of economic instruments in environmental policy have begun. Early examples of the use of economic instruments include the industrial sewage fees based on pollution load that have been, or are being, implemented in some states. In São Paulo, a sewage fee has been in effect since 1983 and was revised in 1990. These charges have led to a very significant drop in pollution loads in several sectors. A similar pollution charge is in effect in Rio de Janeiro and has been proposed in the Minas Gerais and Paraná states.

Cleaner Production Developments

The transition of the Brazilian economy to more private sector involvement, deregulation, and openness has had important consequences for environmental management. Several government-owned companies used to be among the largest sources of industrial pollution (for example, PETROBRAS, CVRD, and CSN, the largest steel mill in South America), and state environmental agencies had very limited enforcement authority over them. In some cases privatisation has led to significantly better environmental performance, due to more effective enforcement of environmental regulations and mobilisation of private capital for environmental improvements.

One of the main channels for government promotion of CP is directed credit. BNDES, the development bank of the national government, used to be the main source of long-term credit in Brazil. Since 1986, BNDES has offered credit lines for industrial pollution control. Environmental lending by BNDES, under a variety of programmes, increased from $202 million in 1990 to $304 million in 1994. Projects eligible for financing include end-of-pipe controls, process changes, and recycling/waste recovery projects. Financing of investments is complemented by financing of EIA's and staff training. Beyond its strictly environmental programmes, BNDES finances industrial investment in areas such as energy efficiency. Environmental projects constituted 6 per cent of BNDES lending in 1993, with the expectation of reaching 20 per cent in ten years.

The government is supporting quality management through information dissemination and a large-scale training programme. A government finance agency, FINEP, offers financing through its

Linhea de Apoio a Gestão de Qualidade to assist companies to set up a quality management programme. Lending under this financing facility increased from $6 million in 1992 to $16 million in 1993 and reached $62 million in 1994. Together with other FINEP programmes that support technological innovation, total FINEP lending in 1994 was $285 million. FINEP is currently creating a new financing line that would support environmental audits, environmental life cycle analysis, environmental management systems, environmental certification, and evaluation of environmental performance. One of the key objectives of this financing line is to support SMEs in obtaining ISO certification.

A wide range of other government institutions is involved in promoting cleaner production in Brazil. For example, the Instituto de Pesquisas Tecnológicas (IPT, a technological research institute of the São Paulo state government) has a variety of research activities with the objective of encouraging pollution control and integrated pollution management. IPT has its own laboratory for the treatment of industrial effluents, a research project for environmentally friendly materials such as biodegradable plastics, and analysis of recycling projects. IPT is increasingly directing its activities at SMEs.

The first National Center for Clean Technologies in Latin America will be established in the south of Brazil in Porto Alegre (Rio Grande do Sul). The centre, which is a joint initiative of UNEP, UNIDO and the state industry federation, will have an initial investment of $440,000. This centre will promote technology transfer through pilot and demonstration projects, environmental audits, training, and information dissemination. A particular focus will be to assist companies in receiving ISO 14000 certification. After three years, the objective is that the centre will be self-financing through charging consultant fees.

Brazil takes an unusually active interest in the development of international standards such as ISO 9000 and now ISO 14000. The adoption of ISO 9000 certification for total quality management is proceeding very rapidly in Brazil. While about 600 organisations (about 90 per cent of which are in industry) met ISO 9000 standards in March 1995, it was expected that 1,300 organisations would be certified by the end of 1995. At the end of 1994, 80 per cent of all certified firms in Latin America were located in Brazil. Industrial sectors with the highest participation are the electric, chemical and metal industries. Clearly, the recent opening of the Brazilian economy has provided the major push for companies to adopt international quality standards. While large export-oriented firms have been the first to seek certification, these companies are now requiring the same of their suppliers, thus pushing smaller companies to raise their performance.

Through the Grupo de Apoio a Normalicão Ambiental (GANA), Brazil has been actively participating in the development of the ISO 14000 standards for environmental management. GANA is mainly composed of industry representatives, but is also supported by government environmental agencies. Already, interest by Brazilian industry in ISO 14000 certification is high and rapid dissemination of the standards is expected.

In some states, there is active collaboration between government agency and industry representatives in CP initiatives. The industry federation of São Paulo (FIESP) awards an environmental prize to companies with particular achievements in environmental management. In São Paulo, the state environment secretary and the state environment agency (CETESB) are working together with the FIESP in a project for reducing industrial solid waste. CETESB is also establishing sectoral councils for 26 different industries with the objective of developing and defining new instruments for achieving sustainable development. A particular emphasis will be placed on the role of cleaner production. These councils include representatives from industry, unions, research institutes, and the occupational health and safety field.

The Brazilian national industry federation is assisting companies through seminars and training programmes in environmental management. The industry federation is also undertaking various initiatives to explicitly promote CP. It operates 30 technology centres, each of which has an environment group to support industry in environmental management. In Curitiba, Paraná, a national centre for environmental technology was established by SENAI, an organisation associated with the national industry federation.

Large companies with an orientation towards international markets have taken the initiative by voluntarily adopting measures to introduce cleaner production. Nine out of 23 Brazilian firms with sales above $200 million have adopted environmental auditing as part of their management routine.[5] A recent survey shows that the principal reasons for undertaking environmental audits in these firms were improved image of the enterprise (43.5 per cent), differentiation from competitors (30.4 per cent), improved relations with enforcement agencies (26 per cent) and greater access to external markets (21.7 per cent).[6] Not surprisingly, those companies that are focused on exports to Europe, such as in the steel and cellulose branches, are leading many of these activities.

2.3   Chile[7]

The Macroeconomic Framework

After profound economic, political and social changes, it is widely recognised that Chile today has the most stable and liberalised economy in Latin America. Sound macroeconomic policies and declining inflation have attracted domestic and foreign investment and led to high and sustained economic growth over several years. There is broad-based national support for a market-based economic system. Importantly, much of the economic growth is generated by expansion of the mining, forestry and fishing sectors, whose operations have often been linked to serious environmental problems. Interestingly, Chile's desire to enter into free trade arrangements with OECD countries, such as the North American Free Trade Agreement (NAFTA), has been an important driving force in the domestic discussion of improved environmental management.

Chile's capital markets are deeper than those of several other Latin American countries, making the mobilisation of financial resources for domestic investments easier. Price controls, subsidies, and other distortions of the economy have been removed earlier than in many other Latin American countries. In general, there are no subsidies, for example on energy or water, but also no mechanisms to fully internalise environmental costs, for example the costs of inadequate wastewater treatment.

---

[5]   Survey by Boucinhas e Campos Consultores, reported in Serôa da Motta and Reis, 1994.

[6]   Veiga, P.M., 1994: Evidências sobre as relações entre comércio e meio ambiente no Brasil. *Revista Brasileira de Comércio Exterior*, 41.

[7]   This section draws from comprehensive information kindly provided by the Comisión Nacional de Medio Ambiente (CONAMA) and from World Bank, 1994: *Chile – Managing Environmental Problems*, Washington, D.C.

Major Pollution Problems

Chile's major pollution problems are concentrated in the Santiago Metropolitan Region (SMR). Santiago's serious air pollution problems are caused by emissions from industry and transport, aggravated by the city's location in an enclosed valley with limited winds, little rain, and thermal inversion throughout a large part of the year. Water pollution is caused by industrial effluent and the virtual absence of domestic wastewater treatment. Chile also has pollution problems in secondary cities with industrial centres, such as Concepción-Talcahuano.

There are other serious but more localised environmental problems surrounding major industrial sites, primarily in the mining but also the fish processing and pulp and paper industries. In the case of the mining industry, the main problems relate to the older operations of the government-owned CODELCO and ENAMI companies, while more recent mining sites, usually operated by private investors, follow much stricter environmental standards. The problems are thus more closely associated with the stock of old investments rather than with new incoming investments.

Environmental Policy

Fragmented sectoral environmental regulations, which were rarely enforced, have existed for some time in Chile. The establishment of a more systematic environmental policy in Chile began with the transition to a democratic government in 1989/1990. In 1989 the government created a special commission for the decontamination of Santiago (CEDRM), and in 1990 a national environmental commission (CONAMA) was set up. In 1994 an environmental framework law was passed by Congress which has created the basic pillars of a national environmental policy. This law establishes a permanent structure for CONAMA and 13 regional environment commissions (COREMAs). CONAMA has a co-ordinating function for national environmental policy, while most regulatory and enforcement functions rest with the sectoral agencies, such as the Ministries of Transport, Health, and Mining. In reflecting the political constitution of the country, environmental management is highly centralised.

To mitigate potential pollution problems from new investments, a comprehensive requirement for Environmental Impact Assessment (EIA) of all new private and public sector industrial projects is applied. To address pollution problems from existing facilities, the main instrument is the development of pollution prevention and decontamination plans in areas where ambient environmental standards are either being approached or exceeded. These plans create the framework for implementing pollution control and prevention measures, including emission standards and tradable emission permits.

Many of the regulations and corresponding policy instruments under the new framework law are still under preparation or in early implementation. Therefore, experience with these instruments is limited so far. However, significant experience already exists with the use of decontamination plans for some areas heavily polluted by mining operations. In these cases, the one (or two) operators of emission sources in an area that has been declared saturated for specific air pollutants (in general, fine particulate matter and/or sulphur dioxide) have prepared and negotiated with the government a timetable for emission reductions. The agreed decontamination plans have then been decreed by the government. The pollution control investments in the public mining sector corresponding to these decontamination plans are estimated to reach $1 billion for the years 1992-2000, mostly for the construction of sulphuric acid plants.

A very interesting experience with the use of economic instruments in pollution control predates the environmental framework law. In 1992, the government began implementation of an innovative compensation system for the control of particulate emissions from fixed sources in the Santiago Metropolitan Region. An emission standard for existing fixed pollution sources was combined with a credit trading scheme that required the acquisition of compensating credits for any new emission sources. Actual trading so far has been very limited. The government has decided to improve the legal foundation of the compensation system, leading to further delays. Even though lack of enforcement and uncertainty about the initial endowment of pollution credits have hampered the system, it is an important experience that has increased the acceptability of economic instruments for pollution policies and will be further pursued.

Cleaner Production Developments

Overall, Chilean environmental regulations and policies are neutral towards technology choices. There is no explicit policy requiring best available technology, nor are their sectoral or technology-specific standards. Emission standards are generally defined as uniform concentration standards. With its inclination to use economic instruments in environmental policy (another example is the Chilean system of tradable water rights), Chile leaves more technology choices to the polluters and thus avoids a bias in its policy against the use of CP approaches.

There is no explicit government policy aimed at promoting cleaner technologies, for example through credit lines or grants directed exclusively at CP approaches. However, a range of government programmes is directed at industrial development or technological innovation in general. Some of these programmes include environmental improvements and pollution reduction in their objectives, or require minimum environmental performance by supported projects. Thus, some of these programmes are supporting initiatives that will lead to the adoption of cleaner production.

The "Fondo Nacional de Desarrollo Tecnológico y Productivo" (FONTEC) is a public fund created in 1991 and aimed at promoting, guiding, financing and subsidising the development of projects that incorporate innovative technologies in the private sector. Although this programme is not explicitly directed at clean technologies, such projects are eligible within the programme. FONTEC provides financing for projects proposed by the private sector. Financing consists of credit and subsidies of up to $100,000 for individual enterprises or groups of enterprises, and up to $300,000 for technology infrastructure and centres for technology transfer.

The "Fondo de Fomento al Desarrollo Cientifico y Tecnológico" (FONDEFF) is administered by the National Council for Science and Technology within the Education Ministry. FONDEFF financially supports projects that increase competitiveness in sectors such as mining, forestry and fisheries. Out of 99 projects approved so far, 61 are classified as having neutral or acceptable environmental impact and 38 are identified as having positive environmental impact. Approved projects receiving FONDEFF funding amount to $61 million and total investments are $134 million. FONDEFF contributes to both the development of clean technologies and the strengthening and consolidation of environmental research and development capabilities.

INTEC, a government technology research agency, is currently developing a specific project that aims at strengthening national technological capacities for the treatment of liquid industrial effluents. This project assists SMEs in pollution reduction through either end-of-pipe or cleaner production solutions. In its current first phase, information on characteristics of selected industries – tanning, painting, textile, and agro-industries – is gathered. This phase will be followed by concrete assistance programmes for the application of clean technologies.

INTEC itself does not provide financing for enterprises. However, together with the implementing enterprises, INTEC seeks funding for individual projects through government funds such as FONTEC. An interesting case of INTEC's experience in CP approaches was an investigation of wood-burning bakeries in the Santiago Metropolitan Region (SMR). Following the introduction of tighter emission regulations, INTEC worked with bakeries in the measurement of their emissions and in experiments on oven design and combustion. This work led to a project proposal to convert the bakeries from wood-burning to gas stoves. The conversion is now being implemented by about 700 bakeries. Moreover, participant bakeries have realised that, due to rising fuelwood prices, the conversion to gas generates not only environmental but also financial benefits.

A technical assistance project between Chile and the Hesse State of Germany explicitly seeks to establish the permanent transfer of clean technologies to Chile. The project is financed by the Hesse State of Germany through the Carl Duisberg Foundation and co-ordinated in Chile by the industry federation, SOFOFA. The Chilean government is represented on the consultative council of the project through CONAMA and the Economics Ministry. During the first phase, environmental audits will be conducted in several enterprises of the metal and metal processing industry. During the second phase of the project (1996-1998), implementation of projects resulting from the environmental audits and a training programme for cleaner production is foreseen.

The "Propel Chile" initiative is aimed at assisting SMEs in the development and implementation of projects that enhance the competitiveness and environmental management of these enterprises. The programme assists SMEs through seminars, training, consultancies, and also in seeking financing for projects from government programmes or the private capital market. Initiatives are aimed at, *inter alia*, increased energy efficiency and the minimisation of emissions.

The EP3 Chile technical assistance programme of USAID provides assistance to SMEs with the objective of introducing cleaner production approaches. So far, environmental audits have been conducted in 20 enterprises of the tanning, painting, textile and meat processing industries. During the next phase, the project will support the establishment of an information centre for clean technologies in a well-established Chilean NGO.

Finally, there are a number of cleaner production initiatives by universities and industry. These include the Programme for Sustainable Development at the Universidad de Chile, the Industrial Corporation for Regional Development of the Bío-Bío (CIDERE BIOBIO), and the Unit for Technical Development at the Universidad de Concepción.

Currently, a major private sector project with significant implications for the use of cleaner fuels and the air pollution problem of the SMR is being discussed. Also, the government is creating the legal and regulatory framework for the import, transport and distribution of natural gas through one or several gas pipelines from Argentina to Chile. This project is mainly driven by commercial interest in a cheaper source of energy. However, the tightening air emission regulations in the SMR contribute to the attractiveness of the project. While natural gas will likely be used first in large industrial operations, discussions on converting vehicles to compressed natural gas (CNG) are underway.

3.0   Lessons and Conclusions

The practical experience with CP approaches in Argentina, Chile and Brazil is still quite limited, and its systematic assessment is hindered by incomplete documentation of their impacts. While an overall evaluation of the effect of government policies on CP is therefore hardly possible, some interesting conclusions can nevertheless be drawn from the experience. Specifically, the limited experience with government approaches towards CP in these three countries suggests there is a hierarchy of policies that should begin with reforms towards a sound macroeconomic framework, then the development of a systematic environmental regulatory framework, and finally targeted measures to promote CP (see Figure 1). This approach does not suggest that CP would not be suitable in countries that still have macroeconomic distortions or lack a systematic environmental management framework. However, in that situation policies to address the more fundamental deficiencies would be expected to have higher returns in terms of achieving low-cost pollution reduction through CP approaches.

Figure 1: Hierarchy of CP-promoting Policies

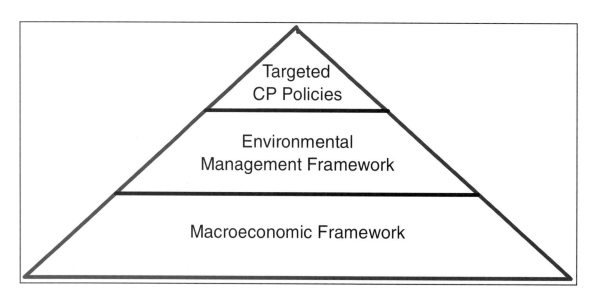

3.1   Important Non-environmental Policies

The rapid diffusion of CP approaches after economic reforms that led to increased investment and orientation towards export markets is the most notable feature of the experience presented here. From a country-wide perspective, the influence that general economic policies have on the adoption of cleaner production, and thus pollution reduction, seems to clearly dominate the effect of specific initiatives that encourage the adoption of CP. Generally speaking, the experience could be described as follows:

- Macroeconomic stability is a precondition for governments and enterprises to take environmental policy seriously.

- Measures that lead to increased investment will speed up the diffusion of cleaner technologies.

- The privatisation of state enterprises often increases the ability to raise capital required for investment and to improve the environmental performance of the enterprise.

- Trade liberalisation and increased openness of the economy facilitate faster diffusion of foreign technologies and increase the demand for environmentally benign production from international markets.

- Liberalisation of capital markets and other measures to deepen financial markets will improve enterprises' access to commercial credit and thus improve their ability to adopt environmental innovations.

- The removal of subsidies on, and possibly taxation of, inputs that are associated with pollution, such as energy, water and some raw materials, creates powerful incentives for energy and materials efficiency and cleaner production.

3.2   A Predictable and Flexible Regulatory Framework

Improved general economic policies allow polluters to adopt measures that pay for themselves (win-win options) and respond efficiently to regulatory incentives from environmental agencies. However, good environmental regulation is the critical contribution that governments need to make to improve environmental performance. An effective environmental regulatory system that is not biased against CP would include the following important considerations:

- At the low levels of current pollution control in most developing countries, the clarity and predictability of the environmental regulations is more important than the absolute level of environmental quality desired. Many companies are bothered more by inconsistent application of existing regulation, and by regulatory uncertainty, than by the specific level of pollution reduction required. In an uncertain regulatory environment, polluters are unlikely to commit their resources to long-term investments, such as those required for many CP approaches.

- Flexibility in environmental regulation is critical for the adoption of CP approaches. Polluters should be left free choice of technology and only be regulated with respect to their final emissions. Flexibility in the timing of pollution reduction is critical for the adoption of new processes that are connected with major investments. Economic instruments, such as pollution charges and marketable permits, will usually best allow this flexibility, but the application of other instruments such as standards and licenses can also be made more flexible.

- Environmental regulation cannot be effective without enforcement. Polluters will not adopt costly CP measures without facing a credible enforcement system that is linked to the threat of sufficiently high fines or closure. Self-reporting systems can reduce administrative costs and have proven to be effective where they are linked to spot-checks and high fines for misreporting.

3.3   Differentiated Approaches to Cleaner Production

Cleaner production and pollution prevention should be seen as integral additions to the menu of pollution reduction options that are available for selecting the most cost-effective pollution reduction strategy. CP options have often been neglected in the past and, therefore, deserve particular attention by governments. However, it would be erroneous to make the opposite mistake and bias policies artificially in favour of CP options, which in some cases may not be cost-effective.

Targeted measures to aid enterprises in the adoption of CP approaches have to address the different constraints that different types of enterprises face. Clearly, a broad distinction needs to be made between large and efficiently managed firms in dynamic sectors with access to capital and know-how, and small firms in mature sectors with limited access to these resources.[8] A more detailed differentiation of groups of enterprises may later evolve and would allow more precise targeting of policy approaches.

For larger enterprises with an international orientation, good macroeconomic policies and a reliable environmental regulatory framework are a necessary, and usually also sufficient, condition for stimulating interest in CP. The environmental decision-making by these companies is often influenced by developments in international markets and in the countries of their headquarters. Companies are sensitive to their environmental image and the demand from international markets for environmentally sound production practices. These enterprises usually have the financial and technical resources to adopt financially beneficial solutions on their own. Given a clear regulatory framework, they will also adopt the socially efficient approach to pollution reduction.

The situation is entirely different in the case of SMEs. In small enterprises, good housekeeping measures often have high theoretical financial payoffs as well. However, the constraint often lies in the lack of managerial attention to pollution problems. Managerial attention is a scarce resource that is undervalued in a typical environmental audit. In the case where these enterprises operate in mature industries with low capital renewal, and in countries in which SMEs have limited access to capital, a sound regulatory framework may be insufficient for the implementation of a low-cost pollution reduction strategy.

To overcome their lack of know-how, technical assistance in the form of environmental audits and training can be critical for implementing low-cost CP approaches in SMEs. In addition, assistance in obtaining environmental certification can be important to offset the advantage that large firms would otherwise have in international and other image-sensitive markets. In the case of capital-intensive process changes, credit facilities that are carefully designed and closely targeted would be an important transition measure until capital markets have developed such that SMEs have sufficient access to funds provided by the financial markets.

REFERENCES

Bercovichand, N. and M. Chidiak, 1994: *Restructuración industrial y gestión ambiental en el sector de celulosa y papel en Argentina.* Centro de investigación para la transformación. Buenos Aires.

Hanrahan, D., 1995: *Putting Cleaner Production to Work.* Environment Department Discussion Draft Paper. The World Bank. Washington, D.C.

Margulis, S., 1994: "The Use of Economic Instruments in Environmental Policies: The Experiences of Brazil, Mexico, Chile and Argentina," in: OECD (1994): *Applying Economic Instruments to Environmental Policies in OECD and Dynamic Non-Member Economies.* Paris.

---

[8] See Hanrahan, 1995.

Serôa da Motta, R. and E. Reis, 1994: *Uso de Instrumentos Economicos para Gestão Ambiental: Teoria e Práctica no Brasil. Mimeograph. Instituto De Pesquisa Economica Aplicada.* Rio de Janeiro.

World Bank, 1994: *Chile: Managing Environmental Problems – Economic Analysis of Selected Issues.* Report No. 13061-CH. Washington, D.C.

World Bank, 1995a: *World Development Report 1995. World Development Indicators.* Washington, D.C.

World Bank, 1995b: *Argentina: Managing Environmental Pollution – Issues and Options.* Report No. 14070-AR. Washington, D.C.

CLEANER PRODUCTION AND WASTE MINIMISATION: EXPERIENCE FROM MEXICO

Luis Guadarrama
Ministry of Environment, Natural Resources and Fisheries, Mexico

1.0   Introduction

This paper first provides a brief introduction to Mexico's industrial structure, with special emphasis on policies for hazardous waste management. Mexico's integration into the world economy, and membership of bodies such as OECD, WTO and NAFTA, pose major challenges to Mexican industry to improve its competitiveness. Many obstacles have hindered domestic industry's competitiveness and environmental performance. These obstacles have been met by authorities and industrialists alike with efforts to create an institutional basis for the promotion of competitiveness, environmentally friendly processes, and specifically the promotion of clean production and waste minimisation. Though these efforts are quite promising, they need to be complemented by specific instruments to promote greater environmental protection. Economic instruments can be very helpful when used with the existing regulation. One example will be put forward, with its potential for aiding in hazardous waste management. The paper will end by pointing out certain obstacles to the implementation of economic instruments, and to environmental policy in general.

2.0   Industry structure

Industry in Mexico has played an important role in the country's growth since the beginning of the century. It is since the 1940s, and until recently, that the industrial sector has been the major contributor to growth and employment, though several changes occurred during the process. A brief enumeration of how industry has evolved follows:

- Composition of activities. Initially centred on food processing and textiles, industry has now become more diversified through the development of the chemical, metallurgy, and machinery and equipment manufacturing industries.

- Increased participation by the private sector. This has been in response to the increase in the number of foreign firms, the *"maquiladora"*[1] *scheme,* and the shift from public to private involvement in some industrial activities.

- Size of firms. Large firms increasingly dominate production, but micro, small- and medium-sized enterprises account for almost 90% of all establishments.

- Orientation. Industry is focused on the external market, as opposed to the tendency from the 1940s to the early 1980s to focus on the internal one.

In the last decade and a half, industry has been replaced in importance by the service sector. In spite of this, industry's role in any growth perspectives the country may have is undeniably important. With a labour force that will grow in the next decade at 2.5-3.0 per cent annually, the task of growing in per capita terms is by no means easy. Moreover, jobs for the increasing number of Mexicans have to be provided in accordance with greater competitiveness and better environmental performance.

Mexico's industrial structure is defined by four types of industry (Table 1).

Table 1: Types of Industry that Define the Industrial Structure

Type of industry	% of industrial production	% of all industrial establishments	% of GDP
Extractive industry	9	1.6	3
Manufacturing industry	73	94.8	24
Construction industry	15	3.6	5
Electrical industry	3	0.0	1
Total	100	100	
Total for industry as % of GDP			33

Source: Department of Business Information of BANAMEX and the Industrial Census of 1993.

2.1   Manufacturing

Most industrial establishments are in the manufacturing sector, which includes most of the jobs, almost three-quarters of production, and over 70 per cent of total national exports. As will be seen later, some manufacturing sub-sectors stand out from the point of view of hazardous waste generation. Several sub-sectors (with their code numbers) are listed in Table 2, together with the percentage of total manufacturing establishments and of total manufacturing employees in each sub-sector.

---

[1]   A type of industry which imports its raw materials, uses Mexican labour to assemble them into a finished product, and then exports this product.

The geographical distribution of manufacturing industries in Mexico observes an important centralisation. Thirty-one states and one Federal District form the whole of the country. Table 3 shows participation by states in manufacturing, in value added terms.

More than 40 per cent of the country's manufacturing production, in value added terms, takes place in the Metropolitan Zone of Mexico City (MZMC), which spans the Federal District and parts of the State of Mexico. Two other cities have important shares: Monterrey, in the northern state of Nuevo Leon, and Guadalajara, in the central state of Jalisco. Finally, there is the northern border region, which covers all the zone bordering the United States and has almost all the *maquiladora* type of plants. This zone has been growing at rates that double the national rates.

Table 2: Selected Manufacturing Sub-sectors

Subsector	% of all manufacturing establishments	% of all employees in manufacturing
31 Food, beverages and tobacco	24.05	18.13
32 Textiles, leather and shoes	16.92	17.73
33 Wood products	8.1	3.93
34 Paper and printing	9.57	5.89
35 Chemical industry	6.93	11.92
36 Ceramics, glass and non-metallic minerals	4.91	4.24
37 Steel and non-ferrous metals	1.03	2.2
38 Metal products, automobiles, machinery and equipment	24.61	32.94
39 Other manufactures	3.89	3.03

Sources: Bases para una estrategia ambiental para la industria en México, INE, 1993, and Instituto Mexicano del Seguro Social.

Table 3: Participation in Manufacturing by State

State	Participation (% of national value added)
Federal District	29.5
State of Mexico	18.1
Nuevo Leon	9.1
Jalisco	6.7
Veracruz	5.3
Northern border states (Baja California, Chihuahua, Coahuila, Sonora, Tamaulipas)	9.9
All other states (22)	21.4

Source: Bases para una estrategia ambiental para la industria en México. INE, 1993.

2.2   Size of Firms

The manufacturing industry in Mexico is made up of a small number of conglomerates and transnational firms and a great many micro, small and medium-scale firms (Table 4). Although the large firms represent less than 2 per cent of all manufacturing establishments, on average they represent half of total manufacturing production and half the total number of employees. Just to give two examples: the steel industry, in which only two producers are responsible for almost 60 per cent of total production in that industry, and the cement industry, in which eight producers are responsible for nearly all of that industry's production.

The micro scale is by far the best represented in terms of number of establishments. Almost 80 per cent of all the manufacturing establishments in the country belong to this category.

Table 4: Number of Firms of Different Sizes in the Mexican Manufacturing Sector

Size	Number of establishments	Number of employees
Micro industry	97,996	394,145
Small industry	18,070	673,779
Medium industry	3,230	506,204
Large industry	2,347	1,646,369
Total	121,643	3,220,497

Source: Instituto Mexicano del Seguro Social.

2.3 Hazardous Waste Generation in MexicoE

Efforts to compile a comprehensive inventory of emissions in Mexico have been ongoing. In the recently launched Programme for the Integral Management of Industrial Waste, the National Institute of Ecology estimates that approximately 8 million metric tonnes of hazardous wastes are generated annually in Mexico; of this total approximately 65% is sourced from central Mexico (which includes the Metropolitan Zone of Mexico City (MZMC) and its environs.) Other important source areas are northern Mexico, which accounts for 24% of the total, and the Gulf of Mexico region, with 7%. The northern border region, by contrast, only generates 1% of the hazardous wastes total.

Approximately 12% of the hazardous waste generated is adequately managed, either in certified facilities or by some means of reuse or recycling.

A small number of sub-sectors account for a large volume of hazardous waste generation. Table 5 shows hazardous waste generation by sub-sector (with the four-digit MSIC codes of each) as a percentage of total hazardous waste generation, estimated on a national basis.

Table 5: Hazardous Waste Generation by Sub-sector

Sub-sector with code number	% of toxic waste generated
3512 Production of basic chemical substances excluding petrochemicals	25
3511 Basic petrochemicals	12
3530 Petroleum refining	10
3513 Synthetic fibres	9
3522 Production of other chemical substances and products	5
3410 Cellulose, paper and their products	4
Total for these sub-sectors	65

Source: World Bank and SEMARNAP, 1995.

3.0 Industrial Policy

Different programmes have been developed since the 1940s to foster industrial development. They include the adoption of fiscal incentives, political protection against external competition (through customs tariffs), legal instruments that introduce tax exemptions, import substitution, orientation towards investment through interest rates, public investment to create infrastructure, and low internal prices for energy (fuel and electricity). Among some of the side effects of these measures, there is the lack of incentives for innovation, the very high intensity in the use of energy, low competitiveness, and governmental deficits.

Therefore, since the mid 1980s, major restructuring has occurred in order to reinsert Mexico's industry into the world market. Early trade liberalisation policies in the 1980s included Mexico's entering the General Agreement on Tariffs and Trade (GATT) and many examples of unilateral lowering of trade barriers. In 1994, the North American Free Trade Agreement (NAFTA) went into operation and Mexico also became a member of the OECD.

It is under these new circumstances that industry faces the challenge of greater competitiveness and better environmental management. Co-operation between industry and government should be consistent with the new commitments made in diverse international and multilateral fora. In this context the government, along with the private sector, has devised a set of institutions and initiatives designed to help industry cope with the open market and adopt cleaner and more competitive technologies (Table 6).

Table 6: Institutions, Initiatives and Their Objectives

Institution and Initiatives	Objectives
National Centre of Metrology	· Establish national patterns and verify international compatibility · Harmonize the National System of Calibration · Certify laboratories
Mexican Institute of Industrial Property	· Register, protect and provide industrial property rights · Give proper diffusion to new inventions · Assist technology transfer · Integrate directories of different institutions dedicated to innovation
Mexican Society for Normalisation and Certification	· Study, propose, elaborate and provide diffusion of Mexican private and non-obligatory norms; also verify their compliance
Mexican Institute for Normalisation and Certification	· Act as a national organism for certifying quality systems · Make available instruments that help improve competitiveness and quality
Certified Mexican Quality	· Audit and verify quality systems
National Quality Prize	· Awarded to industries pursuing Total Quality
Unit for the Transfer of Technology	· Provide technological management services · Finance research projects oriented towards modernisation and technological development
Mexican Foundation for Innovation and Technology Transfer in Medium-sized and Small Industry	· Support initiatives towards technological innovation in medium and small-sized industries

Events stemming from the 1994 economic crisis have impacted on all sectors of the economy, but especially in the industrial sector. For example in the 1995 report by the World Economic Forum[3] Mexico dropped from 26th place in competitiveness (in a survey of 48 countries) to 44th place. Recognising that the challenge of creating jobs while protecting the environment has become more difficult in this context, earlier this year government and industry developed the Environmental Protection and Industrial Competitiveness Programme.

---

[3] *World Competitiveness Report*, 1995.

The Programme's main objectives are to:

- Enhance industrial competitiveness. A long-term commitment of industry and the authorities, based on mutual understanding and clear rules, includes:

- Improve environmental regulation and industry competitiveness. Based on a normative framework that promotes efficiency and total quality in processes, improvement focuses on prevention and minimisation of wastes and emissions;

- Promote self-regulation. Develop and promote voluntary programmes by making commitments to environmental audits, input substitution, technological modernisation, energy efficiency and recycling;

- Reduce the administrative burden. Minimise any bureaucratic burden in favour of all industry, but mostly in favour of small and micro industries;

- Strengthen environmental information systems. Access to information about processes, regulation, the norm, and technological change;

- Improve environmental education and capacity building efforts. To create the human resources needed for environmental management;

- Promote technological upgrading and co-operation. Promote the use of clean technologies and access to needed financing from development and commercial banks;

- Support decentralisation. Promote regional centres for industrial environmental management with the participation of industrial chambers, authorities at all levels of government, academic institutions and consulting firms;

- Establish an Institute of Environment and Industrial Development. Institutionalise any environmental management and information programmes; this in order to help the interaction between industry, authorities and international bodies;

- Access more fully potential financing sources. Promote access to international financing of projects; and

- Strengthen environmental infrastructure. Promote private investment in environmental infrastructure.

Another important initiative is the establishment of the Mexican Centre for Cleaner Production, a joint venture between the Transformation Industry Chamber of Mexico, the National Polytechnic Institute of Mexico, UNIDO and UNEP. The main objective of the Centre is to promote the dissemination of clean technology schemes throughout Mexican industry. Through a series of pilot projects it is hoped to demonstrate to industry the economic and environmental benefits of cleaner technologies. The Centre has recently completed a pilot programme in the metal finishing industry and is in the process of disseminating the results.

4.0   Waste Management

In spite of all the efforts that have been made, there has been little progress with respect to the adoption of waste minimisation and cleaner technologies. Among the reasons is the lack of ambient quality regulations and the focus on more restrictive emissions regulations. Banning or restricting the production or use of a certain substance, requiring new formulations, mandating recycling of a substance and/or its container, and other restrictions have been the norm in hazardous waste management. These restrictions normally favour end-of-pipe measures, equipment for pollution control, and recycling facilities instead of better production methods.

In late 1996 the Programme for the Integral Management of Industrial Waste (Instituto Nacional de Ecologia "Programa para el manejo integral y aprovechamiento de los residuos industriales en la region central de Mexico 1996-2000") was launched by the National Institute of Ecology to promote a comprehensive policy framework for hazardous waste management. The main elements of the Programme are:

- to enforce the regulatory framework in order to promote waste minimisation and recycling;
- to ensure that all relevant information is readily available; and
- to promote the participation of the private sector in waste minimisation schemes and to provide an economic incentive for the proper final disposal of hazardous wastes.

To understand how waste minimisation and cleaner technologies can be promoted, we can use the marginal cost curve approach. Waste management is divided into five different alternatives (for analytical purposes only), each with different marginal costs curves.

Empirically[4] the cost curves (when costs are internalised) for each alternative behave as shown in Figure 1:

- Minimisation: The first units to be minimised have relatively little cost, but, as the units to be controlled grow, minimisation becomes more costly;

- Recycling: The first units to be recycled cost more than minimisation, but, as these units grow, the cost doesn't grow as fast as minimisation costs;

- Incineration (or another option): The first units to be incinerated are more costly than either minimisation or recycling, but eventually this becomes the least costly option;

- Other treatment: This becomes a less costly option when the percentage of reduction becomes very high;

- Confinement: The most costly option, but probably the only feasible one when the amount of risk should be reduced to a maximum.

Using this approach, the potential of waste minimisation and cleaner technologies is defined by a cost curve. If the cost curve of each alternative behaves as shown in Figure 1, the percentage of

---

[4]   See Goddard, H.C., 1993: *The Benefits and Costs of Alternative Solid Waste Management Policies.* Washington D.C.

units (or risk) reduced by waste minimisation and cleaner technologies lies between points A and B. Any measure that can promote cleaner technologies and waste minimisation should bring the cost curve down, and therefore lead to a greater distance between A and B.

Figure 1: Marginal Cost Curves for Waste Management Alternatives

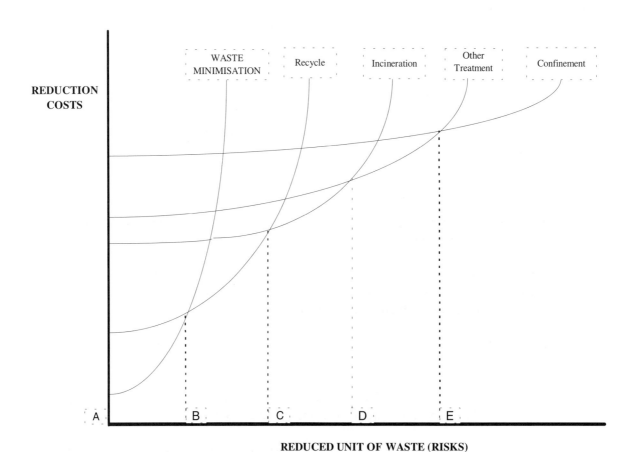

Source: Goddard, H.C. (1993): <u>The Benefit and Costs of Alternative Solid Waste Management Policies.</u>

4.1 Economic Instruments

There are many instruments and actions that could lower the cost of cleaner technologies and waste minimisation. A better regulatory framework in which certainty is guaranteed, and easy and cheap access to financing, are two of them. Another is the use of economic instruments. By using economic instruments to complement other policy instruments, the whole framework of waste management can benefit from, among others: cost-effectiveness; flexibility; continued incentives to reduce waste; and, in some cases, the generation of public funds. A brief description of a particular instrument being considered for application in Mexico, and how it works, will illustrate this point.

4.2 The Pollution Prevention Guarantee Scheme (PPGS)

This scheme is defined as a financial guarantee by a firm that demonstrates a commitment to sound management of its hazardous wastes. Based on the Polluter-Pays Principle and on deposit-refund systems, the scheme requires that at the beginning of each given time period (it could be a year, six months, or any other) a firm deposits a financial guarantee of compliance with the regulatory agency. This guarantee is based on an estimation of the amount of hazardous wastes the firm is going to produce. The amount deposited is a given percentage of the whole estimated cost of managing the wastes. At the end of the period, if the firm can demonstrate that all of its wastes were reduced or handled according to the law, the total amount of the guarantee is returned to the firm (with the opportunity cost of the money included). If the firm cannot demonstrate that all of the wastes generated were safely managed, it loses an amount proportionate to the cost of managing the wastes, which is calculated on the basis of the guarantee itself, not just the amount of the deposit. With the moneys retained, the regulatory agency pays for the administrative infrastructure to monitor firms' waste generation and treatment and can create an environmental fund.

In this scheme firms have the incentive to reduce waste generation in the most cost-effective ways, as the guarantee is calculated on a fixed cost per tonne for treatment; this cost per tonne is derived from the cost of all the available policy options. The generator would choose the least costly option, and would also try to find better methods by innovating. Since the firms are the ones who provide the information on waste generated and on control of this waste, the administrative costs for the authority are relatively low and tend to diminish as time goes by.

One disadvantage does appear when the authority has to calculate the guarantees. Difficulties arise when differences in toxicity have to be considered. A better understanding of the differential in costs related to exposure to different substances with different properties should alleviate this problem.

4.3 Obstacles to Implementing Economic Instruments

The benefits of using economic instruments have been discussed in many fora, but not much has been said about the obstacles faced in implementing them. The following list shows many of the perceived obstacles in Mexico to the implementation of economic instruments such as the Pollution Prevention Guarantee Scheme. This list is relevant in that many of these obstacles are also obstacles to all environmental policy making (although here they are addressed specifically in regard to the implementation of clean technologies and waste minimisation measures).

Obstacles to the implementation of economic instruments include:

Economic

- They raise costs: we have to consider the economic situation a country faces, and the competitiveness of its industry.

- There are monitoring costs.

Political

- If taxes are the relevant economic instrument, we have to consider that new taxes are unpopular, independent of the fact that they raise costs. People's perception of new taxes is that they normally mean actual, or future, problems in public administration.

- An economic instrument might reduce the legal responsibilities of environmental groups and NGOs.

- Related to all the other barriers is the non-attainment of consensus.

- There are different impacts on different groups and sectors.

- The non-credibility of measures taken by the government is a problem resulting from bad precedents. For example, in the late 1980s the government established a voluntary audit scheme, which some firms adopted. Unfortunately for them, the information they provided about their environmental performance was used to put them on a "black list" which was used whenever an environmental problem arose. The firms which did not adopt the audit scheme were not included in the "black list"as the authorities had no information on them, although they might have contributed to pollution.

- People perceive that these instruments might generate inflationary pressures.

Technical

- For tradable permits, there is no certainty regarding the quantity of emissions to be considered as a base.

- For emission charges, there is no certainty regarding the degree of control to be attained.

Cultural

- There is a lack of information on how the instruments work.

- There is a lack of information on the expected results.

- There is little confidence in the expected results.

- Pollution is the problem. It does not appeal to people as being morally, or ethically, correct to "sell rights to pollute".

Administrative

- There is a need to create new administrative institutions;

- There is a strong tradition of, and experience with, "command and control" policies.

Legal

- Mexican law did not previously make provision for the use of economic instruments; in the 1996 review of the General Law for the Protection of the Environment, a section defining the status of economic instruments has been added under the chapter on instruments.

5.0   Conclusions

The characteristics of Mexico's industrial base, in the face of both an economic crisis and the new international obligations and opportunities, call for innovative approaches in order to keep it working. The right blend of policy options for environmental protection can enhance industrial competitiveness. A review of industry's position in the national economy, its regional development potential, and its capacity to contribute to sustainable development, along with the ongoing changes in the institutional and instrumental framework on which it is based, would show that, even though there is much to do, the future looks quite promising.

ANNEX: MEXICO'S INSTITUTIONAL FRAMEWORK FOR ENVIRONMENTAL MANAGEMENT

The Federal Public Administrative Act (La Ley Orgánica de la Administración Pública Federal) establishes the responsibilities of the different ministries in charge of the regulation and control of chemical substances (materials and hazardous wastes) in Mexico. The following table summarises the responsibilities of the relevant ministries concerning hazardous waste management.

Ministry of Environment, Natural Resources and Fisheries	Establish the Official Mexican Norms (NOMs) for dangerous materials, solid and hazardous wastes. NATIONAL INSTITUTE OF ECOLOGY
	Enforce relevant laws, NOMs, and programmes related to the environment. ATTORNEY GENERAL FOR THE PROTECTION OF THE ENVIRONMENT
	Manage the environmental impact process, as well as programmes for the prevention of accidents with an ecological impact. NATIONAL INSTITUTE OF ECOLOGY
Ministry of National Defense	Monitor and issue permits for trade, transportation and storage of weapons, bullets, explosives, chemical substances, and strategic materials.
	Control and monitor the import and export of eleven kinds of weapons, bullets, chemical substances and strategic material.
Ministry of Commerce and Industrial Promotion	Establish policies for industrialisation, distribution and consumption of agricultural, cattle, forest, mineral and fishing products in co-ordination with the appropriate federal agencies.
	Study and determine restrictions on the import and export of goods.
	Regulate and promote the development of the power generation industry and discharge responsibilities for the supply of electric energy and gas distribution.
Ministry of Health	Direct the general health policy of the country, except for agricultural health policy in which the preservation of human health is not involved.
	Direct the special health policy for ports, coasts and border zones, except for agricultural health policy in which the preservation of human health is not involved.
	Implement the necessary measures to secure the well-being and health of rural and city workers, and industrial hygiene, except for issues concerning social insurance in the workplace.
	Act as the principal sanitary authority, and ensure compliance with relevant legislation and controls.
Ministry of Labour and Social Insurance	Assess and implement any security measure to ensure the safety and industrial hygiene of workers in the workplace. Assure compliance with these measures.

PART II:

CLEANER PRODUCTION
AND THE PRIVATE SECTOR

IMPLEMENTING WASTE MINIMISATION AND ECO-EFFICIENCY IN THE PRIVATE SECTOR

Joel Hirschhorn
Hirschhorn and Associates, USA

1.0　　What is Eco-efficiency?

Over the past 15 years many different terms have been used to describe a strategy for obtaining environmental improvements while simultaneously obtaining economic benefits for industrial companies. It is more important to recognise this general commonality than to be concerned by possible narrow technical differences among terms such as eco-efficiency, pollution prevention, waste minimisation, cleaner production, clean technology, industrial metabolism, design for the environment, environmentally conscious manufacturing, toxics use reduction, waste reduction, and others. All share a prevention or precautionary approach to environmental protection, in comparison to addressing wastes and pollutants after they are created.

The essential historical significance of this still emerging global movement is that it gives substance and a means of implementation to goals of sustainable economic development. Moreover, eco-efficiency recognises that in the long run it is more effective to emphasise how industry can obtain economic benefits from actions that produce environmental benefits than to rely solely or predominantly on government laws, regulations, and enforcement actions (penalties) to force industry to control pollution and waste. The theoretical basis of eco-efficiency is that industry should do what is in its economic self-interest, while it may not do what government and the general society demands it do to protect public health and the environment if this requires increased costs. It is the convergence of economic and environmental goals that is the essential significance of eco-efficiency and similar terms.

Technically, eco-efficiency covers a very broad range of possible industrial actions. There are three basic technical components of eco-efficiency and similar terms: (1) the more efficient use of materials to produce more products and less waste and pollutants; (2) the substitution of less toxic materials to reduce the toxicity of wastes and pollutants where the materials are first produced and then used elsewhere in industry; and (3) the redesign of products to reduce waste and pollutant generation over the entire life cycles of products.

1.1   Incentives and Rewards for Adopting Eco-efficiency in Industry

The fundamental need for translating eco-efficiency from a concept into a new form of industrial society is to clearly define, identify and quantify specific economic benefits to industrial firms that must take the actions that produce specific environmental benefits. Economic benefits must become quantitative, attractive, and – most importantly – competitive with alternative opportunities for companies to reduce their costs and increase their profits. It is not enough to theorise about potential economic benefits, but to begin a process of identifying low-risk actions that can produce significant economic benefits in the near term, so that more difficult and higher cost investments will be made over the longer term. These economic benefits can be seen as internally generated "push" factors that drive companies to eco-efficiency.

The following list presents a summary of the major forms of economic benefits that must be considered for providing concrete incentives and rewards for companies:

- reducing the direct costs of production by decreasing the amounts of purchased raw materials and other inputs (for example, energy, water);

- increasing the productivity of an existing plant operation; that is, reducing the amount of waste and defective products and increasing the amount of products from existing equipment;

- increasing the quality of existing products or adding an environmental performance characteristic to them (i.e. making products "green"), or creating entirely new products, that can be used to improve sales, particularly for export markets in developed countries with heightened environmental consciousness among consumers and commercial customers;

- increasing the economic value of the company to owners, shareholders and society by reducing actual and potential economic liabilities resulting from poor environmental performance, including costs for compliance with laws and regulations, such as investments in pollution control equipment, clean-up of contaminated land and water, and payments for injuries to workers and others impacted by environmental pollution.

As important as the internal "push" incentives and rewards are, it is also important to recognise that external "pull" factors can also contribute to the nucleation and growth of eco-efficient firms and industrial sectors. The most basic reason for the importance of external factors is that in the ordinary course of conducting any business, small or large in any sector, the management of a firm always has several alternative means of sustaining or improving its economic or financial performance. Companies also perceive many demands from government and society that often are seen as conflicting and burdensome messages. It is the external factors that can draw attention to the economic, environmental and social benefits of eco-efficiency and shift difficult management decisions to explore and invest in eco-efficiency opportunities rather than, or in addition to, more traditional alternatives that generally are seen as more familiar and less risky.

Therefore, a host of actions by governments, NGOs and business organisations can promote eco-efficiency as a general strategy and movement by offering incentives, rewards, and assistance. The following list presents a brief summary of some external "pull" factors:

- government policies embodied in laws and statements of high officials that communicate a clear preference for eco-efficiency in industry as a means of achieving national, and even international, economic and environmental goals, and programmes of important government agencies that offer diverse forms of assistance to companies to implement eco-efficiency actions;

- government policies and actions, particularly through legislation and administrative programmes that send a clear message that environmental pollution and harm will not be tolerated and that conventional "polluter pays" penalties will be vigorously and consistently imposed;

- government policies that remove disincentives for eco-efficiency, particularly subsidised (low) prices for production inputs such as raw materials, water and energy, or even for pollution control facilities;

- general advocacy for and continuing education about eco-efficiency by many diverse NGOs, including environmental and consumer organisations, academic and professional groups, business and trade organisations, student organisations, etc.;

- sustained attention to eco-efficiency benefits, methods, programmes, and success stories by the general news media and in business publications;

- recognition by organisations in the financial community (for example banks, insurance firms, donor agencies) that firms with commitments to eco-efficiency are seen as more proactive, pioneering, innovative and successful in the domestic and global marketplaces and, therefore, are more highly valued and will receive specific benefits.

2.0 Application Issues, Obstacles and Successes

Turning eco-efficiency concepts into actions continues to pose a major challenge worldwide, in both industrialised and developing countries, for all sizes and types of industrial companies. Two major application issues are summarised below:

Need: Maximising implementation requires various types of assessments or audits at specific industrial facilities, so that opportunities can be identified, assessed, quantitatively evaluated for costs and benefits, and then implemented.

Problem: Assessment activities require the time of company employees and often of outside experts on eco-efficiency in general, and on the specific industrial operation, and therefore impose costs; implementation of even the most beneficial and practical actions often does not occur; various programmes often focus on only a small number of industrial sectors.

Solution: Government programmes (often with external financial assistance from international donor agencies for developing countries) can offer free site assessments, especially for smaller companies; business, academic and professional organisations can have training programmes to educate personnel about conducting assessments and using appropriate methodologies for evaluating actions. Much more attention must be given to follow-up assistance and support to ensure that technically feasible and economically practical opportunities are actually implemented; for example, by developing implementation plans through partnerships between companies and agencies providing technical assistance. Also, such programmes must not only pay attention to implementation of specific actions in the near term, but also to assisting companies to develop permanent company eco-efficiency programmes that address the need to train workers, obtain senior management support, and continuously assess existing and planned new facilities for additional eco-efficiency actions. Existing industry associations must be used to broaden coverage to all industrial sectors.

Need: Engineers in companies need considerable reliable and detailed information about technologies and materials that they might use within existing facilities in order to accurately assess specific costs, benefits, and risks of actions.

Problem: Although there is a large and growing literature on case examples and various success stories in almost all industrial sectors from many different types of organisations (for example, UNEP, U.S. EPA), databases with the very latest data on specific vendors offering newer clean technologies and materials are generally lacking or are not user friendly or generally accessible.

Solution: More attention is needed by national and international programmes to gathering and dissemination clean technology information for specific industrial sectors and major categories of generic engineering unit operations necessary for making concrete engineering and investment decisions on implementing eco-efficiency actions requiring new equipment, processes or materials.

There are other significant bottlenecks and obstacles that must be given continuing attention. Many national and international programmes assume that the largest companies, including multinationals, have the resources and commitments to maximise the application of eco-efficiency principles. Nothing could be further from the truth. While in theory large companies have the technical and management resources to apply all the various forms of eco-efficiency, they do not necessarily do so. Some examples of impediments in large companies include:

- Older large plants producing well-established products, in which huge sums of money have been invested, often only accommodate the very simplest, low-cost and low-risk actions (so-called "low hanging fruit" such as improvements in housekeeping and maintenance), but not more fundamental changes in raw materials or process technology. Engineers often believe that technology has already been fully optimised. Many companies are not receptive to changing the design of well-established products to make them "green".

- The construction of entirely new large industrial facilities often is seen as presenting major new opportunities, but the latest technological innovations may not necessarily be implemented because of poor information, judgements that insufficient experience poses high risks, needs for raw materials that may not be locally available, and, in many developing countries, serious concerns about using proprietary technologies and intellectual property that cannot be effectively protected with patents and other conventional means.

- There is a general instability in many large companies because of rapidly changing markets and products, rapidly changing manufacturing technologies, mergers and acquisitions, changing management, perceptions of changing government policies, and other factors that all lead to limited funding of programmes associated with eco-efficiency and similar terms. Corporate policies remain extremely positive, with seemingly strong commitments to environmentally conscious strategies, but actual investments often lag and are minimal.

There are special problems in developing countries that require continuing attention. A largely overlooked condition, for example, is that rapidly rising rates of industrialisation in many developing countries impose conditions in which the owners and managers of successful industrial enterprises simply do not have the time for or interest in eco-efficiency. When companies are undergoing very rapid growth and can barely maintain production to satisfy rapidly rising demand for their products, the opportunities to make large profits through familiar and low-risk actions reduce interest in eco-efficiency. Company owners know that even low-quality products may be accepted on the market, that very large profits can be made by expanding production capacity even with the oldest technology, and that their technical staffs lack the time, education and expertise to examine and implement more sophisticated technologies.

Time and time again owners of highly successful companies in developing countries show little interest in technological improvements associated with even the most proven forms of eco-efficiency methods and technologies. And their attitudes and decisions are logical, given their specific circumstances. This situation is often aggravated by perceptions that the government will not necessarily impose or enforce strict environmental regulations that require investments in pollution control equipment. And, all too often, this is a correct perception.

However, there are certain conditions that can change this situation. For example, when companies shift from production for domestic markets to international ones, the interest in eco-efficiency rises substantially because of the need to produce higher quality products and meet international standards of practice (for example, ISO standards). And when there are clearer signals from government that current polluting plants will no longer be tolerated, companies show more interest in avoiding investments which, unlike eco-efficiency actions, only add to costs and do not increase net profits. The external "pull" factors discussed above are especially important in these circumstances.

Another interesting and largely ignored problem is that owners of companies in developing countries often purchase older, used equipment for existing and new plants. There is a long history of exporting used manufacturing equipment from industrialised to developing countries. Not only do the inefficiencies of such equipment lead to high rates of waste generation, but they also may preclude using newer types of raw materials and newer types of process control instruments. Many older types of manufacturing equipment require the use of the most toxic raw materials. For example, older types of printing equipment may not easily allow the use of water-based instead of solvent-based inks. More attention is required in both developed and developing countries to the longer-term consequences for both developing countries and the rest of the world of this familiar strategy of exporting the most "eco-inefficient" equipment to developing countries.

Another problem is that in many developing countries there are industries that rely on locally available raw materials that are not used in industries making similar products in industrialised countries. For example, in some developing countries paper and paper products are not made from tree pulp but from locally grown grasses and other materials. Or some types of material-intensive industries no longer exist in industrialised countries. The problem is that technological advances have not necessarily been made in such industries in developing countries and, therefore, major eco-efficiency opportunities do not exist. Hence there is a need in many cases for clean technology research and development for industries unique to certain developing countries.

There are now literally hundreds and hundreds of success stories about implementing eco-efficiency and cleaner production methods and technologies worldwide in every conceivable type of industry. The UNEP Cleaner Production Programme, the U.S. EPA, and the U.S. Agency for

International Development's Environmental Pollution Prevention Project, for example, have made many case studies available to countless companies worldwide. Some industrial sectors that are present in many developing countries have received especially intense attention in the past decade and therefore present especially important opportunities for further application of well-proven methods. Several of these sectors are briefly addressed below. All are usually targeted for attention by pollution control programmes, meaning that the use of clean technologies can help companies avoid spending on pollution control equipment:

Leather Tanning

Leather tanneries have traditionally caused serious water pollution and also produced large quantities of noxious solid wastes. There are several technical strategies now available to either eliminate the use of chromium in tanning or greatly improve its efficient use, through internal reuse and recycling, so that no pollution control equipment is necessary to meet stringent effluent standards. Investments in new equipment offer very fast paybacks, generally less than a year. Moreover, solvent-based dyes and coatings can be replaced by water-based ones, and most solid wastes can be used to produce other products. In leather tanneries throughout the world the use of eco-efficiency concepts has produced operations that are lower in cost, able to produce higher quality products, and environmentally benign and safer for workers. Interestingly, because industrialised countries have relatively few tanneries, most of the success stories have been in developing countries.

Textiles

Textile dyeing operations have been transformed in many countries through the use of improved methods of dyeing, techniques to recover and reuse dye bath solutions, improved process control instrumentation, and methods to conserve energy and water which are used in large quantities. Literally any textile dyeing operation can make use of multiple cleaner production methods to cut costs without any sacrifice of product quality. Although new equipment can often be justified, it is possible to make substantial improvements in existing companies without major investments, and with paybacks in weeks or months. However, some testing is necessary to assure that changes to production methods do not adversely affect product quality.

Electroplating and Metal Finishing

These industrial operations are ubiquitous in both large and small companies in every country. Positive experiences in industrialised countries are a sound base for greatly improving highly inefficient, polluting, and unsafe operations in developing countries. Generally speaking, the consumption of metals in electroplating and of paints and coatings in finishing can be greatly reduced, even using existing manufacturing equipment, through relatively modest investments as well as worker training. Moreover, high water use can usually be greatly reduced through improved practices. Applying eco-efficiency concepts can easily improve production output by reducing rejects and also improve product quality. Although proven methods are available, it can be difficult to convince owners and operators of very small companies of the net economic benefits of investing in making the necessary improvements. Part of the problem is that very small shops have little if any professional technical personnel, making it difficult to conduct site assessments and communicate the results.

In the finishing of metal and wood products with paints and other coatings there are enormous opportunities to improve transfer efficiencies, so that less waste and pollution are generated and production costs are reduced. Worker exposures to toxic chemicals can also be greatly reduced. There are major opportunities to replace solvent-based paints and coatings with water-based ones, but this poses greater challenges in developing countries because of the need to change equipment, conduct thorough testing, and have access to different raw materials.

3.0　　Opportunities for Accelerating Eco-efficiency Actions in Industry

3.1　　Technology and Information Transfer

All organisations interested in accelerating eco-efficiency in industry should understand that past efforts have largely concentrated on educating and motivating people concerning the broad principles of eco-efficiency and similar strategies. Anyone who travels globally quickly discovers that in virtually every country the leaders in industry and government are very familiar with the language and concepts of the new paradigm. However, the greater need now is to focus on the more practical challenges of transferring clean technology and the types of detailed information necessary for maximum implementation in all industrial sectors. The rapid rates of industrialisation in developing countries, and the rapid rates of product and process technology change in industrialised countries, pose difficult challenges for efficiently transferring technology and information. For the most part, the information and electronics revolution has not been effectively utilised for promoting eco-efficiency. There is an enormous opportunity to use the emerging global information highway linking computers everywhere, such as through the World Wide Web on the Internet, to accelerate adoption of eco-efficiency concepts. What is most needed is detailed data from companies offering new technologies and material, sufficient to allow engineers anywhere to make a thorough evaluation and know exactly where to seek further technical and cost data.

3.2　　Life Cycle Approach with More Emphasis on Raw Materials and Product Design

Intellectually, it is important to emphasise a life cycle approach in industry so that the maximum amount of eco-efficiency applications are used. The life cycle way of thinking – more than any formal, quantitative life cycle analysis – is critically important to not becoming dependent solely on trying to increase the efficiency of manufacturing operations. It is just as important, but more challenging technically, to also focus on changing the types of raw materials used in industrial operations and to reconsider the design, composition and packaging of products. So many environmental problems occur through the use and consumption of products after they are manufactured. Yet traditional thinking has generally meant that companies are unconcerned about those problems, resulting in impacts and costs for the general society. No better example exists than the mounting problem of solid waste in urban centres in developing countries, resulting from the massive increase in modern consumer products. Enormous amounts of post-consumer solid waste are causing problems for large cities in developing countries everywhere. With life cycle thinking, companies can discover means of improving the environmental performance of their products, making them safer to use and less polluting in use, and creating less waste when they are consumed and disposed. Other companies may be able to define new business opportunities from, for example, recycling discarded materials.

3.3 Government Policy

Governments everywhere can do much more in directly supporting eco-efficiency and in establishing more certain avoidable costs for pollution control investments. Much of the economic case for eco-efficiency in industrialised countries rests on avoidable spending on regulatory compliance, pollution control equipment, and clean-up costs. In developing countries the economic case must now rest nearly entirely on direct production cost savings or more uncertain means to improve sales. This makes it more difficult to economically justify all actions for maximum eco-efficiency. For those actions with greater investment costs, many will not be implemented in developing countries if there are not avoidable spending costs related to pollution control requirements by the government. It is important, therefore, for governments to establish certainty for pollution control spending and enforcement of environmental standards and regulations if the best possible climate for eco-efficiency is to be created.

Secondly, governments can generally do a much better job in articulating and widely communicating a clear national preference for eco-efficiency over conventional pollution control solutions, and in supporting that policy through various technical assistance and education programmes for industry. No one should underestimate the competitive struggle in the commercial marketplace being faced by the pollution control and waste management industry. It has already faced declining business because of the emergence of the new pollution prevention paradigm and reduced rates of hazardous waste generation, for example. This means continuing pressures on governments to favour conventional end-of-pipe pollution control over eco-efficiency.

3.4 Reviews of Plans for New Plants

Local and national governments, as well as international donor agencies and banks, can greatly accelerate eco-efficiency by requiring that all plans for new industrial plants be reviewed to assess whether maximum use has been made of eco-efficiency technologies and methods. Environmental impact assessments and reviews for loans should explicitly address the issue of whether raw materials, production processes, and product designs have captured eco-efficiency opportunities to the maximum extent. If not, then companies should be required to seek assistance in formulating improved plans. Companies should also be required to demonstrate that new plants will have management and worker programmes for permanent eco-efficiency efforts.

3.5 Global Sunsetting of Highly Toxic or Harmful Chemicals

As the global programme on finding replacements for CFCs and many national programmes for banning various toxic chemicals have shown, it is feasible to send clear messages to industry that they will be required within certain times to use alternatives to particularly harmful materials used in industrial operations. The historical record shows that although industry has a tendency to predict the most dire consequences of such government restrictions, they do not come true because of technological innovations and the commercialisation of safer substitutes. While many environmental benefits will result from other forms of eco-efficiency, in the long term it is necessary for the global economy to shift its use of toxic chemicals to more benign materials.

3.6 Policy on the Export of Older Equipment

It is appropriate for OECD and perhaps other international organisations to seriously examine the need to take steps to stem the export of older industrial equipment from the industrialised countries to developing ones. There are obvious economic benefits to those companies able to sell used equipment, to those companies specialising in finding customers in developing countries, and to buyers of old equipment. But there is a larger need to examine the longer term penalties, both competitiveness and environmental penalties, paid by developing countries. Moreover, many of the savings anticipated by buyers might be offset by buying new equipment that captures the benefits of cleaner production in newer designs. Governments in industrialised countries could consider the use of tax credits or export taxes, and governments of developing countries could consider special import duties for older industrial equipment that is associated with waste and pollutant generation.

4.0   Conclusions

The global eco-efficiency movement, with its many different names, is maturing after over a decade of building interest in its general concepts.

The main challenge now is finding more effective ways to expand the range of applications and to accelerate adoption within all industries worldwide.

While the basic concept is that industry will do what is in its economic self-interest, in reality there are many obstacles standing in the way of using proven clean technologies to gain positive economic rewards.

External factors are necessary to channel industrial interests and actions into greater and faster adoption of eco-efficiency methods. These are particularly needed in developing countries, where company owners and managers have many attractive investment alternatives to using eco-efficiency to improve economic performance.

There remain many opportunities for examining how eco-efficiency in industry can be more effectively supported, encouraged and accelerated. As the new paradigm movement has matured, there is greater need to focus on quantitative measures of the extent of implementation within sectors and countries so that a higher level of application can be defined and numerical targets established. Advocates of eco-efficiency should recognise the need to shift from philosophical rhetoric to measurable results. We need global competition for eco-efficiency performance.

CLEANER PRODUCTION IN SMALL AND MEDIUM-SIZED ENTERPRISES: THE ROLE OF CLEANER PRODUCTION PROGRAMMES

C.M. Lin
Hong Kong Productivity Council, Hong Kong

1.0 Introduction

Pollution is an unwanted by-product of industrialisation. Due to our past ignorance or negligence, we have made quite a number of environmental mistakes, inflicting serious harm on our environment. Some notable examples of environmental disasters include the London smog episode caused by air pollution, the Minamata disease caused by water pollution, and the more recent depletion of the ozone layer caused by CFC emissions.

It is true and gratifying that environmental awareness has grown considerably in recent years. In addition to the developing end-of-pipe pollution control technologies to mitigate the effects of pollutants, the concept of sustainable development was also promulgated, and this laudable concept represents a more holistic approach to tackling our environmental problems. A number of companies, especially the big international corporations, were quick to realise the importance of sound environmental management and sustainable development. For example, the International Chamber of Commerce launched the Business Charter for Sustainable Development in April 1991 at the Second World Industry Conference on Environmental Management to assist enterprises in fulfilling their commitment to environmental stewardship.

To bring about sustainable development, the adoption of cleaner production is an extremely important tool that can augment or replace the traditional tool of end-of-pipe treatment. Whereas the large corporations have more resources and, thus, are better equipped to handle cleaner production, the small and medium-sized enterprises (SMEs) have a different set of characteristics and it is unrealistic to assume that they would be able to achieve cleaner production on their own without much difficulty. Before designing ways of facilitating the adoption of cleaner production by SMEs, it will be useful to closely examine the profile and characteristics of these companies in order to understand the problems and barriers they face.

2.0 Characteristics of SMEs

Typically, SMEs vastly outnumber large corporations. In Hong Kong, over 30,000 factories are packed into a small city with an area of about 1,000 km^2, and more than 95 per cent of these factories employ fewer than 50 workers. It is not too difficult to imagine how small these businesses are. This is also true in many other Asian countries, such as India, Thailand and Indonesia, where over 90 per cent of companies are SMEs.

Although SMEs are small in size, their importance should not be disparaged. Their smallness gives them the advantage of being flexible, enabling them to respond quickly to meet changes in production as demanded by their clients, who are often the larger corporations. Thus, many SMEs are providing crucially important linkage support to the large enterprises.

Despite their contribution to the economy, however, SMEs can create very severe problems in terms of environmental degradation. Being large in number and usually widely dispersed throughout a country, SMEs are extremely difficult for the environmental authority to check to ensure their compliance with requirements. In contrast with the larger corporations, SMEs generally lack a sense of commitment to be environmentally responsible. It is usually when SMEs are faced with stiff fines for non-compliance that they become more ready to install environmental improvement measures.

In the past, these environmental improvement measures were usually end-of-pipe pollution treatment facilities to mitigate the effects of pollutants arising from production processes. Recently, the practice of cleaner production has also been recognised by factories as a cost-effective way of mitigating environmental impact, which not only improves environmental performance but also reduces production costs and results in financial return.

3.0 Examples of Cleaner Production

Cleaner production is applicable to different sectors and companies of all sizes. Several examples will be discussed to examine how cleaner production can be practised in different types of SMEs. The first example is a small electroplating company employing 30 workers. This company installed in its factory two barrel nickel-plating lines. Barrel-plating is a plating operation in which the small mass-produced components are loaded into a tumbling barrel, and the whole barrel is immersed in the plating baths. The barrels are perforated to allow free movement of plating solution through the barrels, while securely retaining the small workpieces within them. The workpieces are immersed in a nickel-plating bath for the electrodeposition of nickel on the surface of the workpieces. A dragout tank is provided immediately after the nickel-plating bath to serve as a "still" rinse. The workpieces are then rinsed again with running rinsing water before they are dried at an elevated temperature as finished products. After this stage of rinsing, the running rinse water contains nickel, which is a source of pollution. Instead of installing end-of-pipe equipment to treat the nickel, the factory decided to install a nickel recovery unit to recover the nickel for reuse.

The nickel recovery unit has been in service for about two and a half years. It is estimated that a total of 65 kg of nickel sulphate is recovered per month and is reused in the plating bath. The company mentioned that the nickel recovery system not only completely eliminated their pollution problem but also brought them economic savings. The nickel recovery unit costs about US$20,000 and the payback period is about four years. As the recovery process removes pollution and brings economic benefits, it can be classified as a beneficial cleaner production process.

A second example is a metal-painting factory that uses electrostatic spray for surface painting instead of the conventional air-atomised spray. With air-atomised spray, the paint is carried by compressed air onto the surface of the workpiece to be painted. The transfer efficiency of this conventional process is about 40 per cent, and the paint that is not coated onto the workpiece becomes pollutant. With electrostatic spray, paint is supplied to the nozzle of the spray gun at high pressure to achieve atomisation instead of using compressed air to achieve atomisation. A high voltage charge is also applied to the nozzle to assist atomisation. The workpiece is earthed, and when the charged paint is sprayed towards the workpiece, an electrostatic field is formed to attract the paint particles onto the surface of the workpiece. The transfer efficiency of this process is about 90 per cent, resulting in paint savings and a significant decrease in pollutants. The payback period is less than a year.

A further example is a small textile finishing factory employing 50 workers. This factory developed an automated low-pressure kier to replace the traditional kier in performing scouring of cotton. In a traditional kier, sodium hypochlorite is used as the scouring agent and close control of the process operation is required to avoid the undesirable occurrence of scouring spots on the product. By automating the kier, operator error is eliminated and wastage of scouring chemicals is avoided. By lowering the operating pressure which reduces the rate of spot-damage occurrence, the factory is able to replace sodium hypochlorite with hydrogen peroxide, a chemical which is much more environment-friendly but could not be used previously because of the danger of causing scouring spots. By using the automated lower pressure kier, the factory is able to achieve a saving of 20 per cent in chemical and energy costs, and a 60 per cent saving in labour costs, together with a reduction of harm to the environment.

These examples appear to illustrate that cleaner production can offer an answer to pollution problems and should gain ready acceptance by SMEs. Unfortunately, this is not yet the situation because of the many barriers to introducing cleaner production to SMEs. This paper aims at constructing a theoretical model to explain the nature of these barriers and gives suggestions on how these barriers can be removed.

4.0   A Conceptual Model of Barriers to Introducing Cleaner Production in SMEs

The many barriers to introducing cleaner production to SMEs can be broadly classified into two categories:

- the internal barriers, and
- the external barriers.

The internal barriers are those limitations inherent in the SME itself and include the management barrier and the organisational barrier. Theoretically these internal barriers can be removed by improving the internal operations of the SME, either out of its own volition or through the encouragement and support of an external agency. The external barriers are limitations external to the SME and beyond its control. External barriers include the technology barrier and the enforcement barrier. These external barriers must be removed by external agencies.

4.1   Management Barrier

This is related to the knowledge, aptitude and attitude of the management of SMEs. Many decision-makers in SMEs are not qualified managers, and they are not familiar with modern management practices involving corporate environmental policy or cleaner production. They are more familiar with the traditional production process itself, and hence their attention is usually drawn to securing more job orders and increasing their production capacity as the major way of maintaining or increasing their profit level. Very few of them pay attention to process upgrading or quality improvement, or to clean technology as another option that could prove to be more profitable and strategically superior. They know little or nothing about cleaner production and are not aware of its availability and the possible associated benefits. When confronted with an environmental problem that can no longer be ducked, the first solution that comes into their minds is how to install end-of-pipe treatment systems that can neutralise or contain the pollutants. Even when the methodology and merits of cleaner production are explained to them, SMEs have considerable difficulties in understanding the concept and making reasoned judgements on the suitability of using cleaner production in their operations. The natural tendency is for them to resist something which they cannot understand well and take the more familiar end-of-pipe option. This tendency is often reinforced when SME management seek advice from their staff, who are usually equally uninformed and lack knowledge about cleaner production practices.

4.2   Organisational Barrier

This is related to the organisational structure and characteristics of SMEs. Because SMEs are small in size, they are more vulnerable to risk. A single mistake may not do much harm to a large corporation, but the same mistake may cost an SME very dearly. It is therefore not surprising that SMEs are generally more risk-averse. Because cleaner production practices are often an integral part of an operation, SMEs may be fearful that if something goes wrong, the problem will affect production as a whole and seriously endanger the existence of the SME itself. On the other hand, conventional end-of-pipe treatment is separate from the production process, has been practised for many years, and has proved its usefulness. It is therefore difficult to convince SMEs to adopt cleaner production as an alternative to end-of-pipe treatment methods.

Another organisational barrier is the lack of technical support within SMEs. While larger companies can assign their staff to investigate in detail the feasibility and merits of adopting cleaner production, SMEs do not have the necessary staff resources to undertake this task and the option of cleaner production is simply not considered.

The non-availability of funding for implementing cleaner production is also a potential barrier. Although the cost of cleaner production may be lower than the cost of end-of-pipe treatment, it is paradoxical that obtaining funding for cleaner production can be more difficult. As end-of-pipe treatment usually involves the use of tangible pollution control equipment, financial institutions have less difficulty in assessing and recognising the value of this piece of equipment. Cleaner production, on the other hand, may involve a combination of measures such as improving factory layout and housekeeping, acquiring some minor equipment to improve the production flow, training workers, using better and more expensive raw materials. SMEs will find it much more difficult to gain the support from financial institutions in implementing these beneficial measures because, from the financier's perspective, they are not related to tangible assets. SMEs will then need to finance cleaner production measures on their own, and they may not have sufficiently high liquidity or a strong enough cash flow position to afford these measures.

4.3 Technology Barrier

This is related to the beneficial value of the cleaner production measures. It is postulated that cleaner production can be classified into two main types according to the extent of its benefits. Type 1 cleaner production is the highly beneficial type that can both eliminate pollution control costs and reduce manufacturing costs. Type 2 cleaner production is the marginally beneficial type that can reduce pollution control costs but increases manufacturing costs, although the overall cost of production is still marginally reduced. These two types are at opposite ends of the benefit spectrum, and there is no absolute dividing line where one type finishes and the other begins. There are bigger incentives to adopt cleaner production that is closer to the Type 1 category. SMEs require a higher degree of motivation, and only cleaner production that is close to Type 1 will be adopted by SMEs. This is because SMEs require more high-level management involvement in making a decision on the acquisition of cleaner production, and this opportunity cost of high-level involvement has to be offset by a more favourable return. Furthermore, a higher return is also required to justify a clean technology investment that is seen to be more high-risk in the perspective of the risk-averse SMEs. It is necessary to develop more cleaner production technologies that are closer to the Type 1 category.[12]

4.4 Enforcement Barrier

This is related to the adequacy of environmental legislation and the extent of enforcement. Without effective enforcement of environmental legislation, the driving force for SMEs to adopt cleaner production will be considerably weakened. Whereas the larger corporations may have an environmental policy independent of legislative requirements, SMEs are influenced to a large extent by government pressure to comply with statutory regulations. If SMEs are not required to improve their environmental performance, they would most likely continue to channel their attention and resources into other areas. After all, environmental consideration is usually only a matter of secondary importance for SMEs. Lacking a suitable environmental driving force, even a truly Type 1 cleaner production will not be able to attract the attention it well deserves, not to mention the complicating fact that it is possible for Type 1 cleaner production to be downgraded to Type 2 when there is inadequate environmental legislation or enforcement.

The above conceptual model aims at providing a simplified theoretical framework in understanding the barriers to SMEs' introduction of cleaner production and designing appropriate strategies to overcome the barriers. However, it should be stressed that this model is simplistic in nature: barriers can be interrelated, and some barriers can bear the dual characteristics of being both external and internal. For example, the technology barrier, which is classified as an external barrier, can also be viewed as a partly internal barrier because it is related to the organisational structure of an SME. Another barrier, the cost barrier, is classified as internal because it is caused by the smallness of SMEs. However, it can also be viewed as external in the sense that it is external financial institutions which refuse to lend financial support and so give rise to this barrier. Nevertheless, the broad classification of barriers into internal and external can help us give proper focus in designing the intervening strategies.

---

[12] For a more detailed discussion, see C.M. Lin, "Cleaner production in small and medium-sized industries," in *Industry and Environment*, Vol. 17, No. 4, October-December 1994. This quarterly review, published by the UNEP Industry and Environment Office, often contains articles related to cleaner production including in SMEs. The newsletter of UNEP's Cleaner Production Network also appears regularly in the review. For more information, contact: UNEP IE, 39-43 quai André-Citroën, 75739 Paris Cedex 15, France; email: unepie@unep.fr; http://www.unepie.org; fax: (33) 01 44 37 14 74.

If the barrier is internal in nature, we should pay more attention to improving the internal management and structure of the SME. If the barrier is external, emphasis should be given to improving support mechanisms that are beyond the control of SMEs.

5.0   Designing Strategies for Cleaner Production in SMEs

Having discussed the various types of barriers to introducing cleaner production to SMEs, it can be readily seen that SMEs cannot be expected to take a proactive approach to implement cleaner production on their own initiative. A set of coherent strategies designed to remove these obstacles will be needed.

The recommended strategies are listed below:

- developing highly beneficial cleaner production;
- formulating appropriate environmental legislation and implementing it efficiently;
- removing the organisational barrier through the provision of adequate support schemes;
- enhancing management capability and facilitating the management process.

5.1   Developing Highly Beneficial Cleaner Production

This is an essential step in removing the technology barrier. SMEs do not have research and development capabilities and they cannot afford to experiment to discover the truly beneficial cleaner production methods. Proven, highly beneficial cleaner production methods must be readily available for SMEs to decide whether or not it is worth their while to adopt them. The responsibility for developing such highly beneficial cleaner production methods must fall upon research institutions or the government, not the SMEs. The initial development cost will need to be defrayed by the government, although the cost can be recovered later by imposing a charge on SMEs that choose to adopt the developed cleaner production technology. Although the developmental cost is recoverable, it is unlikely that commercial research organisations would want to take up this task because of the inherent uncertainties and risks involved. Success in developing a sound and beneficial technology is no guarantee that the technology will be adopted: successful marketing of the technology will still be required. Many hurdles will be encountered in this marketing process – the hurdles being those other barriers that we have already discussed. Commercial research institutions are likely to be dissuaded by this marketing uncertainty. Thus, the government will need to provide initial funding to support a research institution or a cleaner production development centre to undertake this task. It is entirely possible that this institution can become self-supporting financially after a period of time.

5.2   Formulating Appropriate Environmental Legislation and Implementing It Effectively

As noted previously, SMEs seldom place top priority on environmental management. A driving force is needed to coerce them into environmental compliance before these companies will turn their attention to cleaner production. There must be appropriate environmental legislation, enforced effectively, to provide this driving force.

5.3   Removing the Organisational Barrier by Providing Adequate Support Measures

The organisational barrier, or the organisational weaknesses of the SMEs, are difficult to remove because they are related to characteristics inherent in SMEs. The government will need to design support schemes to mitigate the effects of these organisational weaknesses.

Regarding the lack of technical support and environmental experts within SMEs to assess and implement cleaner production, it is impractical to expect an SME to recruit its own expert to undertake this task. SMEs do not have the financial resources to afford this, nor do they possess the capability or time to select the right expert. The government needs to intervene again. A possible solution is for the government to sponsor the training of cleaner production professionals to serve SMEs. These professionals must be practitioners who are able to provide a complete package of service in the assessment, selection and, most importantly, implementation of cleaner production methods. The professionals should preferably not be government officials but private consultants from government-related organisations, such as the national productivity organisations or trade associations. They should charge a fee for the provided service, probably at a subsidised rate initially, but should be able to get full cost recovery or better eventually. For similar reasons discussed above, commercial companies are unlikely to be interested in providing this kind of service initially. The government has to take the initiative by liaising with suitable organisations or sponsoring the setting up of a cleaner production consultancy centre to take up this task.

The SMEs' lack of funding is another organisational barrier, and some form of government assistance is required. Assistance can be direct financial aid, such as providing an interest-bearing loan for the implementation of cleaner production measures. The terms of the loan need not contain a subsidy element, although such an element would definitely help to attract SMEs in the initial stages. The subsidy element is not too important, as the purpose of the loan is to help SMEs that would otherwise have difficulty in convincing financiers that cleaner production is a worthwhile investment. Alternatively, the government could provide indirect assistance by making arrangements with the private financiers to help them understand the merits of cleaner production, thus enhancing their willingness to provide loans for these beneficial activities that could ultimately generate returns for both the borrowers and the lenders.

6.0   Enhancing Management Capability and Facilitating the Management Process

This is the most important strategy, aimed at influencing the SME management to make a positive decision on the adoption of cleaner production. Although there are many negative barriers to introducing cleaner production to SMEs, there is a very important positive factor which must be noted. The management structure of SMEs is extremely simple: usually there is only one dominant decision-maker – the SME owner himself – and the decision-making process can be very quick and efficient once the decision-maker is convinced. Great emphasis must, therefore, be placed on persuading the SME management to make the decision to acquire cleaner production.

The establishment of a cleaner production demonstration factory is a direct and effective way of making SME management understand the benefits and removing their unfounded fears about possible adverse consequences of cleaner production. The government should assist a number of SMEs to implement cleaner production measures in their factories and provide them with incentives to open their factories to other SMEs on a regular basis to share their experience. Follow-up interactions with the SME visitors should be made to encourage and assist them to adopt cleaner production. Of course, adequate technical support must be available from cleaner production professionals to overcome the organisational barrier and sufficient financial support must be available to overcome any possible cost barrier.

There should be other types of cleaner production marketing to arouse the awareness of SMEs. Information about cleaner production should be made readily available to SMEs in the form of concise booklets, videos and case studies. Talks and seminars on cleaner production for SMEs should be organised. The information dissemination process would increase the knowledge of SME management about cleaner production and facilitate their decision-making process on adopting cleaner production. A cleaner production marketing group should be set up to do this type of marketing work.

In the longer term, cleaner production should be introduced into the education curriculum, and more management training for SMEs on the interaction of environment and production should be organised to remove the management barrier.

7.0   Key Factors for Implementing Cleaner Production in SMEs

From the above discussion it can be seen that government support is crucially important in removing the cleaner production barriers, especially in the initial stages. Once the ball is rolling, cleaner production can be a self-supporting activity. The priority is to mobilise the relevant government departments. Departments concerned with environment must ensure that companies give proper attention to environmental management while carrying out the production process. Only when this has been accomplished can cleaner production have a chance to compete with end-of-pipe treatment to gain the acceptance of SMEs as a suitable candidate for environmental improvement. Departments concerned with industry must then help the SMEs to recognise the benefits of cleaner production and make the right choice. Action is also needed to facilitate the introduction of cleaner production to SMEs. To this end, it is necessary for the government to co-ordinate with all related parties, such as the national productivity organisations, trade associations, research institutions, training institutions and financial institutions, to dismantle the barriers and start the ball rolling. It will be particularly helpful for the government to formulate a detailed cleaner production policy, perhaps taking into consideration the above conceptual model and the suggested strategies. The government will then be able to design an action plan in the form of a cleaner production programme, the details of which will depend on the policy. However, the cleaner production programme must fulfil functions of cleaner production technology development, cleaner production consulting, and cleaner production marketing. It would be ideal for the government to set up a cleaner production centre that can, possibly in association with other suitable government departments and organisations, play a co-ordinating role and perform all three functions.

8.0   Conclusion

Cleaner production is a valuable tool that can help companies to improve their environmental performance and enhance their productivity. There are internal and external barriers to overcome, however, before cleaner production can be successfully introduced to SMEs. The government is in the best position to initiate policies to assist SMEs in overcoming the barriers, although the actual implementation of the cleaner production programme does not need to be carried out by the government. In fact, it is more appropriate for other non-profit agencies, such as the national productivity organisations or cleaner production centres, to take up this task. A good cleaner production programme must encompass the development of cleaner production technology, provision of comprehensive consultancy services and proactive marketing, which are the three essential pillars for gaining SMEs' acceptance of cleaner production and achieving green productivity.

THE ENVIRONMENTAL GOODS AND SERVICES INDUSTRY IN OECD AND DYNAMIC NON-MEMBER ECONOMIES

Graham Vickery and Maria Iarrera
Directorate for Science, Technology and Industry, OECD

1.0   Introduction

The environmental goods and services industry is defined as comprising activities which produce goods and services to measure, prevent, limit or correct environmental damage to water, air and soil, as well as problems related to waste, noise and ecosystems. It includes suppliers of equipment, materials, and services for air and water pollution control (for example, chemical and biological recovery systems, sewage treatment, wastewater reuse equipment); solid waste management and some recycling; protection of soil and water; noise pollution control; pollution monitoring; special environmental services (for example, engineering design/specification/project management, environmental impact assessment, environmental audits, environmental research and development, education and training). To some extent, natural resources conservation and protection services, renewable energy equipment, cleaner production equipment, and cleaner products are included, although this last group poses boundary problems and measurement difficulties despite their acknowledged importance and major contribution to achieving sustainable development. Since cleaner technologies, processes and products are often difficult to define and identify, data in this paper will mainly refer to suppliers of pollution control, reduction, clean-up and waste handling equipment and related technology, materials and services. It will be indicated when cleaner technologies and products are considered.

Recently, the environmental goods and services industry has received attention for two main reasons: its rapid rate of growth and its strong contribution to sustainable development. The industry is characterised by a global environmental market which is estimated to be of the order of US$250 billion (placing it between the pharmaceutical industry and the information technology industry in size, excluding most clean technologies), and is growing at around 5 per cent per year.

Growth in the environment industry is highly dependent on public awareness of environmental protection and environmental regulations. Introduction and enforcement of measures for environmental protection (environmental laws, regulations and standards, taxes, tradable permits, charges, fees, etc.) largely determine the market development, growth and characteristics of the environmental industry. An increasing number of firms appear also to be incorporating environmental factors into their development strategies as a source of competitive advantage. It is by anticipating and meeting these demands that the environment industry can play a significant role in improving environmental performance.

Governments are experimenting with mixed approaches to environmental management, involving the use of economic instruments in support of command-and-control regulations, voluntary agreements and broad strategic environmental planning. Waste minimisation and cleaner production are receiving greater attention, because they appear to be more efficient in yielding economic benefits and improving environmental performance. They encourage the industrial sector to increase environmental effort and expenditures, raising the demand for environmental goods and services.

This mixed approach to environmental management by governments has direct impacts on the environment industry. Flexible environmental measures and economic instruments often force the industry to be more innovative and switch from supplying end-of-pipe equipment to cleaner technologies and productive processes. Induced innovation also has an impact on the environment industry. Companies, by upgrading their competitive advantage through the use of cleaner processes, boost demand for new, cleaner environmental goods and services. As this demand increases, research and development and technological innovation become of paramount importance for sustaining growth and competitiveness in the supply industry.

In light of these considerations, this paper will discuss the features of the environment industry in OECD countries and in the Dynamic Non-Member Economies (DNMEs: Argentina, Brazil, Chile, Hong Kong, Korea,[1] Malaysia, Singapore, Thailand, Chinese Taipei) and China. Prospects and challenges for the environmental goods and services industry in the DNMEs and China will be evaluated on the basis of the characteristics of these economies (for example, features of the production structure, the state of environmental regulation, and forecast economic growth) and of OECD experience.

2.0   The Environmental Goods and Services Industry in OECD Countries: Situation and Prospects

In most OECD Member countries, the environment industry has shown rapid growth in the last ten years. Even though economic conditions recently slowed its growth, the environment industry has been one of the best performing sectors along with biotechnology and communications.

The OECD environment industry employs approximately 1 per cent of the labour force, with a market estimated to be of the order of US$200 billion. It is estimated to grow at an average rate of 5-6 per cent up to the year 2000 (see Table 1).

The international market for environmental goods and services is growing rapidly. Estimates of total exports of environmental goods and services are in the range of 5-10 per cent of production, similar to exports in the pharmaceutical industry, but smaller than exports in automobiles and computers where products are more standardised. Trade in environmental goods and services will accelerate to Eastern European countries, East Asian countries and Latin American DNMEs.

It is expected that the industry will become increasingly internationalised and trade-oriented as it develops, particularly in more mature areas such as solid waste and water management and air pollution control. This is due to adoption of world-wide environmental standards, which will open more international markets, to greater privatisation and deregulation of utilities such as water and electricity which expands opportunities for participation by foreign firms, and to consolidation of the supply industry as it matures. Further significant changes in the industry can be expected from the expansion of

---

[1]   Korea became an OECD Member country in 1996.

global operations of major firms, as they set up foreign operations to enter markets and seek foreign partners to develop new technologies in areas such as biotechnology and bioremediation, and renewable energy.

Table 1: Projections of the Global Market for Environmental Goods and Services (US$ billion)

	OECD		ECOTEC			ETDC		Environmental Business International	
	1990	2000	1992	2000	2010	1990	2000	1992	1998
OECD countries									
North America	85	125	100	147	240	125	217	145	199
Europe (1)	51	78	60	89	144	63	188	94	132
Japan	24	39	30	44	72	24	65	21	31
Australia/ New Zealand	2	3				2	4	3	5
Subtotal	**164**	**245**	**195**	**289**	**456**	**214**	**474**	**260**	**367**
Eastern Europe/NIS	15	21	5	9	23	15	25	14	27
Asia(2)			8	19	77	20	69	6	13
Latin America	–	–	2	5	15	–	–	6	10
Rest of world	21	34				6	12	6	9
Total world	**200**	**300**	**210**	**320**	**570**	**255**	**580**	**295**	**426**

Notes

(1) All Western Europe.

(2) East and Southeast Asia: Chinese Taipei, Hong Kong, Korea, Singapore, Malaysia, Thailand, rest of Asian Pacific, China, India.

Sources: Reproduced from OECD, 1996a. OECD (1992) not including "clean" technologies; ECOTEC (1994) not including "clean" technologies; ETDC (Environmental Technologies Development Corporation), in Higgins (1994) including replacement "clean" technologies only, excluding entirely new "clean" processes, "clean" and alternative energy generation, and "clean" products; Environmental Business International, in OTA (1994) including some "clean" technologies such as alternative energy sources.

The environmental goods and services industry is highly dependent for development on environmental regulation, on increased corporate and public awareness of environmental protection, and on technological innovation. Policy and instruments for environmental protection in OECD countries have a strong impact on its size and structure. There has been a shift in focus towards using economic instruments and regulations in combination, as well as voluntary agreements, which concentrate more on overall environmental performance and provide greater flexibility in achieving environmental goals.

Consequently, the environment industry is changing configuration in most OECD countries. In the past, environmental goods and services suppliers focused on stand-alone and end-of-pipe equipment, but the trend has now shifted towards providing integrated solutions.

Important barriers to development of the industry have been uncertainty regarding environmental regulations, and related uncertainties in the supply and demand of new technologies. There are considerable barriers linked to poorly developed markets, differences among national regulations, and technical regulations and specifications which have inhibited flexibility, innovation and scale economies on the supply side. There may also be financial barriers to development, particularly for start-ups and small businesses in new areas which combine different technologies to provide new environmental solutions

General industrial policies and programmes in the areas of R&D and technology, investment incentives to stimulate demand, small firm support, export promotion, etc. have major impacts on the industry. Targeted support for environmental R&D is an important development tool. All OECD countries have identified pollution control and environmental improvement as important socio-economic objectives and provide considerable government R & D resources to meet these objectives (almost US$2 billion in ppps – purchasing power parities – in 1992). Government purchasing and procurement has major impacts in many countries, as about one-half of environmental investment depends on government expenditures.

3.0   The Environmental Goods and Services Industry in the DNMEs: Situation and Prospects

3.1   General Features

Most DNMEs enjoyed high growth rates during the last 20 years. However, the Dynamic Asian Economies (Chinese Taipei, Hong Kong, Korea, Singapore, Malaysia and Thailand) and the reforming economies of Latin America (Argentina, Brazil and Chile) differ in their economic development path, structure and culture. They are therefore discussed separately below.

The Dynamic Asian Economies (DAEs) have followed a more balanced development path, characterised by a stable economic framework. Governments have adopted policies based on outward-oriented industrialisation, liberalisation of financial markets, investments in education and skills upgrading, and incentives to domestic and foreign investments, which have facilitated rapid economic growth without widening income inequality.

In contrast, in the reforming economies of Latin America (Argentina, Brazil and Chile) economic growth was not accompanied by macroeconomic stability. During the 1970s, governments of these countries adopted an import substitution strategy to promote economic development and industrialisation. This strategy required high levels of protection, which in the presence of relatively small domestic markets facilitated the creation of monopolies. As a consequence, the absence of domestic and foreign competition provided little incentive to upgrade technology. In the 1980s, the Latin American DNMEs started a process of reforms based on macroeconomic stabilisation (debt and inflation) and public sector reforms (privatisation, reallocation of subsidies). These reforms have resulted in relative economic stability characterised by a more balanced private-public industrial structure.

Both "regions" have experienced rapid industrialisation and urbanisation, with attendant high levels of pollution. In response, all countries have developed comprehensive environmental regulations which have helped create markets for the environmental goods and services industry. Stronger economic development and increasing environmental awareness may boost further growth in the environmental markets in these regions.

It has been estimated that the Asian economies will increase their demand for water and wastewater disposal equipment in the next few years by about 30-40 per cent, and that the demand for environmental monitoring will increase by 30 per cent. Harmonization of national environmental standards and the pusuit of international environmental agreements may also have considerable impacts by stimulating investment by industry to achieve new standards and by setting common technical targets for environmental quality.

3.2 The Dynamic Asian Economies (DAEs) and China

Despite many differences in natural resources, culture and political institutions, the DAEs all enjoy high rates of economic growth, relatively low income inequality, high rates of growth of manufactured exports, all accompanied by increasing levels of pollution. In the last ten years, they experienced an average 6-10 per cent annual economic growth and an average 10-20 per cent annual growth in pollution levels.

China has enjoyed even higher growth rates (average rate of 10-11 per cent in the last five years). Economic reforms, including special economic zones where conditions are similar to free markets, have provided incentives for foreign business to operate in China as well as dramatically boosting local industry. Industrial development has been very rapid in coastal regions compared with the internal agricultural regions, and has concentrated most environmental problems in the coastal areas.

Like the Central and Eastern European (CEE) countries, the DAEs are seeking to reduce their pollution load. Two distinctions from the CEE countries, however, are that the DAEs enjoy a stable economic framework which will allow them to tackle their environmental problems, and they have a smaller legacy of accumulated environmental degradation.

All of the DAEs have developed rather comprehensive environmental regulations. Their governments are also employing economic incentives as complements to regulations. The Polluter-Pays Principle is increasingly applied to encourage pollution prevention; this indirectly may catalyse development of cleaner technologies and products. There are also comprehensive plans for government environmental expenditure in most of these economies.

Consequently, most of these economies have developed an end-of-pipe equipment industry and a small environmental services supplier industry. The environmental market in the DAEs and China was estimated at US$6 billion in 1993 with projected 6-12 per cent (or more) annual growth up to the year 1997, taking it close to US$10 billion (see Table 2). Water and wastewater treatment and air pollution control are the principal sectors, and they will attract increasing expenditures for environmental protection.

Table 2: Projected Market for Environmental Goods and Services in the DAEs and China (US$ million, 1993)

Economy	Market size	Growth rate (%) (1993-1997)	1993 GDP (US$ bn)	% of GDP
Chinese Taipei	1,700	8-12	208	0.8
Korea	1,600	8-12	321	0.5
Hong Kong	800	8-12	85	0.9
Thailand	500	20-25	103	0.5
Malaysia	350	20-25	124	0.3
Singapore	300	6-10	55	0.5
China	700	10-15	505	0.1

Note: Estimates include some "clean" technologies, such as alternative energy sources.

Source: Derived from Environmental Business International, Inc. (1995).

In principle, stronger environmental regulations and the region's rapid economic growth should boost the demand for environmental goods and services to focus more on the development of cleaner technologies and products than on end-of-pipe equipment. Rapid economic growth allows a more rapid technological turnover. Older and more resource-intensive technologies can more easily be replaced, helping industrial restructuring and improving competitiveness with reduced environmental impacts. For the next ten years, it has been estimated that in these economies 50 per cent of capital stock will be replaced, much of it incorporating new technologies, which could easily be cleaner technologies. Although cleaner technologies may develop very rapidly because of the high level of technological turnover, the market demand for end-of-pipe equipment will also remain strong.

The major impediment to the growth of this industry is lack of enforcement of environmental regulations. There are opportunities to promote better co-ordination among financial and environmental institutions in order to support environmentally sound investment, and to improve consistency in enforcing environmental regulation.

Chinese Taipei

Following a slow start in the 1980s, the government has seriously committed itself to environmental protection, catalysed by the high level of industrial and urban pollution. New environmental regulation has been enacted, based on applying the same principles as in OECD countries:

- the Polluter-Pays Principle;

- pollution prevention, which promotes programmes for waste minimisation, environmental management systems, and cleaner technologies and products;

- public participation, which promotes the participation of relevant stakeholders;

148

- privatisation, which requires in most cases some industrial restructuring, and facilitates the use of cleaner production and treatment processes.

The government has developed a comprehensive plan for environmental expenditures, which allocated US$12 billion for the period 1992-1997 (see Table 3). Municipal solid waste disposal and waste management in state-owned enterprises are recognised as major problems. They were allocated almost three-quarters of total planned expenditures.

This general framework and a market for environmental goods and services of US$1,700 million annually, the biggest in the Asian region with projected annual growth around 8-12 per cent, suggest that the environment industry in Chinese Taipei is in a good position for broader development and that it will develop even faster in the future.

Table 3: Environmental Expenditure Programme 1992-1997: Chinese Taipei

Sector	US$ billion	% of total
Municipal solid waste	4.80	40
State-run corporations	4.08	34
Other public	1.32	11
Pollution of rivers	0.72	6
Air/noise pollution	0.48	4
Industrial wastewater	0.24	2
Drinking water	0.12	1
Industrial solid waste	0.12	1
Others	0.12	1
Total	12.0	100

Source: Environmental Protection Administration, in OTA.

In 1992, there were 370 pollution control companies, which supplied 35 per cent of the domestic market. To fill the gap between domestic supply and demand, local companies are trying to establish technology transfer agreements and joint ventures with foreign companies (especially US companies). For this reason, building domestic engineering capability in the environmental field has been strongly promoted.

Recently, the Ministry of Economic Affairs has changed its critical attitude towards environmental regulation and begun supporting the commercialisation of pollution control technologies and helping industry to meet regulations. Furthermore, the Industrial Technology Research Institute established the Centre for Pollution Control and Technology, which co-ordinates research and development and provides assistance to private environmental firms.

The main environmental problems in Chinese Taipei are related to enforcement of environmental regulations. This is attributed to inadequate infrastructure, insufficient administrative and information systems, and lack of skilled personnel. Furthermore, recent lower private investment rates have reinforced continuing worries among business that environmental protection and remediation policies hold back international competitiveness, particularly because the economy is highly dependent on exports.

Korea

Korea is highly industrialised, with a focus on heavy industries. The industrial sector produces more than 40 per cent of GDP, of which 30 per cent is related to machinery and equipment production. Agriculture contributes 7 per cent to GDP and the service sector 50 per cent. Rapid industrialisation accompanied by urbanisation has rapidly increased levels of air, water and solid waste pollution.

Korea has developed the most comprehensive environmental regulation among the DAEs. Since 1978, with the enactment of the first Environmental Preservation Act (EPA), the Korean government has dedicated a large amount of resources to environmental protection. The environmental regulations include standards and economic incentives which have been developed on the basis of the American and Japanese environmental laws. The Polluter-Pays Principle has been endorsed and emission charges, deposit fees to cover the costs of waste recycling, and a liability system for pollution damage by industrial enterprises implemented.

Recently, the government has enacted a law to support the environment industry and to establish an institute for environmental research and technology consulting. This institute, the Institute for Environmental Policy and Technology Development, aims to undertake research on environmental technologies and science development. Furthermore, the Ministry of Environment has been standardising environmental facilities since 1987 to help industry improve pollution control and to assist trade with other countries. Besides these initiatives, Korea developed an environmental investment plan totalling US$12 billion (see Table 4).

The environmental market is estimated to be US$1.6 billion and it is expected to grow at around 8-12 per cent annually. Estimates indicate that 60 per cent of the market is related to pollution prevention activities. There are currently 38,000 people working in the field of environmental science and technologies.

Table 4: Environmental Investment Plan in Korea (US$ million)

	1991	1992	1993	1994-95	Total (%)
Air pollution	1,384	1,342	599	1,094	4,419 (37)
Water pollution	622	872	1,110	1,624	4,229 (36)
Waste management	204	364	494	1,890	2,952 (25)
Soil conservation	12	15	18	48	93 (0.7)
Marine conservation	21	25	24	13	84 (0.7)
Nature conservation	0.3	0.7	1	3	5 (0.04)
R&D	3	12	13	26	53 (0.4)
Total	2,248	2,632	2,258	4,698	11,838 (100)

Source: Ministry of Environment, white paper in OTA, *Industry, Technology, and the Environment: Competitive Challenges and Business Opportunities* (1994).

The technological level of the environmental industry lags that of the Japanese or the American industries. Technology for air and water protection is middle to top class, but waste incineration and global environmental protection technologies, such as for CFC substitutes, have a rather weak competitive position.

As a consequence, air and water protection equipment are supplied domestically, while more advanced environmental technologies are normally imported from either Japan or the USA (import costs were estimated at US$98.3 million in 1992). For this reason the Ministry of Environment enacted a ten-year plan to support the development of environmental technologies, which aims to increase the competitiveness of these technologies (Long-term Master Plan for Environmental Technology Development 1992-2001, with an estimated budget of US$1 billion) and accelerate the use of cleaner processes in industry. Some results have already been achieved, since industry is spending less on pollution control equipment and more on recycling and cleaner technologies (Korean Chamber of Commerce, 1995).

Barriers to the development of cleaner technologies and to the environmental goods and services industry are related to weak enforcement of legislation, partially due to the lack of the necessary authority being given to the responsible agents, and to the organisation of environmental regulations by media, which makes it difficult for SMEs to comply with laws and regulations.

Hong Kong

Hong Kong is predominantly a services-oriented economy. Almost 80 per cent of its GDP is produced by the services sector, and only 20 per cent by the industry sector. Most of the environmental problems in Hong Kong are related to water and solid waste management, as a result of a highly urbanised development pattern.

Like other DAEs, Hong Kong has developed a relatively comprehensive framework of laws, standards and economic incentives for environmental protection. Recent public expenditures for environmental infrastructure are focused in two specific areas: sewage systems (US$2.5 billion) and solid waste management projects (US$1.6 billion.)

The environmental market in Hong Kong is estimated at around US$800 million and is expected to grow at a rate of 8-12 per cent. In recent years, the environment industry partly relocated to the southern region of China, with the prospect of becoming a major supplier of environmental goods and services in China.

Growth in the environmental industry will especially favour the environmental services sector, stimulated by a strong demand for environmental assistance from the more than 40,000 small and medium-sized enterprises in Hong Kong. The potential of the Chinese market will augment this demand. Increased concern for greater environmental regulatory compliance by SMEs has prompted the government to establish a Private Sector Committee for the Environment which, in collaboration with the Centre of Environmental Technology, is promoting and demonstrating cleaner production programmes to SMEs.

Thailand

The Thai economy is characterised by a strong services sector (51 per cent of GDP) and an industrial sector (39 per cent of GDP) concentrated in what are currently highly polluting activities (19 per cent in textiles and clothing and 40 per cent in machinery and equipment). The agriculture sector produces 10 per cent of GDP. The industrialisation process has resulted in a rapid and unbalanced increase in the demand for water and energy, and generated huge quantities of waste and pollution. Growing amounts of municipal and industrial waste, in combination with the lack of centralised and organised water collection and waste disposal infrastructures, are underlining demands for much more effective pollution control management.

To fulfil this need, the Thai Government has re-oriented environmental regulation towards incentive measures and developed a plan for environmental expenditure (see Table 5). This plan covers three main areas: environmental management, environmental quality promotion, and pollution control. The major investments are focused on wastewater treatment, urban solid waste management, and industrial infrastructure upgrading. Expenditures on the monitoring and enforcement of environmental regulations are modest and probably inadequate.

The market for environmental goods and services is estimated to range from US$0.5 billion (see Table 2) to US$3.2 billion (DEG-European Union, 1994). Most of the demand is concentrated in water supply and wastewater treatment and disposal (75 per cent) (see Table 6). The demand for recycling and materials recovery is also rapidly expanding. Opportunities for advanced cleaner technologies are expected to emerge at a later stage, when there is sufficient information on cleaner productive technologies, and the environmental costs of production are fully understood and internalised by industry.

The domestic environment industry supplies only 20 per cent of the total demand, while 25 per cent is supplied by American firms, 25 per cent by Japanese, 20 per cent by European and 5 per cent by Singapore firms. The domestic industry has, however, a track record in supplying end-of-pipe environmental technology.

Table 5: Government Expenditure on the Environment in Thailand, 1991-1994 (US$ million)

	1991	1992	1993	1994
Environmental management	4.9	6.4	8.7	30.0
Environmental quality promotion	13.5	91.7	178.5	219.7
Pollution control	6.2	4.6	4.6	18.7
Total	24.6	102.7	194.9	268.4

Source: Environmental Business International, Inc. (1995).

Table 6: Environmental Technologies Market Segmentation in Thailand, 1994 (% of total)

Clean water supply treatment and distribution	40
Wastewater collection, treatment, reuse and disposal	35
Solid and hazardous waste collection, treatment and disposal	15
Air pollution control equipment	10

Source: DEG-Commission of the European Union (1994).

More recently, the environment industry has developed domestic consulting and engineering services. Some of the largest Thai engineering, property development and financial companies have acquired significant stakes in local environmental services and technology supply companies.

The industrial location of enterprises, which are regrouped and concentrated in specific territorial areas, has facilitated the development of centralised waste treatment facilities. This is particularly true for small and medium-sized enterprises with similar waste streams.

Like most Asian countries, Thailand hopes to attract foreign investment through joint ventures, foreign direct investment and technology transfer programmes, in order to develop more advanced environmental technologies and upgraded know-how. Major obstacles to international co-operation by foreign firms are related to cost competitiveness and limited local technical skills for production or operation.

Malaysia

The Malaysian industrial sector has a number of major polluting industries, such as palm oil mills and rubber processing plants. Food processing, electronics, and chemicals and petrochemicals are increasingly important contributors to national production, and all have potentially high environmental impacts.

The first comprehensive environmental regulation, the Environmental Quality Act, was enacted in 1974. In 1976 the general regulatory framework, including environmental management objectives, was formalised. In 1991, the government reinforced its commitment to promoting environmental protection in the Sixth Environmental Plan (1991-1995), including encouragement for private sector involvement in environmental management. Co-operation between the public and private sectors was to be developed and promoted in priority areas: water treatment technologies; site remediation; air pollution control; commercial production of pollution control equipment; total quality management; resource management; training and development; R&D; promotion of energy efficiency and conservation programmes.

Furthermore, having recognised that regulatory enforcement is the major obstacle to compliance, the government reinforced efforts to support the implementation of environmental regulation. For example, from 1992 the Department of Environment increased the number of court sanctions brought against companies which were not complying with environmental regulations.

The environmental market is estimated from various sources to be of the order of US$500 million and it is expected to grow at a rate of 20-25 per cent annually. The environment industry is focused on traditional environmental problems such as wastewater treatment, solid and hazardous waste disposal, and air pollution control. In the future it will probably increasingly enter new sub-sectors, in collaboration with foreign companies.

Singapore

Singapore's structure of production is composed of strong services (63 per cent of the total GDP) and industrial (37 per cent of the GDP) sectors. Machinery and equipment manufacturing is the largest industrial sub-sector. The major environmental problems are related to energy efficiency and consumption.

The small domestic market, and strict environmental regulation and enforcement, have allowed Singapore to balance economic development and environmental protection. Singapore claims to be the cleanest country of the Asian region. Annual environmental expenditure was estimated to be around 1 per cent of GDP (US$350-390 million annually during the 1980s), which is in line with the average environmental expenditure in OECD countries.

Environmental market estimates range from US$300 to 670 million in the early 1990s (see Table 2 and Table 7). Singapore is developing a strong environment industry and hopes to become the regional centre for technology transfer in Asia. Its Ministry for Environment has formed a commercial division to provide environmental consulting to countries like Malaysia and Indonesia, and has established environmental technology co-operation through joint ventures with Germany and other EU countries to develop technologies, and with Vietnam and China to supply technology.

Table 7: Environmental Goods and Services Market in Singapore, 1992

Sub-sectors	US$ million	%
Industrial waste management equipment	370	55
Wastewater treatment equipment and services	200	30
Air pollution equipment	102	15
Total	672	100

Source: Park (1994), *Assessing the Environmental Market in the East Asian Region.*

The Singapore government has set up a Regional Institute of Environmental Technology as a joint venture with the European Union. It is the first of its kind in the Asian region; Singapore provides US$3.6 million and the European Union US$2.9 million to support its operation. This is a three-year project initially, which aims to develop and market advanced environmental technologies. It is expected to become self-financing.

The Singapore environment industry is highly competitive and innovative. It is well-connected with developed countries (including Canada, Member States of the European Union, and Australia) through joint ventures for environmental technologies.

China

Economic reforms have had a strong and continuing impact on the Chinese structure of production. China is becoming a highly industrialised economy, with the industry sector producing almost 50 per cent of GDP, the services sector contributing 33 per cent, and the agriculture sector 19 per cent. The major environmental problems are related to polluting industrial processes and low energy efficiency, which results in acid rain, toxic waste, water pollution, and increasing amounts of CO_2 emissions.

The Chinese government has recognised that improvement of environmental quality is of paramount importance. Pollution prevention and waste minimisation programmes were included in environmental regulations, together with economic instruments and other incentive measures.

The Chinese government enacted a five-year programme (1991-1995) for environmental protection with a projected budget of US$15 billion. Even if its target had been achieved, it would not have been sufficient to adequately improve environmental quality, as estimates show that US$34.7 billion would have been needed to retrofit all factories with pollution control equipment (International Environment Reporter, 1993). Most environmental projects are financed by local governments and concern basic urban sanitation, recycling, water purification, and garbage disposal. At present, 10 per cent of these projects are financed by foreign investors either through multilateral aid (World Bank) or through joint ventures between firms.

At present, the Chinese environmental market is estimated to be around US$700 million. The environment industry is still young and is not able to satisfy the total domestic market demand. For example, in 1991 China had a trade deficit in environmental protection equipment of US$91 million, with $119 million of imports and only $28 million of exports.

Nevertheless, the environment supply industry is expected to grow very quickly (due to 10-20 per cent annual demand growth), with most of the demand concentrated on simple and inexpensive environmental equipment. It has been reported that for the moment foreign technologies are either too expensive or too advanced for the Chinese market (International Environment Reporter, 1993). Furthermore, 80 per cent of wastewater and 70 per cent of solid waste are treated by using end-of-pipe equipment (estimates as at 1990). Overall, it is expected that cleaner processes and technologies will need more time before being broadly used in Chinese industry.

On the other hand, the potential for improvement is very large. It has been estimated that a 10 per cent improvement in energy and resources efficiency, through cleaner production and environmental management programmes, will save approximately 20 per cent of the new capital investment requirement. Furthermore, the Chinese Environmental Protection Committee has estimated that annual losses due to waste and inefficiencies in the production processes amount to about 18 per cent of the national budget.

Major obstacles to better enforcement of environmental regulations, improved environmental performance, and demand for environmental goods and services are related to the industrial structure. Large and inefficient state-owned enterprises and numerous small enterprises, especially township and village firms, are not easy to supervise and control. Furthermore, weak public pressure to promote environmental protection constrains the development of an environmental market and the local supply industry.

3.3   Latin American DNMEs

Industrial dynamism in Latin America was held back by the predominance of the public sector, monopolies, limited competition, and import substitution strategies coupled with reliance on foreign investment in some sectors. In the 1980s, most Latin American economies undertook economic reforms to promote stable economic conditions, control high inflation and increase investment, domestically and from overseas. The endorsement of privatisation reforms has opened the possibility for restructuring and investment in the industrial sector as well as in utilities and many services. Furthermore, positive results from the process of macroeconomic stabilisation suggest favourable growth prospects overall.

Poor enforcement, more than lack of legislation, is the main institutional obstacle to development and growth of environmental demand. Lack of resources and technical skills constrains growth of the supply side potential. Nevertheless, estimates for the environmental market range from US$2 to 6 billion (see Table 1 and Table 8) and suggest that it is growing at around 10 per cent annually. The market is driven by infrastructure-related projects (for example, sewage systems) and privatisation programmes.

The region's environment industry is still weak. It relies on foreign companies for products and innovation, and well over one-quarter of the domestic demand is satisfied by foreign companies. In the future, the local environment industry will need to improve its performance by training and skill development and by encouraging local entrepeneurs and universities to develop technologies. Privatisation programmes and the presence of numerous small and medium-sized enterprises will create a large market for environmental consulting services. Moreover, emphasis on pollution prevention programmes will create opportunities for cleaner process technologies.

Table 8: Environmental Markets in the Latin American DNMEs
(US$ million, 1992)

Country	Water and wastewater treatment	Air pollution control	Waste management	Total	% imported
Brazil	845	120	50	1,015	19
Chile	350	195	15	560	89
Argentina	100	53	15	168	25

Source: OTA (1994).

Brazil

In 1993, the Brazilian agricultural sector accounted for 11 per cent of GDP, industry contributed 37 per cent, and services 52 per cent. In 1994, the economic stabilisation programme, emphasising price stabilisation, deregulation of the economy and increased foreign investment, was implemented and was yielding promising results.

Environmental regulation in Brazil has been developed under the influence of the 1992 UNCED outcomes. Nationally, Agenda 21 was endorsed and regulations enacted in line with it. Brazil has the most advanced environmental regulation in the region, but it needs to be improved through better enforcement and a more comprehensive approach.

Most environmental investment is directed to water and wastewater treatment. Solid and hazardous waste and air pollution control are also important. Investment in the environmental field is assisted by loans from international financing institutions (for example, Interamerican Development Bank, World Bank): US$100 million was committed to the construction of a major wastewater plant in 1995.

The environmental market is the biggest in the region, with demand estimated at US$1015 million (see Table 8). Demand for environmental goods and services will grow, stimulated by increasing public pressure, an increasingly market-oriented economy, stronger enforcement of regulations, and privatisation of industry.

Brazil has developed relatively strong domestic capabilities, mainly through licensing of foreign technology, rather than relying on imports and other forms of technology transfer. In the future, it was expected that the environment industry will focus on environmental equipment and services for water and wastewater treatment. Particular opportunities include measuring equipment, pumps, filtering equipment, and water purification equipment. Waste management and air pollution control also represented good opportunities for the environment industry. Most of the local environment firms will provide end-of-pipe equipment, rather than cleaner process and product technologies.

Chile

Much of Chile's recent industrial growth has been founded on pollution-intensive industries. Inadequate environmental regulations provided a competitive advantage for its exports. Since 1990, the government developed the legal and institutional framework for environmental protection, and in 1994 it enacted the first general and comprehensive environmental law. The approach followed by the Chilean government focuses on measures which promote efficient management of resources and energy, pollution prevention, and participation of both the private sector and the community in decision-making.

The Chilean environmental market is evaluated at US$560 million (see Table 8). The mining and fishing industries are investing substantial sums to recover materials and reduce pollutant emissions. The paper industry is also investing heavily in recycling technologies and facilities. The environment industry is in an embryonic state, although local capabilities are expanding steadily. Equipment for water and wastewater treatment and air pollution control are supplied by domestic firms, superseding an earlier reliance on imported technologies.

In the future, opportunities for the environment industry will be concentrated in air pollution control equipment and water and wastewater treatment systems. Technology transfer will be facilitated by a good understanding of sophisticated environmental technologies

Argentina

Over the last few years, the economy of Argentina has started to recover. The economy is stabilising, although growth may be lower than in the preceding years. GDP is split among agriculture (6 per cent), industry (31 per cent) and services (63 per cent). The major manufacturing industries are motor vehicles, textiles and durable goods.

Argentina has only recently developed comprehensive environmental regulation for water and wastewater, solid and hazardous waste, and air pollution control. The government plans to supply potable water to 90 per cent of the population by the year 2000. As far as solid waste management is concerned, regulation controlling liability and clean-up of past pollution is weak. Environmental regulation for air pollution control focuses on three areas: electric power, industrial production and transportation.

The environmental market is very small. It is estimated at US$168 million (see Table 8). As a consequence, the environment industry is not very developed, but it is expected to grow as new environmental regulations are enacted and as public awareness of environmental issues grows. Areas of major growth should be air and water treatment. The major obstacle to the development of the environment industry is weak enforcement of environmental regulations.

4.0   Conclusions

Most of the DNMEs have experienced rapid industrialisation and urbanisation, with attendant high levels of pollution. All these economies have developed comprehensive environmental regulations which have stimulated the emergence of markets for the environmental goods and services industry.

Governments have reoriented environmental policies by promoting mixes of regulatory and economic instruments and incentives, and waste minimisation and cleaner production programmes. Private sector participation has also been strongly encouraged in these initiatives. This new approach, with sustained economic development and increasing environmental awareness, will probably accelerate growth in environmental markets in these regions.

The environment industry in these countries will develop along different paths. In the DAEs, the environmental goods and services industry will probably emphasise cleaner production and waste minimisation, since high rates of investment and rapid economic development will provide favourable conditions for technological innovation. Moreover, in a few of these economies, support for the development of R&D for cleaner technologies will strengthen prospects and opportunities for this industry. Although cleaner technologies may develop very quickly, the market demand for end-of-pipe equipment will also remain strong, for example, in China.

DAEs' governments have recognised the importance of foreign investors in the environment industry. Through measures to facilitate joint ventures and technology transfer (for example, in Singapore and Thailand) with more advanced countries, the DAEs aim to fill technological gaps and open opportunities for development of the environment industry, domestically and internationally.

In the Latin American DNMEs, the process of privatisation and economic stabilisation will provide good opportunities for the development of a domestic environmental goods and services industry. The growth of this industry will mainly rely on foreign know-how, and will focus more on end-of-pipe equipment. Joint ventures, technology transfer, and co-operation with foreign enterprises will assure technological innovation and market opportunities.

In both "regions" the development of the environment industry will rely on stricter enforcement of environmental regulation and on building local capacity through education, training, and extension programmes.

Looking to the future, favourable economic conditions in the DNMEs suggest that industries could identify important economic benefits from implementing waste minimisation programmes and investing in cleaner technologies to improve their environmental performance. The evidence, however, suggests that industries still largely prefer end-of-pipe solutions, as they are perceived as easier and cheaper to apply.

Waste minimisation programmes and cleaner technologies are of paramount importance for the development of a cleaner industrial sector in the DNMEs. It is suggested that governments can help support the implementation of these programmes in industry by:

- recognising the important role played by the environmental goods and services industry. It supplies equipment, consultancy services and technologies which are instrumental to the improvement of environmental performance. If governments encourage the environment industry to develop a broad range of new and cleaner solutions, this may extend their implementation in industry;

- encouraging improved environmental performance as a strategic necessity for firms. If government policy clearly states the importance of improved products in economic and environmental terms, they may encourage firms to make cleaner production part of their normal business;

- making environmental regulations clear, and enforcement consistent. Governments should combine environmental regulation with economic instruments and voluntary agreements to give firms a range of possibilities to reach the best environmental performance. By being flexible, environmental regulations will facilitate compliance in industry;

- making price signals clear, for example by removing distortions in, and subsidisation of, input prices. Opening markets to international competition encourages and underpins the removal of price distortions;

- supporting: technological innovation; small and medium-sized enterprises, which have the most problems implementing cleaner technologies and waste minimisation programmes; and education and training programmes;

- improving the measurement of the extent of application of cleaner technologies. It is important to measure the use of cleaner technologies more clearly, in order to identify their environmental economic benefits separately from general economic benefits.

BIBLIOGRAPHY

Chiang, P.K., 1994: *The Economic Development of the Republic of China on Taiwan: Issues and Strategies*. Ministry of Economic Affairs, Taiwan.

Conama (Commission Nacional del Medio Ambiente), 1995: *Environmental Progress in Chile.*

DEG-Commission of the European Union, 1994: *Thailand Environmental Technology Study*. German Investment and Development Company, Cologne, Germany

ECOTEC-JEMU, 1994: *The UK Environmental Industry: Succeeding in the Changing Global Market.* HMSO, London.

Environmental Business Journal, 1994: "The Global Environment Industry". Environmental Business Journal Inc., San Diego California.

Environmental Business Journal, 1995a: "ASEAN Countries" (April). Environmental Business Journal   Inc., San Diego, California.

Environmental Business Journal, 1995b: "Latin American DNMEs" (July). Environmental Business Journal Inc., San Diego, California.

Higgins, J., 1994: "Global Environmental Industry", in <u>Ecodecision</u> (January 1994), pp. 20-22.

Hunter, B., 1995: *The Statesman's Year-Book 1995-1996.*

International Environment Reporter, 1993: "Pollution Control Industry Mushroom, Enters Alliance with Foreign Partners" (February).

International Finance Corporation, 1992: *Investing in the Environment: Business Opportunities in the Developing Countries.* World Bank and IFC, Washington, D.C.

Kosowatz, J.J. and D.K. Rubin, 1995: "Big Contracts Mark Hong Kong Water and Solid Waste Clean Up," in <u>Engineering Review</u> (29 May, 1995).

Newman, M., 1995: "Message Received," in <u>Far Eastern Economic Review</u> (June 22, 1995).

OECD, 1992: *The OECD Environment Industry: Situation, Prospects and Government Policy*, Paris.

OECD, 1995: *Economic Outlook* (June), Paris.

OECD, 1996a: *The Global Environmental Goods and Services Industry,* Paris.

OECD, 1996b: Interim Definition and Classification of the Environment Industry. OCDE/GD(96)117, Paris.

O'Connor, D., 1994: *Managing the Environment with Rapid Industrialisation: Lessons from the East Asian Experience.* OECD Development Centre Studies, Paris.

OTA (Office of Technology and Assessment), US Congress, 1994: *Industry, Technology, and the Environment: Competitive Challenges and Business Opportunities,* Washington, D.C.

Park, J., 1996: "Assessing the Environmental Market in the East Asian Region" <u>in</u> OECD, 1996: *The Environment Industry. The Washington Meeting.* OECD Documents Series, Paris.

Schmid, A. and D.K. Rubin, 1995: "Brazil Emerges as Latin America's New Environmental Hotshot," in <u>Engineering Review</u> (29 May, 1995).

US EPA, 1993: *International Trade in Environmental Protection Equipment: An Assessment of Existing Data,* Washington, D.C.

World Bank, 1995: *Annual Report 1995*, Washington, D.C.

PART III:

ASSESSING THE COST-EFFECTIVENESS OF CLEANER PRODUCTION

ASSESSING THE COST-EFFECTIVENESS OF CLEANER PRODUCTION

Harvey Yakowitz
Environment Directorate, OECD

1.0   Realising the Cost-effectiveness of Implementing Cleaner Technologies

There have been hundreds of published examples showing how good housekeeping actions have avoided waste of feedstocks, cut pollutant releases, and reduced variable costs of production. These outcomes have been put forward as "proof" that cleaner technologies and cleaner production actions are cost-effective. But good housekeeping is only one step on the path to realising the full potential of cleaner technologies to boost market share and profits while at the same time reducing environmental releases.

In order to realise the full potential of cleaner technologies, both government and the private sector need to take certain actions. For a firm, a key action is to develop a managerial accounting system which consistently isolates and quantifies environmental costs. A number of firms in the OECD area are developing these systems. Findings are that the bulk of environmental costs occur as out-of-pocket fixed costs; environmental components attributable to variable costs are almost always much smaller [1].

Good housekeeping actions usually help to cut variable costs; they do not much affect fixed costs. Hence, unless out-of-pocket environmental components of fixed costs are identified and attacked, the full potential of cleaner production to reduce total costs and environmental releases while improving market share and profitability cannot be realised. And the key means to attack these fixed cost items is by means of investment in cleaner technologies. Thus, to realise the full cost-effectiveness of cleaner production, a firm must be able to identify its environmental costs, act to reduce them in the short-term by good housekeeping actions and then attack them in the long-term through judicious investment in the most effective cleaner technologies.

These facts indicate that firms must take positive actions to determine their environmental costs on both a product-by-product basis as well as on a technology of production basis. In practice, this means firms must take the time, trouble and resources to develop and implement an appropriate managerial accounting system to isolate and quantify environmental costs consistently. This system will almost certainly include some means of physically auditing operations to identify opportunities to reduce feedstock and energy use, cut releases and wastes. The outcomes of the auditing exercise can then be used to provide a foundation for the numerical accounting exercise to pinpoint current and probable future sources of environmental costs. In turn, these results can be used to identify "best" capital investments to reduce environmental costs and releases and improve profits.

In realising the full cost-effectiveness of moving towards cleaner technologies and cleaner production some important points for firms to consider include [2]:

- Upstream changes linked to cleaner production techniques by definition create complex and disparate repercussions mid-stream and downstream. Changing inputs from more to less toxic substances, for example, necessitates careful consideration of how such changes will affect equipment performance and product quality. In the same vein, product redesign likely requires equipment modifications within a process line. Accompanying these technology adjustments will be a set of capital and operating costs and savings which may be far-reaching, indirect, and not immediately evident. Thus, in evaluating the profitability of such investments, compiling and analysing operational and capital costs becomes that much more complicated and prone to error and/or omission of potentially significant cost items. Accurate costing quickly moves beyond the capabilities and data sources of a single staff person such as the environmental engineer, the materials manager, the production engineer, or the financial officer. Contributions from multiple, rather than, single departments will be necessary to assemble such data;

- Cleaner technologies are associated with certain contingent benefits which often are difficult to predict and quantify. Avoided liability is a prime example of this situation. The firm examining a potential project aimed at eliminating a hazardous waste stream or emission maybe motivated by a desire to eliminate certain risks of litigation linked to personal or property damages. However, such risks are probabilistic in nature, that is, they may materialise if and when an accident occurs or a claimant sues the firm for such damages. This could occur next week, next month, next year, or never. Thus, incorporating the full estimated future monetary benefits may depend on if, when, and how much liability cost is avoided;

- Cleaner technology profits may materialise well beyond the two- to five-year time frame commonly applied in investment analyses. Though the savings of some practices – such as improved inventory control – may accrue in the short term, major and more costly changes to processes, materials, and products are likely to extend well beyond the two- to five-year time period. Analytical methods which fail to capture this steam of savings contain inherent biases against cleaner technology investments. In the competition for limited capital resources, such investments are likely to be rendered non-competitive with more traditional pollution control projects and projects which are primarily driven by non-environmental objectives; and

- The need to track the performance of any cleaner production actions and investments is crucial. A post-investment assessment is needed to evaluate the effectiveness of decision-making and business processes after the fact. Integrating environmental costs and performance into this assessment provides a basis by which a firm can measure its decision-making and business process effectiveness relative to its competitors. The assessment allows the firm to make improvements on a real-time basis as well. Finally, any effects of government actions, such as new regulatory requirements, could also be incorporated in order to help future planning.

Government has an important role to play in encouraging sustainable development founded upon cleaner technologies and cleaner production. Indeed, governments must take a leadership role in creating demand for cleaner technologies and in clearly ensuring that the cost advantages of these technologies are maximised. To do this government must identify the best mix of economic, regulatory and information exchange policies which will promote long-term implementation of cleaner technologies and cleaner production [3, 4].

A key role for government is likely to involve actions to promote implementation of cost-effective cleaner production actions among SMEs. This role may involve training, advice, financial incentives and so on. Demonstration projects may also prove useful to show the cost-effectiveness of cleaner production actions to SMEs. A more general comment is that all state-owned enterprises whether large, medium or small should be pioneers in acting to demonstrate the cost-effectiveness of cleaner technologies and cleaner production and in implementing them.

In sum, cleaner technologies and cleaner production are cost-effective. But unless an effort is made to determine precise costs in firms, full knowledge of how cost-effective will not be available. Since certain cleaner production investments are far more beneficial than others, it is important to be able to set priorities in order that investment decisions are most cost-effective in reducing environmental costs and releases while promoting realisation of national and individual company goals for sustainable economic development over time.

2.0   Current Situation

Cleaner technologies reduce pollutants and the amounts of energy and natural resources needed to produce, market and use products by introducing changes to the core production technology. Cleaner technologies contribute to optimise the use of resources; thus, environmental benefits may be achieved in conjunction with financial and economic benefits as well as technological improvements. Implementation of cleaner technologies includes goods, services, equipment, technical and organisational know-how, worker skills, managerial skills and procedures. The installation of hardware without the capacity for technical know-how, organisational, worker and managerial skills has not proven very successful in practice. Moreover, strong capacity in these areas can often identify more effective and less costly technological solutions and can lead to indigenous capabilities and new business opportunities.

In contrast, end-of-pipe (pollution control) technologies are those which involve the installation of equipment for treatment of pollution after it has been generated. These technologies usually add to production costs without adding to productivity. Moreover, end-of-pipe technologies often create new environmental problems such as the disposal of wastes from end-of-pipe treatment facilities. In practice, however, the two strategies, pollution prevention and pollution control, are complementary, since it is not possible to prevent all pollutants and wastes from being generated. EOP controls have great power to diminish direct point sources of waste and pollution; they are indeed indispensable for many applications such as flue gas desulphurization from power plants or municipal and industrial wastewater treatment. Policies strongly favouring EOP controls can be viewed as a way to reduce impacts on the environment without affecting products other than their cost. But, policies favouring EOP devices alone are not adequate as a strategy for attaining sustainability [5].

For purposes of this paper, "cleaner technologies" will be broadly taken to include technologies that extract and use natural resources as efficiently as possible at all stages of their lives;

that generate products with reduced or no potentially harmful components; that minimise releases to air, water and soil, i.e. which minimise wastes during fabrication and use of the product; and that produce durable products which can be recovered or recycled so far as possible. And at all stages of the life cycle, these technologies are energy efficient, i.e. output is achieved for as little energy input as is practical.

The market for cleaner technologies is already growing. For 1990, OECD exports of cleaner technologies from the electrical and non-electrical machinery sectors to developing countries were estimated at $9 billion; the environmental production sector (mostly EOP devices) exported $6.7 billion. Hence, cleaner technologies apparently already outstrip EOP devices in export value [6]. This trend and its momentum need to be maintained and increased. Governments will need to understand how their private sector firms – particularly small and medium-sized enterprises (SMEs) – can co-operate and supply these cleaner technologies to potential customers.

So, cleaner technologies can reduce cost of producing goods, cut wastage of energy and raw materials and generally improve profitability while lessening pollutant releases. But, if this statement is true, why is the implementation of cleaner technologies proceeding at a relatively slow pace? For example, the U.S. Environmental Pollution Prevention Program (EP3) has found that conducting a pollution prevention assessment and presenting the findings to company managers is not sufficient to get them to implement the recommendations, despite the potential for reducing costs to produce their products. Staff of the EP3 programme must spend significant time with each facility to help them implement cleaner technology recommendations and to monitor progress [7]. According to one representative of industry in India, there are some basic reasons for this difficulty [8]:

Plant managers think that a shift to cleaner technologies may somehow impair product quality;

- Cleaner technologies may take a long time to implement and do not eliminate the need for EOP devices required for compliance with government regulations;

- Cleaner technologies are thought to cost much more than "dirty" technology plus EOP devices; and

- Plant managers are convinced that their current operations are efficient enough.

In order to dispel these myths, better managerial accounting systems are a key way forward. Since competitiveness and profitability objectives call for tighter controls over operations to cut resource wastage and releases to the environment, management and accounting systems are needed that fully reflect the value of these actions. Lacking them, personnel from top management to process engineers have little incentive to change towards cleaner technologies.

Bluntly put, a firm cannot really know about the effectiveness of cleaner technologies without a consistent managerial accounting scheme which enables all components and magnitudes of "environmental" costs to be identified as unambiguously as possible. This scheme needs to be incorporated into the cost-volume-profit (C-V-P) considerations of the firm as it seeks to gain market share, increase profits and cut costs of making and marketing its products.

There are a number of actions that the private sector and government can take to pinpoint the most cost-effective means to promote transformation towards cleaner technologies as ways to improve competitiveness and profitability while reducing environmental burdens. The cases of large firms and

166

SMEs will both be considered in the analysis. The main results indicate that transformation to cleaner technologies almost always results in avoiding certain fixed and variable costs of production, but these must be able to be put in priority order so as to maximise the value of specific investment decisions by a firm. Moreover, unless government enacts and enforces appropriate environmental and economic approaches, incentives to invest in and implement cleaner technologies may be greatly reduced or even eliminated.

3.0   Managerial Accounting for Environmental Costs

In order for the full cost-effectiveness of cleaner technologies and cleaner production to be apparent, a consistent foundation for isolating and quantifying total environmental costs is necessary in order to understand how much is being spent and why . This knowledge will aid in better control of environmental costs and motivate mangers to act to reduce them – good for the bottom line and good for the environment.

The key first step is to convince top management that a managerial accounting system must be implemented which seeks to pinpoint all environmental costs of producing each product. The next step is to assemble a team, for example, accountants, engineers, managers, administrators, marketers, to develop a pilot system and test it. The ultimate aim is to provide valid and timely information to decision-makers about environmental costs now and their probable costs in the future. This information will allow management to make investment decisions consistent with company objectives and environmental imperatives. In almost every case, investments in cleaner technologies can provide the best approach towards increased profitability and market share with reduced environmental costs and releases.

3.1   Purpose and Uses of Managerial Accounting Systems

Managerial accounting deals with information which is needed for planning and control decisions within a firm. Data such as resource capacity and consumption as well as about regulatory requirements imposed by various levels of government may be needed to support these decisions. The emphasis of a good managerial accounting system is to lessen the risks of decisions affecting the competitiveness or profitability of the firm. The value of the managerial accounting information is in its ability to improve the decision making process so as to achieve the objectives of the firm efficiently, effectively and consistently.

When environmental costs are to be taken into account, the firm must define these costs to suit their intended uses, for example, capital budget allocations, cost control, product pricing, etc. There is simply no universal approach or definition concerning environmental costs. In sum, an effective managerial accounting system can help decision-makers co-ordinate environmental and other activities within the firm. The system can be used to collect and monitor relevant environmental cost information and to further the objectives of the firm in this area.

Tracing costs directly to specific decisions can enable managers to learn about both the financial and environmental consequences of their actions. Choosing which products to market and which technologies to use to manufacture them can affect the environmental cost burden on the firm. But, if these costs only appear in a general maintenance budget, managers will systematically underestimate the potential benefits of cleaner technologies and cleaner production in general whether attained by "good housekeeping" or by investment in new equipment or processes or both [1].

For example, under typical accounting practices, many costs avoided by using cleaner technologies are not directly credited to the unit responsible. Hence, cleaner technologies often compete at a disadvantage with EOP units [9]. Still, quantifying the real costs of controlling releases or the potential benefits in terms of costs avoided over time of implementing cleaner technologies is usually not simple. How then can this problem be attacked in a rational and consistent fashion by a firm?

3.2   Examples of Managerial Accounting for Environmental Costs

Accounting information, including environmental information, is costly to develop. The benefit of this information is determined by the relative value of the information in arriving at a specific decision. If management does not find an item of accounting information relevant or useful in reaching a particular decision, then the value of that information to management is zero [10]. The managerial accounting system should therefore:

- inform decision-makers of the environmental costs of their operations;
- increase accountability of managers for environmental costs and benefits;
- create incentives to address the causes of current and future environmental costs;
- develop approaches to help anticipate future environmental costs; and
- incorporate environmental cost accounting into ongoing business processes and practices.

The effort invested in developing managerial accounting systems incorporating environmental costs has created surprising results for a number of important manufacturing firms in a variety of businesses. For example, at a major petroleum refinery, managers estimated annual environmental costs at three per cent of non-crude oil operating costs. Careful accounting revealed that these costs were, in fact, about twenty-two per cent of non-crude oil operating costs [11]. For a pharmaceutical firm, environmental costs for one important product were at least nineteen per cent of total production costs and probably higher than this [12]. A large chemical company found that nearly twenty per cent of manufacturing costs for an agricultural pesticide product were environmental costs [9].

Even more surprising was the finding in each of these cases that a large majority of the environmental costs fell into the category of fixed rather than variable costs. In the case of the agricultural chemical, almost one-third of the manufacturing costs were environmental out-of- pocket fixed costs as compared with about seven per cent arising from environmental components of the variable costs. Fixed out-of-pocket costs of interest include such items as:

- materials handling;
- direct labour;
- overhead;
- administrative, for example, reporting to authorities;
- maintenance;
- energy (electricity and steam);
- laboratory analysis services;
- "green" marketing actions;
- waste recovery and/or disposal;
- taxes; and
- insurance against environmental damage and liability.

Historical costs, such as building depreciation, also can contribute to environmental costs but only out-of-pocket fixed and variable costs can be reduced. But, for planning and control purposes – particularly in capital investments – historical cost items may indicate important trends [12]. This point can play an important role in deciding on investments in cleaner technologies.

Out-of-pocket variable costs include such items as:

- raw materials;
- certain waste treatment;
- packaging of the product; and
- some energy costs.

Note that labour is not included in the variable cost list since labour usually cannot be removed except in cases of plant closings and consolidations. Unless labour is specifically hired to produce a given line of product(s) and labour inputs vary with volume of those products, labour is properly accounted as an indirect out-of-pocket fixed expense.

In using the managerial accounting approach to identify and to try to isolate and quantify environmental costs, four items are possible contributors:

- the direct out-of-pocket costs associated with fixed and variable cost items, for example, capital expense for a cleaner technology or EOP device,

- indirect costs arising from requirements to monitor releases, submit to government inspections, report to public agencies, etc.;

- added costs of insurance against environmental releases and damages; any penalties levied for non-compliance with regulations and costs of internal auditing; and

- costs of "green" marketing, obtaining an eco-label, training an on-site environmental cadre, community relations, etc.

The key points for the managerial accounting systems are:

- Are the costs of environmental activities properly and consistently identified?

- Is the financial nature of such costs preserved for managerial decision-making?

For example, if some environmental costs, including capital expenditures for pollution controls, are included in generic property accounts, the environmental attribute is lost. If capital investments in cleaner technologies meant to prevent releases and perhaps increase product yields are not offset against out-of-pocket fixed and variable costs reduced as a result of this investment, then managerial incentives to place high priority on identifying and developing approaches using cleaner technologies are substantially limited [11].

The managerial accounting system needs to divide environmental costs into controllable and non-controllable categories. For example, most fixed costs -- where the bulk of environmental costs seem to lie -- are not controllable in the short run. They can only be reduced by means of capital investments or long-term utilisation decisions. Thus, we see that almost all "good housekeeping" approaches -- which reduce environmental costs in the short-run -- primarily affect variable costs. They cut use of raw materials or energy; they ensure that waste streams are not mixed and hence can be disposed at lower cost per unit of product manufactured and so on.

Some examples of relatively small "good housekeeping" investments with large financial and environmental benefits are described in Table 1.

Table 2 lists the payback period or break-even time for a variety of cleaner technology investments implemented in the United States.

The environmental components of fixed costs can be reduced by investments in cleaner technologies. Note that since fixed costs remain constant despite changes in production, environmental costs are not likely to be an important factor in decisions to increase, lower or cease production. Rather, once the production decision is made, experience suggests that environmental and other manufacturing costs tend to follow technologies. Thus, to better monitor and control technology driven costs, the managerial accounting reporting system should be segmented along the lines of the main manufacturing technologies being used [9]. In addition, the managerial accounting system could also include an "environmental profile" of each product including the environmental costs of each step in the production process [12].

4.0   Cleaner Technologies and the Capital Allocation Process in a Firm

4.1   Large Multidivisional Firms

Unless managers are aware of the full environmental costs of their actions and where, when and how those costs occur, they will have little incentive to propose investments in cleaner technologies. As noted, an appropriate managerial accounting system can provide this awareness. The question then is how the capital allocation process of a firm can act to favour investment in cleaner technologies. The size of the capital allocation is related to the growth desired by a firm. Usually depreciation plus retained earnings plus deferred taxes represents the pool available for capital investment. If this pool is not sufficient to meet growth goals -- or to meet imposed requirements such as regulatorily mandated EOP pollution devices -- the firm must borrow and debt-to-equity will rise.

Clearly, imposed requirements to install EOP devices affect the freedom of the firm to invest to improve market share and profits; these requirements may also force the firm to borrow, thus further reducing its financial freedom. This situation in itself argues for considering investments in cleaner technologies in general. However, in practice, Division heads tend to expect an allocation from the pool which is more or less consistent with the Division's contribution to the goals of the firm. Division heads need to be able to demonstrate that environmental costs and potential future liabilities are well understood and that any new investment in cleaner technologies will reduce these such that the financial and environmental benefits significantly outweigh the costs.

Typical issues in the decision-making process are whether competitors have adopted the cleaner technology approach. If so, have the competitors results hurt Division market share and profits? If not, what business advantages can be anticipated by investment in the cleaner technology over time? Also, will regulatory changes possibly render investment in a particular cleaner technology obsolete prior to the end of the anticipated life of the investment?

Table 1: Selected Good Housekeeping Contributions to Cleaner Production and Processing Cost Avoidance

Facility	Activity	Investment	Releases reduced	First-year cost avoidance
Oil refinery	Leak detector to pinpoint volatile organic compound (VOC) fugitive emissions and capping of leaks	$16,000	2,800 tonnes per year of VOCs	$570,000
Chemical factory	Modify processor to reduce losses of vinyl chloride monomer	$30,000	54 tonnes per year of vinyl chloride	$2 million
Chemical factory	Recover heat from wastewater system (saves 11000 tonnes/year steam)	$22,000	NO_x and SO_2	$243,000
Cement factory	Reduce fuel consumption by pyrometer-gas analysis installation	$55,000	No_x and dust	$150,000
Detergent producer	Monitor water level in scrubbers to prevent loss of detergent product	–	250 tonnes of detergent	$330,000

Source: World Environment Center, New York.

Table 2: Payback Periods for Selected U.S. Pollution Prevention Technologies

Technology	Payback period
Low-cost technologies	
Use high-volume, low-pressure paint spray guns	6 months or less
Implementation of improved cleaning process for reaction tanks	immediate
Recycle solvents, use water-based cleaners	5 months
Medium-cost technologies	
Install floating roofs and solvent conservation units	6-12 months
Install cryogenic vapour recovery systems	6 months
Install a wastewater recycling system in fertiliser manufacturing plants	3 years
Higher-cost technologies	
Install a hydrochloric acid and caustic soda recovery system for the textile industry	2.5 years
Install a chrome recovery system in tanning mills	2.5 years
Conversion of spent phosphoric acid into trisodium phosphate crystals	2 years

Source: Hirschhorn and Associates, Inc., USA.

This latter point tends to make voluntary agreements with government attractive to some firms in order to avoid the risk of environmental regulatory actions reducing the value of an investment. With a voluntary agreement in place, these firms have much more control concerning targets for environmental releases as a function of time. On balance, firms which invest in processes having a long anticipated lifetime might well be those who most favour voluntary approaches.

In the final analysis, capital allocation choices are made on such bases as a five year average return-on-investment or a payback period of say two or three years. Proponents of various possible capital investments are usually required to provide estimates of revenues, costs, market share and profits over, say, a five year time horizon. In other words, the proponent must work out an estimated C-V-P projection over time. Unless, environmental costs are properly taken into account, the chances for cleaner technologies to be proposed severely diminish. The benefits of the investment which is made may then be dramatically reduced as compared to competitors who do choose to invest in cleaner technologies.

A managerial accounting system which allows for isolation and quantification of environmental costs is crucial for developing the appropriate C-V-P projections in the competition for capital investment allocations. If, as demonstrated in the cases of several firms [1], most environmental costs are in the "fixed cost" domain, then only investment in cleaner technologies is likely to address these costs properly. For example, DuPont was able to identify over 700 separate investments which reduced wastes and costs. These were then set in priority order to compare the benefits and costs of each investment. The results ranged from as little as a few pennies per kilogram of waste reduced to over $2000 per kilogram. Hence, managers could propose the most effective investments in cleaner technologies [9].

4.2   Small and Medium-sized Enterprises (SMEs)

In small firms, where key investment decisions typically reside with one or a few owners or managers, formalised budgets and procedures for project prioritisation schemes are rare. Investment decisions cluster in the profit-sustaining (including compliance and infrastructural) and profit-adding (cost reducing) categories, spurred most often by equipment obsolescence or breakdown, or pressures from regulators to bring a facility into compliance. Small service-oriented businesses tend to have stable markets and repeat customers. Profitability is basically a function of performing an established service with consistent quality while seeking out cost-reducing measures. Where waste generation is concerned, securing transport and disposal services for small volumes is increasingly expensive. Thus, uncomplicated rapid-payback investments such as on-site recycling systems are inherently attractive. Realising such benefits, however, faces perennial capital constraints characteristic of small businesses which generally prefer to borrow rather than to invest from current cash flow for even short periods of time [2].

Medium-sized firms can be characterised by additional layers of project review, but not necessarily more sophisticated analytical methods. A cleaner technology project may originate, for example, with a staff engineer, and proceed through the manufacturing division, and obtain financial and corporate approval. Each of these approvals is likely to be made by an individual, and collectively the handful of reviewers represent key managers within the firm. Capital budgeting is informal; regular review of project proposals is uncommon. The impetus for a cleaner technology project is as likely to come from an equipment vendor as from the firm's environmental staff. This same vendor may provide an initial project financial analysis which, depending on the sophistication of the firm, may turn out to be the only analysis used, or may merely provide a first screening of the project. As in the case of smaller firms, profit-sustaining and cost reducing projects are most common, driven by capital replacement needs or, in the environmental case, mandates by regulators to achieve compliance [2].

For environmental issues, regulations have usually required direct action on the part of industry, reduction of releases of potentially harmful contaminants to specified levels and/or compulsory use of "best available technology" being mandated. SMEs then usually opt for "proven" end-of-pipe control technologies; process changes or in-house recycling are usually not selected since information about them is less readily available, results of applying them are less predictable and their initial costs may be larger than end-of-pipe controls. Since SME managers will tend to avoid any unnecessary risks, the safer investment will be most likely. Moreover, SMEs are often unable to keep up with all of the details of government regulation and may simply make little or no investment either through ignorance or in the hope that their small size will make them unlikely targets for enforcement actions [13].

SMEs need to motivate their employees towards producing products at some pre-determined target cost and to strive to reduce that cost over the lifetime (market demand) of the product. Costs of environmental compliance must be fully factored into determining the target cost of every product offered for sale. Options to reduce these costs to a practical minimum – over the lifetime of the firm – then need to be devised and considered by management. In most, if not all instances, cleaner technologies will be attractive if the analysis is performed properly – especially if the environmental taxes now being considered in several countries are actually imposed.

But, how can SMEs be stimulated towards doing the analysis in the first place since their managers are fully engaged in daily operations? And, even if the analysis is done and the results point towards cleaner production options, how can SMEs identify the proper technologies and afford to deploy them? In the past (and in the present), the first question was not really addressed in any systematic way while the answer to the second question was, more or less, "That is their problem."

There are a number of possible approaches for engaging SME owners and managers in order to acquaint them with the potential financial and environmental benefits of investing in cleaner technologies and cleaner production in general. Here, government and the private sector, for example, trade associations and large firms who are supplied by SMEs could co-operate. Possible approaches might include [13]:

- developing proposals for uniform accounting approaches for SMEs in which the costs of environmental protection are strictly accounted as a production cost;

- publicising actions taken by major industry to cut wastage in production using several major corporations as role models. This step could also include "hands-on" visits by representatives of major industry to volunteer SMEs, perhaps organised under the auspices of a trade association;

- providing a "benign" government inspectorate for SMEs which, with access similar to occupational health and safety officials, might aid industrial SMEs in identifying potential (or actual) problems with respect to environmental protection, for example, by auditing potentially hazardous materials on the SME site. The inspectorate might then suggest appropriate cleaner production approaches;

- provision of low-interest loans or conditional grants to help fund SME investment in cleaner technologies;

- using some of the proceeds of any "green taxes" to help SMEs to implement cleaner production;

- development of training programmes – funded at government expense – for SME personnel concerning cleaner technologies, their deployment and their operation and maintenance;

- critical review of the various compilations of cleaner technologies for applicability to various unit operations used by SMEs and a recasting of these into a form which might be useful in training programmes for SME personnel;

- deploying industry-government assistance teams who at SME request might act as "free" consultants in suggesting pros and cons of cleaner technologies in specific cases;

- ensuring that SMEs that do choose cleaner technologies can, if they wish, seek continuing consultation concerning operations and maintenance;

- ensuring that regulations concerning standards for release of potentially harmful contaminants remain stable for a long enough period that SMEs can realise the full potential of their investment in cleaner technologies; and

- working to harmonize options to promote use of cleaner technologies by SMEs on an international basis.

5.0   Government Actions to Promote Cleaner Technologies

Unless government sends clear signals that transforming to cleaner technologies and cleaner production is a major goal of both economic and environmental policy, then there may well not be very great incentive for firms to investigate and implement cleaner technologies. This is likely to be true despite the financial benefits a firm may eventually realise from cleaner production. In particular, once "good housekeeping" actions are taken to cut variable costs of production and some environmental releases, major investments in cleaner technologies to cut fixed cost components arising from environmental sources are unlikely to compete fairly with other proposals for less clean technology.

Priority areas for government action to promote sustainable development using cleaner technologies and cleaner production as key tools include [14]:

- obtaining and disseminating appropriate information concerning cleaner technologies and their contribution to economic aims;

- developing a baseline state-of-the environment assessment for a region or a country (this information is crucial in order to know how the environment is affected over time as economic development proceeds);

- engendering strong public support for economic development based on cleaner technologies by providing information and educational materials;

- involving individual producers in the private sector and providing them with convincing information that implementing cleaner technologies will improve profitability and competitive position;

- providing information to government decision-makers based-upon results achieved in various industrial sectors so that appropriate policies to create demand for cleaner technology implementation over the long term can be developed;

- ensuring that private sector bodies such as trade associations, scientific societies and local consulting firms are fully aware of the role of cleaner technologies in sustainable development and that these bodies play a major role in creating support for their implementation;

- overcoming financial barriers;

- reducing obstacles to trade in cleaner technologies;

- preparing a national reference document containing plans and policies for implementing sustainable development principles based upon cleaner technologies together with a provisional set of targets and timetables;

- creating a technology centre within countries or regions to act as a transfer point for information about environmental protection, risks, efficient energy and resource use and pricing, cleaner technologies and so on;

- arranging a series of demonstration projects in various industrial sectors;

- ensuring that state-owned enterprises such as power plants, railroads and industrial facilities have a leading role in demonstrating and implementing the use of cleaner technologies. (If public enterprises do not take this role, the private sector receives totally incorrect signals);

- ensuring that financial brokers such as banks, venture capitalists, joint ventures and insurance firms favour cleaner technologies in their investment and other financial decisions;

- establishing a national government commitment to procure cleaner technology based goods and services;

- developing and implementing a cleaner technology certification system for products, processes and services;

- providing training and assistance to SMEs who could implement cleaner production practices; and

- working with universities and the private sector to develop a model managerial accounting system which consistently isolates, identifies and aims to quantify environmental costs in various key production sectors.

In sum, government needs to promote basic changes in awareness and behaviour concerning the environment over the long term, for example, by appropriate educational approaches at all levels, seeking acceptable options to environmentally harmful products or their constituents, assuming a leadership role in purchasing and using cleaner technologies and products for all government activities, and forming partnerships with parties-of-interest (farmers, manufacturers, public-at-large, etc.) to help formulate policies and institutional frameworks to ensure use of cleaner technologies. Government must also establish a framework for creating and implementing future cleaner technologies, for example, by enunciation of strong long-range environmental goals and policies to attain them such as the New Earth 21 Plan (whereby Japan announced approaches seeking to curb global warming) and the National Environment Policy Plan Plus (in which the Netherlands set national environmental quality targets well into the 21st century).

REFERENCES

[1]   Ditz, D., Ranganathan, J. and Banks, R.D., "Environmental Accounting: An Overview" I, in: *Green Ledgers: Case Studies in Environmental Accounting* (Ditz, D., Ranganathan, J. and Banks, R.D., eds.). World Resources Institute, Washington, D.C., May 1995; 181 pp -- hereafter cited as *Green Ledgers*.

[2]   OECD, *Accelerating Corporate Investment in Cleaner Technologies through Enhanced Managerial Accounting Systems*, OECD/GD(94)30. Paris, 1994, 28 pp.

[3]   OECD, *Government Policy Options to Encourage Cleaner Production and Products in the 1990's*, OECD/GD(92)127. Paris, 1992, 40 pp.

[4]   OECD, *Policies to Promote Technologies for Cleaner Production and Products: Guide for Government Self-Assessment*, OECD/GD(95)21. Paris, 1995, 48 pp.

[5]   Ehrenfeld, J., "Industrial Ecology: A Strategic Framework for Product Policy and Other Sustainable Practices;" Keynote Paper for the Second International Conference on Product Oriented Environmental Policy; Stockholm, Sweden, 26-27 September 1994, 37 pp.

[6]   UNIDO, "Cleaner Industrial Production in Developing Countries: Market Opportunities for Developed Countries and Potential Cost Savings for Developing Countries;" OECD Workshop on Development Assistance and Technology Co-operation for Cleaner Industrial Production in Developing Countries; Hanover, Germany, 28-30 September 1994, Paper No. 20, 23 pp.

[7]   Gallup, J., "EP3's Experience in Establishing Sustainable Country Pollution Prevention Programs: The First Year;" OECD Workshop on Development Assistance and Technology Co-operation for Cleaner Industrial Production in Developing Countries; Hanover, Germany, 28-30 September 1994, Paper No. 35, 23 pp.

[8]   Nyati, K.P., "Cleaner Industrial Production in Developing Countries – Prospects, Barriers and Strategies;" OECD Workshop on Development Assistance and Technology Co-operation for Cleaner Industrial Production in Developing Countries; Hanover, Germany, 28-30 September 1994, Keynote Paper, 13 pp.

[9]   Shields, D., Heller, M., Kite, D. and Beloff, B., "Environmental Accounting Case Study: DuPont;" Chapter V in *Green Ledgers* (see Reference 1 above).

[10]   Maindratta, A. and Todd, R., "Environmental Accounting Case Study: Dow Chemical;" Chapter IV in *Green Ledgers* (See Reference 1 above).

[11]   Heller, M.; Shields, D. and Beloff, B.; "Environmental Accounting Case Study: Amoco Yorktown Refinery;" Chapter II in *Green Ledgers* (See Reference 1 above).

[12]   Maindratta, A. and Todd, R.; "Environmental Accounting Case Study: Ciba-Geigy;" Chapter III in *Green Ledgers* (See Reference 1 above).

[13]   OECD, *Promoting the Development and Dissemination of Environmentally Friendly Technologies,* Labour/Management Programme, October 1990; 24 pp.

[14]   Yakowitz, H., "Developed Countries' Views Concerning Environmentally Sound Technology Transfer and Information;" Workshop on the Promotion of Access to and Dissemination of Information on Environmentally Sound Technologies; Seoul, Republic of Korea, 2 December 1994, 40 pp.

IMPROVING CLEANER PRODUCTION IN CHINA

Ning Duan
Environmental Management Institute, Chinese Research Academy of Environmental Sciences, and China National Cleaner Production Center, China

1.0   Introduction

The author of this paper has been participating since 1992 in a National Environmental Protection Agency (NEPA) project on improving cleaner production in China. The project is a World Bank technical assistance project to NEPA and is technically guided by the UNEP Industry and Environment centre (UNEP IE). It is designated as "Subproject B-4". The paper describes cleaner production in China and introduces the overall objectives, framework design and achievements of Subproject B-4. A preliminary analysis is made for the technologies identified by the project. It is found that, on average, no-cost/low-cost technologies reduce COD by 5.4 tonnes/year and generate 30,674 yuan/year economic benefits per 1,000 yuan investment; that equipment update technologies reduce COD by 0.060 tonnes/year and generate 1,076 yuan/year economic benefits (in terms of net present value) for 1,000 yuan investment; and that the payback period is 3.7 months for no-cost/low-cost technologies and 31.8 months for technical update technologies. Based on this analysis and on practical experience with Subproject B-4, the author sets out his preliminary conclusions on the relationships between no-cost/low-cost technologies and the equipment update technologies.

2.0   Factors Promoting Cleaner Production in China

Although China attaches great importance to environmental protection, it is seeing a deterioration of its environmental quality. In 1992, the country (town and village enterprises, or TVEs, not included) discharged 14.4 million tonnes of dust and 16.85 million tonnes of sulphur dioxide. Acid rain has become a serious national problem. Also in 1992, China discharged 36.65 billion tonnes wastewater, of which 23.39 billion tonnes was discharged by industries. Industrial solid wastes are increasing at a rate of 20 million tonnes per year. In recent years, as the TVEs keep growing quickly, pollution is expanding from cities to the countryside. Environmental pollution and degradation have destroyed the living environment for animals and plants.

There are many reasons for serious environmental deterioration, but it appears that a major reason is that China has in practice focused on end-of-pipe controls in the past. Obviously end-of-pipe controls have several drawbacks, such as:

- Capital investment demands are high.
- Operation and maintenance costs are high.
- Residues of pollutants are in most cases unavoidable.
- Secondary pollution may occur.
- In many cases (especially in developing countries) workers who operate end-of-pipe control equipment work in a harmful environment.
- Requirements for operation and maintenance of end-of-pipe control equipment are sometimes too strict.

Most importantly, end-of-pipe control is an add-on for most enterprises. Economically it is just an input without output. Hence it contradicts enterprises' essential and permanent objective of pursuing profits to the extent possible.

It should be pointed out that the consistently worsening situation in regard to China's environment appears at a time when the national pollution control budgets keep increasing. In the Sixth Five-Year Plan (1980-1985) the environmental control budget accounted for 0.5 per cent of national GNP. It increased to 0.7 per cent in the Seventh Five-Year Plan (1986-1990). In the first three years (1991-1993) of the Eighth Five-Year Plan it further increased to 0.7-0.8 per cent. This indicates that China can no longer focus on end-of-pipe controls as in the past.

China sees great potential in cleaner production. In today's China many enterprises still grow based on a pattern of high energy consumption, high materials consumption, and poor management. Not only do the fast-growing TVEs have this problem, but also the state-owned large enterprises. The power generating industry is an example. Not only is the absolute value of coal consumption per kilowatts generated higher than in more advanced countries, but the rate of decrease in coal consumption in China is lower than in most of these countries. Coal consumption dropped by 7.1, 6.5, 5.6 and 5.6 per cent in the United States, the United Kingdom, the former Soviet Union and Germany in 1980-1987. But in 1987-1991 it dropped just 3.6 per cent in China. Since the power generating industry is relatively modern, and its plants are normally big ones, the potential for cleaner production in China is tremendous.

3.0   Subproject B-4 and its Achievements

In order to assist China in implementing cleaner production, the World Bank supported NEPA with Subproject B-4.

3.1   Objectives

Subproject B-4 is designed to meet the following goals:

- develop and test Chinese methods for implementing cleaner production;

- develop and test Chinese training material based on these methods, and train Chinese to be trainers for demonstration projects;

- initiate and carry out several industry demonstration projects to prove:

    -- the efficiency and effectiveness of cleaner production methods in China;

    -- the short-term and long-term economic and environmental benefits of cleaner production for a Chinese industry;

    -- the wide range of non-equipment and equipment options for cleaner production in participating enterprises;

    -- the cost savings resulting from small (if any) investments in end-of-pipe control technologies;

- identify and analyse the obstacles to cleaner production in industry and in governmental policy;

- formulate recommendations for effective policies to implement cleaner production based on specific timetables;

- build a cleaner production network based on existing organisations;

- disseminate the project results among high-level political, governmental and industrial authorities and/or organisations.

- build expertise in cleaner production across China within a variety of institutions.

3.2   Framework Design

The project consists of four phases, to be accomplished over three years:

Preparation Phase

The main tasks in this section are: translation of available materials on cleaner production methods in other countries; and training of selected future trainers in cleaner production, and letting the trainees test and practise cleaner production in Chinese enterprises. During this process the trainees should modify and optimise the translated foreign materials in order to develop preliminarily cleaner production methods specific to China. The period for accomplishing this phase was March 1993 to March 1994.

Demonstration Phase

This section consists of three demonstration projects scheduled for the period March 1994 to March 1995: i) an industry-specific demonstration project; ii) a demonstration project in Beijing; and iii) a demonstration project in Shaoxing.

Policy Studies

Chinese policies to promote cleaner production will be developed throughout Subproject B-4. This will be done by analysing the correlation between existing environmental and industrial policies in China and their effects on cleaner production; effective cleaner production policies in other countries, with a focus on those in Denmark, the Netherlands and the United States; and existing obstacles to implementing cleaner production in enterprises that take part in the demonstration project. In the final report, the components will be integrated and different policy options recommended for implementation.

Dissemination of Results

To promote cleaner production nationally, in the provinces, cities and districts, information about cleaner production and the results of the project will be disseminated in various ways and among a variety of institutions.

3.3   Achievements

Chinese Cleaner Production Methodology

When Subproject B-4 began, translations were made from English to Chinese of UNEP's publication "Audit and Reduction Manual for Industrial Emissions and Wastes", and from Dutch to Chinese of the "Prepare Manual, Part 1, Manual for the Prevention of Waste and Emission" by Sybren de Hoo, et al.   After finishing the first eleven audits in its preparation phase, the "Manual for Enterprise Cleaner Production Audit" was prepared in Chinese. The Manual has been welcomed in China's enterprises. Among the 2,200 copies distributed, most have been directly distributed to enterprises. The Manual has also served as the main teaching material in many CP training workshops.

Capacity Building

The project organised 15 training workshops. Through these workshops, and on-site audit training, some 150 cleaner production professional staff (many of whom participated in three workshops) have learned about cleaner production, including professionals working in organisations at the national, provincial and municipal level as well as in enterprises. Today many of them are actively promoting cleaner production in China and are organisers and trainers in their respective industrial departments, provinces, cities and enterprises.

On-site Audits

Twenty nine audits in 27 enterprises were completed. These audits demonstrated cleaner production's great potential in China. The no-cost/low-cost technologies identified and implemented during on-site audits have generated annual economic benefits of 25 million yuan with a total investment of 0.78 million yuan. They have normally reduced pollution at the plant by 10-30 per cent. Some enterprises have claimed much higher reductions. After screening, the project identified 59 equipment update technologies. It is estimated that, if these equipment update technologies were implemented, with a total investment of 1.7 billion yuan, the economic benefits would be 1.8 billion yuan in net present values each year during the equipment depreciation period.

Policy Recommendations

The project identified several obstacles to cleaner production and proposed preliminary policy recommendations to overcome them.

Although not an exhaustive listing, the major obstacles are captured in the following statements:

- "There is nothing new about cleaner production. We have done it for a long time, and the only difference is that we did not call it "cleaner production.""

- "Cleaner production does not help a lot. If we want to reduce pollution discharge and improve economic benefits on a large scale and drastically, then we have to update equipment."

- "One doesn't achieve anything if there is no money."

- "There aren't any laws that force us to implement cleaner production."

- "I don't get any benefits from cleaner production."

In regard to the first obstacle, the project compared what China has done in pollution prevention in the past with what cleaner production means in terms of pollution prevention. The project has indicated that Chinese governmental bodies have encouraged plants to adopt pollution prevention strategies. But since the encouragement did not include the provision of operational procedures, in practice this amounted simply to telling the plants to "prevent pollution from being discharged into environment." Cleaner production, on the other hand, includes comprehensive operational procedures for plant auditing, so that cleaner production can prevent pollution being generated. Another big difference is that cleaner production is emerging worldwide at a time when environmental consciousness is much greater than ever before. This means the concept and practice of today's cleaner production could not have appeared in the past.

To overcome the second obstacle, the project used as many realistic in-plant examples as possible. These examples convinced most of the plant managers that improving management is a continuous task. In other words, having totally new machines throughout a plant is insufficient if the management is inefficient and ineffective.

The project emphasises repeatedly that the core spirit of cleaner production is "Do it from my plant. Do it from today." So when questioned by the plant managers about the third obstacle, the project managers responded: Should we wait until the money comes and let the pollution continue? How much money is sufficient? Lack of money is also a continuous theme for plant managers. The correct strategy should be: There are ways of implementing cleaner production with more money and there are ways with less money. Do whatever you can do on cleaner production, but just don't wait.

Work is underway on policy recommendations to overcome the fourth and fifth obstacles.

During the project the China National Cleaner Production Center (CNCPC) was established. Most of its staff are the core staff of the subproject. Active participants in Subproject B-4 have set up a CP Training Subcenter in a university and an industry sectoral CP center. CNCPC assisted Shaanxi Province in establishing its provincial subcenter, and is now helping the Shaanxi Province Cleaner Production Subcenter conduct audits at eight enterprises.

Dissemination of Results

Several large cleaner production workshops have been organised by the project. In May 1995, it organised an international symposium on cleaner production. On the Chinese side, officials from important national governmental agencies such as the State Economic and Trading Committee, State Science and Technology Committee, NEPA, etc., officials from municipal environmental protection bureaus, enterprise managers, and CNCPC staff participated in the symposium and made speeches. On the international side, officials from the World Bank, UNIDO and UNEP, and CP experts from abroad, participated in the symposium and made speeches.

The project regularly publishes a CP newsletter. Coloured brochures are also available. CNCPC is now in the process of making a video tape for the purpose of further disseminating cleaner production in China.

4.0   Technologies Identified by Subproject B-4

A "no-cost/low-cost technology" in this paper is defined as one that does not involve any major equipment change and is not expensive. An "equipment update technology" in this paper is defined as a cleaner production technology that involves major equipment changes and is expensive, but would be profitable to install. Note that by definition both types of technologies promote "cleaner production." For example, an equipment renovation technology in the usual sense is not an equipment update technology, as defined here, if it does not comply with the requirements of a cleaner production technology. In fact, all the equipment technologies discussed in this paper are a subset of the equipment renovation technologies proposed by the plants during Subproject B-4. All the equipment update technologies in this subset were identified as cleaner production technologies during the feasibility analysis phase of Subproject B-4. The rest of the equipment renovation technologies proposed by the plants were not evaluated in the feasibility analysis phase and are not considered here as cleaner production technologies.

Tables 1 to 4 summarise relevant information on the cleaner production technologies identified in Subproject B-4. (In these tables "BYPC" stands for Beijing Yanshan Petrochemical Corporation.)

Note that in Table 1 the investment in no-cost/low-cost technologies at the Fuyang Distillery is high. Since the relevant activities mainly involve civil construction and not equipment updating, they are still considered to belong to this category.

Table 2 shows payback periods for no-cost/low-cost technologies. Numbers given under one of the payback periods indicate the number of no-cost/low-cost technologies falling into this payback period. The number of technologies shown in Tables 1 and 2 differ for some plants, as the payback period of some of these technologies is difficult to calculate as reported by the plants.

Table 3 gives a summary of the environmental and economic benefits of equipment update technologies. Note that in this table the net present value is adopted to represent the economic benefits.

Table 4 shows the payback periods for the equipment update technologies. It should be read in the same way as Table 2.

Table 1: Summary of Environmental and Economic Benefits of No-Cost/Low-Cost Technologies

Plant	No. of technologies	Investment (1,000 yuan)	Environmental benefits	Economic benefits (1,000 yuan/year)
1. Beijing Brewery	13	30	COD reduced 357 t/year	3,790
2. Beijing Chemical Factory No. 3	10		Equipment leakages and material losses reduced	240
3. Beijing General Electroplating Factory	12		Wastewater reduced 2,697 t/y; pollutants 24.5 kg/y	160
4. Beijing Pharmaceutical Works Branch 1	13		COD reduced 212 t/y (20%); water saved 3,600 t/y	330
5. Chemical Works No. 1 BYPC	8		COD reduced 128 t/y (13.6%); wastewater 9.7%	253
6. Chemical Works No. 2 BYPC	6		Cleaning water saved completely, dust-cleaning water reduced	1,210
7. Synthetic Rubber Plant BYPC	14		COD reduced 5.1 t/y	1,556
8. Refinery BYPC	21		COD reduced 32 t/y	48
9. Chemical Works No. 1 BYPC	11			6,381
10. Beijing East Chemical Works	12		Wastewater reduced 2,168 t/y; COD reduced 62 t/y	295
11. Beijing Pharmaceutical Works V-C Workshop	13		More than 100 tank leakages eliminated; COD reduced 62 t/y	676
12. Beijing Tannery	17		COD reduced 73 t/y	151
13. Shaoxing General Wool Textile Factory	9	52	COD reduced 0.9 t/y (13%)	33
14. Shaoxing Cereal and Oil Chemical Factory	14	4	COD reduced 14.9 t/y	78
15. Shaoxing General Bicycle Factory	35		Ni reduced 96 kg/y; Cr_2O_3 reduced 3,168 kg/y	690
16. Shaoxing Huasheng Printing and Dyeing Factory	10	43	COD reduced 197 t/y (30%)	137
17. Shaoxing Silk Textile Printing and Dyeing Group	12	2	Wastewater reduced 30%, COD reduced 17 t/y	72
18. Shaoxing Yuejin Printing and Dyeing Company	8		COD reduced 12 t/y (21%)	110
19. Shaoxing Third Printing and Dyeing Mill	15	19	COD reduced 10.8 (10%)	269
20. Shaoxing Dushu Printing and Dyeing Corporation	12	26	COD reduced 22 t/y	118
21. Penglai Brewery	14		COD reduced 5 t/y (12%)	54
22. Yantai Second Distillery	12	13	COD reduced 36 t/y (20%)	504
23. Yantai Seafood Industries	16	34	COD reduced 18 t/y (23.9%)	420
24. Muping Lockware Factory	40		Heavy metals reduced 54%	127
25. Oufu Cement Factory	17		Dust basically controlled below national standards	1,634
26. Dezhou Second Building Material Factory	16		Dust and sold waste reduced	782
27. Ma Anshan Sulphuric Acid Factory	18		Slag reduced 5,624 t/y	349
28. Fuyang Seed Distillery	6	560	COD reduced 30%	1,367
29. Changsha Chromate Factory	7		Chromate slag reduced 420 t/y, chromate wastewater 50,000 t/y	2,184
Total	411	783		24,018

Table 2: Payback Period of No-Cost/Low-Cost Technologies

Plant	1-6 months	7-12 months	13-48 months
1. Beijing Brewery	13		
2. Beijing Chemical Factory No. 3	10		
3. Beijing General Electroplating Factory	12		
4. Beijing Pharmaceutical Works Branch 1	13		
5. Chemical Works No. 1 BYPC	8		
6. Chemical Works No. 2 BYPC	6		
7. Synthetic Rubber Plant BYPC	7	3	4
8. Refinery BYPC	15	6	
9. Chemical Works No. 1 BYPC	9		
10. Beijing East Chemical Works	8	4	
11. Beijing Pharmaceutical Works V-C Workshop	13		
12. Beijing Tannery	9	8	
13. Shaoxing General Wool Textile Factory	7		
14. Shaoxing Cereal and Oil Chemical Factory	11		
15. Shaoxing General Bicycle Factory	35		
16. Shaoxing Huasheng Printing and Dyeing Factory	10		
17. Shaoxing Silk Textile Printing and Dyeing Factory	9	3	
18. Shaoxing Yuejin Printing and Dyeing Company	7	1	
19. Shaoxing Third Printing and Dyeing Mill	15		
20. Shaoxing Dushu Printing and Dyeing Corporation	12		
21. Penglai Brewery	12		
22. Yantai Second Distillery	12		
23. Yantai Seafood Industries	14	2	
24. Muping Lockware Factory	40		
25. Oufu Cement Factory	16	1	
26. Dezhou Second Building Material Factory	12	2	2
27. Ma Anshan Sulphuric Acid Factory	15	2	1
28. Fuyang Seed Distillery	6		
29. Changsha Chromate Factory	7		
Total	363	32	7

Table 3: Summary of Environmental and Economic Benefits of Equipment Update Technologies

Plant	No. of technologies	Investment (1,000 yuan)	Environmental benefits			NPV (1,000 yuan/year)
			Pollutant	t/year reduction	%	
1. Beijing Brewery	2	6,800	COD	20.5	40	3,600
2. Beijing Chemical Factory No. 3	4	5,549	COD	1,026	95	8,655
3. Beijing General Electroplating Factory	1	743	Cu	0.064	26	1,021
4. Beijing Pharmaceutical Works Branch 1	1	1,000	Alcohol	110	90	289
5. Chemical Works No. 1 BYPC	2	2,176	COD	536	57	1,414
6. Chemical Works No. 2 BYPC	2	49,440	Water	653,400	90	84,690
7. Synthetic Rubber Plant BYPC	3	10,680	COD	183	31	7,490
8. Refinery BYPC	3	3,290	COD	92.4	43	3,000
9. Chemical Works No. 1 BYPC	2	1,325	Gaseous emission	72,900 m³/y	3	1,711
10. Beijing East Chemical Works	3	363	COD	12	4	964
11. Beijing Pharmaceutical Works V-C Workshop	2	48,500	COD	245	50	4,055
12. Beijing Tannery	1	480	COD	142	56	161
13. Shaoxing General Wool Textile Factory	1	1,670	Water	45	40	2,565
14. Shaoxing Cereal and Oil Chemical Factory	1	10,182	COD	302		3,488
15. Shaoxing General Bicycle Factory	1	5,000	Wastewater	293 t/y	38	1,802
16. Shaoxing Huasheng Printing and Dyeing Factory	1	1,670	COD	70	42	695
17. Shaoxing Silk Textile Printing and Dyeing Group	1	480	Water	70,000	13	1,012
18. Shaoxing Yuejin Printing and Dyeing Company	1	1,300	COD	6,868	15	1,376
19. Shaoxing Third Printing and Dyeing Mill	1	190	COD	16	15	217
20. Shaoxing Dushu Printing and Dyeing Corporation	1	5,900	COD	158	21	966
21. Penglai Brewery	1	2,725	COD	6	18	3,567
22. Yantai Second Distillery	4	10,148	COD	126	70	18,700
23. Yantai Seafood Industries	3	4,050	COD	47	52	4,766
24. Muping Lockware Factory	1	3,000	Cu	0.414	61	971
25. Oufu Cement Factory	1	6,575	Dust	8,758	98	689
26. Dezhou Second Building Material Factory	8	14,148	Dust	3,360	59	7,773
27. Ma Anshan Sulphuric Acid Factory	3	9,927	Wastewater	8,540,000	87	5,639
28. Fuyang Seed Distillery	3	6,944	COD	1,700	65	3,995
29. Changsha Chromate Factory	1	14,300	Chromate	1,700	68	4,341
Total	59	167,013				179,672

Table 4: Payback Period of Equipment Update Technologies

Plant	1-6 months	7-12 months	13-48 months	49 months and longer
1. Beijing Brewery			2	
2. Beijing Chemical Factory No. 3		1	2	1
3. Beijing General Electroplating Factory				1
4. Beijing Pharmaceutical Works Branch 1				1
5. Chemical Works No. 1 BYPC				2
6. Chemical Works No. 2 BYPC			2	
7. Synthetic Rubber Plant, BYPC			2	1
8. Refinery, BYPC			2	1
9. Chemical Works No. 1 BYPC			2	
10. Beijing East Chemical Works			3	
11. Beijing Pharmaceutical Works V-C Workshop				2
12. Beijing Tannery				1
13. Shaoxing General Wool Textile Factory				1
14. Shaoxing Cereal and Oil Chemical Factory				1
15. Shaoxing General Bicycle Factory				1
16. Shaoxing Huasheng Printing and Dyeing Factory			1	
17. Shaoxing Silk Textile Printing and Dyeing Factory			1	
18. Shaoxing Yuejin Printing and Dyeing Company			1	
19. Shaoxing Third Printing and Dyeing Mill			1	
20. Shaoxing Dushu Printing and Dyeing Corporation				1
21. Penglai Brewery			1	
22. Yantai Second Distillery			4	
23. Yantai Seafood Industries				3
24. Muping Lockware Factory				1
25. Oufu Cement Factory				2
26. Dezhou Second Building Material Factory			6	1
27. Ma Anshan Sulphuric Acid Factory				3
28. Fuyang Seed Distillery			3	
29. Changsha Chromate Factory				1
Total		1	33	25

Table 5: Environmental Benefits of No-Cost/Low-Cost and Equipment Update Technologies

Plant	No-cost/low-cost technologies		Equipment update technologies	
	Investment (1,000 yuan)	COD reduction (t/year)	Investment (1,000 yuan)	COD reduction (t/year)
1. Beijing Brewery	30	357	6,800	20.5
2. Beijing Chemical Factory No. 3			5,549	1,026
3. Beijing Pharmaceutical Works Branch 1		212	1,000	84.7
4. Chemical Works No. 1 BYPC		128	2,176	536
5. Chemical Works No. 2 BYPC			49,440	32.4
6. Synthetic Rubber Plant BYPC		5.1	10,680	183
7. Refinery BYPC		32	3,290	92.4
8. Beijing East Chemical Works		6.6	363	12
9. Beijing Pharmaceutical Works V-C Workshop		62	48,500	245
10. Beijing Tannery		73	480	142
11. Shaoxing General Wool Textile Factory	52	0.9	1,670	45
12. Shaoxing Cereal and Oil Chemical Factory	4	14.9	10,182	302
13. Shaoxing Huasheng Printing and Dyeing Factory	43	197	1,670	70
14. Shaoxing Silk Textile Printing and Dyeing Group	2	17	480	
15. Shaoxing Yuejin Printing and Dyeing Company		12	1,300	6,868
16. Shaoxing Third Printing and Dyeing Mill	19	10.8	190	16
17. Shaoxing Dushu Printing and Dyeing Corporation	26	22	5,900	158
18. Penglai Brewery		5	2,725	6
19. Yantai Second Distillery	13	36	10,148	126
20. Yantai Seafood Industries	34	18	4,950	47
Total	223	1,209.3	167,493	10,012

5.0 Analysis of CP Technologies Identified by Subproject B-4

5.1 Environmental Analysis

Cleaner production technologies may reduce more than one pollutant (some of these technologies produce energy or raw material savings and reduce pollutants simultaneously). There is therefore a need to establish criteria for comparing the environmental benefits of CP technologies. This paper proposes the following criteria.

Representative Pollutant

A "representative pollutant" is the pollutant that appears most frequently in relation to the cleaner production technologies. This definition seems proper for the environmental analysis of the cleaner production technologies identified in Subproject B-4. In other cases the criterion may be changed to representative raw material or representative energy. It all depends on the actual contents of the cleaner production audits done during a particular project.

Inclusion

Where a no-cost/low-cost technology is not explicitly related to reduction of the representative pollutant, but the equipment update technology does explicitly reduce the representative pollutant, the plant and the no-cost/low-cost technology are included in the environmental analysis and vice versa.

Exclusion

Where neither the no-cost/low-cost technologies nor the equipment update technologies of a plant are explicitly related to reduction of the representative pollutant, these technologies and the plant are excluded from the environmental analysis.

Based on the above criteria, chemical oxygen demand (COD) was selected as the representative pollutant. Table 5 is derived from Tables 1 and 3. It is observed that the no-cost/low-cost technologies reduce COD by 5.4 tonnes/year for each 1,000 yuan of investment, whereas the equipment update technologies reduce COD by 0.060 tonne/year for each 1,000 yuan. The former reduction is 90 times higher than the latter.

5.2   Economic Analysis

The economic analysis is used to study both the economic benefits and the payback period. Because cleaner production technologies have different payback periods, a simple formula is used to calculate the average payback period of the no-cost/low-cost technologies and the equipment update technologies:

Average payback period = Σ_i (no. of technologies with payback period i x payback period I)/ sum of technologies

In this formula all payback periods assume their middle terms: for example, one to six months assumes three months, seven to twelve months assumes nine months, etc. For technologies whose payback period is 49 months or longer, their payback period is taken as 54 months and the middle term assumes 51 months.

Using the formula and Tables 1 to 4, the following results can be noted:

- The economic benefits generated by the no-cost/low-cost technologies averaged 30,674 yuan/year for each 1,000 yuan investment. The net present value generated by the equipment update technologies averaged 1,076 yuan/year for each 1,000 yuan investment. The former is 28.5 times greater than the latter.

- The payback period of the no-cost/low-cost technologies averaged 3.7 months, and that of the equipment update technologies averaged 31.8 months. The latter is 8.6 times greater than the former.

5.3   Implementation Analysis

It is important to point out that both the environmental and economic data in Tables 2 and 4 for equipment update technologies mostly represent good intentions. At the time the author wrote this paper, eleven of the 29 audits had been completed more than 16 months before. The other 18 had been finished four months before. However, only eight of the 59 equipment update technologies had been implemented. Subproject B-4 is backed up by a World Bank loan. In other words, plants participating in the project qualify to apply for a share of a lump sum loan from the World Bank to implement equipment update technologies. At the beginning of the project, almost all the participating plants were very active in applying for the loan. However, today only five or six of them are still interested in borrowing the money and buying equipment. Although there are many reasons for this phenomenon, practical difficulties related to implementation of the equipment update technologies definitely constitutes one of the major ones.

On the other hand, implementation of the no-cost/low-cost technologies has been easy. Indeed, most (if not all) the environmental and economic benefits listed in Table 1 were realised while the audits were being carried out. Some plants have obtained even greater environmental and economic benefits from implementation of the no-cost/low-cost technologies than they showed in their reports. Hence, unlike the figures shown in Table 3 for equipment update technologies, the figures shown in Table 1 for no-cost/low-cost technologies are real. This is an important difference.

5.4   Generality and Diversity Analysis

Table 6 shows the sectoral distribution of plants that conducted the 29 on-site audits mentioned above.

It is fortunate that the 29 audits were concentrated in just six industrial sectors. This means that people have a better chance to appreciate the technologies applied in this project. A single sector has more example plants that carried out cleaner production audits, and more plants may have applied the same technologies. If the 29 audits had been done in 29 different sectors, the technologies applied would likely be more scattered.

From Table 6 it can be seen that there were ten audits in the chemical industry. This is the industry in which the most audits were carried out. None of the equipment update technologies applied in the chemical industry were identical. In fact, only four of the equipment update technologies generated by Subproject B-4 are identical.

Table 6: Sectoral Distribution of the Plants that Conducted the 29 Audits

Light industry	Chemical industry	Petrochemical industry	Building material	Textile industry	Electroplating
6	10	2	2	6	3

Subproject B-4 presents a totally different picture when it comes to no-cost/low-cost technologies. This is because all these technologies can be easily grouped into just a few types. Although the contents and formats of the technologies sometimes differ from one plant to another, their basis remains the same and they are being applied repeatedly over time from plant to plant.

6.0   Conclusions

First, as demonstrated by Subproject B-4, cleaner production has great potential in China in terms of both economic and environmental benefits. Cleaner production is the best choice for governmental policies. It is the best choice not only for the administrative agencies responsible for environmental protection, but also for industrial ministries. Because it reduces pollution and increases profits, it will change ways of thinking and play an important role in improving the industrial structure of China.

Cleaner production is also the best choice for enterprises. It increases productivity, improves product quality, saves energy and raw materials, and abates pollution. At the same time, implementation of cleaner production improves the quality of management and operational workers, which is very valuable for the overall enterprise.

Second, it is important to recognise the relationship between no-cost/low-cost technologies and equipment update technologies. No-cost/low-cost technologies have played a crucial role in Subproject B-4. They are more cost-effective from both the pollution abatement and financial perspectives, they are much more practical to implement, and they are much easier to master. These factors will also apply to future cleaner production activities in China, for reasons such as:

- the current status of management in Chinese plants;

- the lack of money at many plants for updating equipment;

- the fact that these technologies are easy to learn, easy to implement, and cost-effective;

Implementation of equipment update technologies in order to reduce pollution and increase productivity on a wide scale is inevitable, but not many plants can afford to adopt such technologies. Plants should actively create opportunities to implement equipment update technologies, for example using no-cost/low-cost technologies to accumulate the necessary capital.

It is essential to emphasise the spirit of "start from my plant and start from today". For a plant that has no money to purchase expensive equipment, polluting as usual while waiting is wrong. Starting from today to implement as many no-cost/low-cost technologies as possible makes economic sense.

Third, no-cost/low-cost technologies are a continuous theme for any plant. Even if plants obtained funds to implement equipment update technologies, plants would still have to attach great importance to the no-cost/low-cost technologies because of their clear advantages.

THE COST-EFFECTIVENESS OF CLEANER PRODUCTION: EXPERIENCE FROM CENTRAL AND EASTERN EUROPE

Olav Nedenes
World Cleaner Production Society, Norway

1.0 Background

1.1 Characteristics of Industry in Central and Eastern European Countries (CEECs)

Industry in Central and Eastern Europe, including the NIS, can with some exceptions be characterised by the following, compared with industry in OECD countries:

- a workforce with very good academic training;

- low efficiency in the use of energy, raw materials and water (usually 20-80 per cent higher consumption of these inputs as compared with factories in OECD countries);

- low operational and capital productivity and lack of capital for modernisation;

- poor environmental management (high emissions and wastes per unit product produced). Industry is by far the most serious contributor to hazardous waste and toxic emissions to the environment;

- centralised management structure and complicated centralised decision-making; limited understanding of the market economy and business analysis principles by senior managers;

- poor quality plant management;

- numerous barriers to innovation and creativity, low motivation and low wages.

In many industrial regions and cities, the industrial pollution load represents a serious threat to human health (for example, the Katowice region in Poland, the Black Triangle and Ostrava regions in the Czech Republic, and Murmansk and Arkhangelsk in Northwest Russia).

1.2 Implementing Cleaner Production in CEECs

The demand for cleaner production in CEECs varies from almost zero in some countries of the former Soviet Union to rather good and rapidly increasing in others (Poland, the Czech Republic, the Slovak Republic, Northwest Russia, the Baltic States). Many governments and industries are still not aware of cleaner production (CP) as a highly cost-effective strategy for restructuring of industry, however.

Consequently, the necessary legislation, and voluntary and economic incentives, from governments to stimulate cleaner production programmes and the dissemination of such programmes to all relevant industry varies from very weak to rather good or rapidly improving. Poland, being the best example due to its early start, with combined train-the-trainers programmes, in-company assessments and demonstration plants, has established the strongest governmental support. A CP declaration signed by the Ministers of Environment and Industry, voluntary agreements between government and industrial enterprises, a revolving fund for demonstration plants, support from the environmental fund for combined assessments in industry, and training of trainers and other economic incentives to stimulate cleaner production are evidence of this commitment. Table 1 provides an overview of the most important policy instruments used in some of the CEECs, compared with some OECD countries. The inventory was prepared in 1994.

Table 1: Policy Instruments to Stimulate Cleaner Production

	Cz	Es	La	Li	Po	Ru	Sl	Uk	Bu	Mo	Cr	Nl	Dk	US
Legislation														
Approval scheme incl. CP	-	o	-	o	x	-	x	x	o	x	o	x	x	x
Voluntary agreements	-	-	x		o	x	-	x	-	-	-	x	x	x
Financial Instruments														
Tax, duties and fees	x	x	x	x	x	x	x	x	o	-	x	x	x	x
Grants and subsidies	-	-	-	-	o	-	x/o	x	o	-	-	x	x	x
Information/education														
Demoprojects processes	x	x	x	x	x	x	x	x	o	o	o	x	x	x
Demoprojects products	-	-	-	-	o	-	-	-	-	-	-	x	x	-
Consultant support	x	o	-	-	x	o	x	x	-	-	o	x	x	x
Centers of expertise	x	o	o	o	x	o	x	-	-	-	o	x	-	x
General manuals	x	o	-	o	x	o	x	-	-	-	x	x	x	x
Industry specific manuals	-	o	-	-	x	-	-	-	-	-	o	x	x	x
Databases	-	o	o	-	o	o	-	-	-	-	o	x	x	x
RD-programmes (research)	-	o	x	o	x	x	x	-	o	o	o	x	x	x

x - "activity fully established"   0 - "under preparation" or "not fully established"
"-" "no activity" or "no information available"

Government efforts to engage industry participation in integrated industrial CP assessments, and demonstration and train-the-trainers programmes, are the single most important policy instrument to support cleaner production. In several of the CEECs a National Cleaner Production Centre (NCPC) has been established, usually as an NGO, to operate such programmes. Possible tasks for such a NCPC are shown in Box 1.

Box 1: Possible Tasks of a Cleaner Production (CP) Centre

* Promote CP as a profitable "win-win" economic-environmental strategy.

* Establish a nation-wide network of CP advisors and resource persons.

* Co-ordinate CP programmes in-country.

* Implement integrated CP train-the-trainers and assessment programmes.

* Conduct examinations and graduate students as CP advisors; train and examine university teachers undertaking CP courses; assist them in developing courses for undergraduate and graduate students.

* Undertake periodic follow-up audits in enterprises and prepare regular reports on progress in implementing firm-level CP action plans.

* Select and monitor the implementation of demonstration projects.

* Establish a national CP database and library comprising national and international materials, case studies, etc.

* Disseminate information on CP to various audiences through publication of a CP newsletter, fact sheets, brochures and sectoral or industrial branch case study results.

* Facilitate a dialogue among industry, local financing institutions, donor agencies, government, NGOs and universities.

One factor in the success of the NCPCs in Central and Eastern Europe is that pollution charges from industry are returned to industry through environmental funds. This may subsidise the operation and dissemination of combined CP programmes, as well as supporting CP investments by industry.

Revolving funds are another instrument whereby industry gets low interest loans for CP investments from government agencies and pays back the loans as soon as it has saved more than two to three times the investment. For larger CP investments, the establishment of "financial intermediaries" such as local commercial banks provides an opportunity to break down loans from international financing institutions such as the World Bank, and to relend money to industry on more manageable terms.

2.0　Assessing the Cost-effectiveness of Cleaner Production Programmes and Technology

2.1　Programme Costs

Experience with CP programmes in CEECs shows that the unit costs per assessment of participating enterprises and per trained CP advisor varies greatly, without a significant difference in results. Of more importance is the fact that the programmes differ greatly in their ability to move from reliance on external help to self-help. A rapid transition can reduce the programme cost to donors by up to 90 per cent, thus increasing the opportunity of using limited external funds to support further CP dissemination activities. Based on several years' experience with western-sponsored CP programmes in different CEECs, the cost of a programme, including all educational facilities and tools, is US$2,000-3,000 per company. This cost includes as an extra benefit two to three certified advisors able to take part in future dissemination programmes to other enterprises.

Experience shows that if US$1-3 million is available as grants provided by a donor country, this can be sufficient to train and certify between 500 and 1,000 advisors/teachers able to carry out CP assessments in companies and to train other trainers. During the period of foreign sponsorship, implementation of from 200 to 500 CP demonstration projects may be expected, with an average of over 40 per cent reduction in emissions after the third year of company assessments. Annual economic savings to the companies on the order of four to five times the total cost of low and small CP investments, including assessments, are also possible. Included in these results are assessments done in a larger number of companies that are trained to do their own CP assessments but not to educate staff in other companies. Figure 1 shows the results of the Norwegian-Polish CP programme as an example.

2.2　Technical and Economic Considerations

To assess the cost-effectiveness of different options, we may first look at the different techniques commonly used when implementing cleaner production action plans in industry. Figure 2 gives an overview of these techniques.

The most cost-effective strategies are usually "source reduction". Good operating practices yield by far the most cost-effective results; usually 20-30 per cent emission reduction can be obtained with no or very low-cost investments. Any investment is fundable from the company's operating budget (i.e. without the need for loans). Good operating practices usually yield annual savings on the order of five to 20 times the investment, and should be implemented immediately.

The basic economic goals of waste minimisation are:

- to reduce or if possible eliminate waste treatment and disposal costs (waste management costs including pollution charges and fees);

- to reduce material input costs (including those of process water, raw materials wastage);

- to improve the efficiency of energy use.

Other important benefits that may accrue include improved product quality, enhanced productivity, decreased worker health risks, reduced environmental hazards, improved credit rating through lowering the potential risk of liability for environmental damage, smaller or fewer waste sites, and an improved corporate image in the community.

Very often many cost-saving factors are forgotten when economic analyses of CP options are undertaken, resulting in smaller savings being calculated than are actually the case. Table 2 is an example of a checklist to help planners conduct a comprehensive analysis.

Figure 1: Implemented and Expected Results of the Norwegian-Polish CP Programme

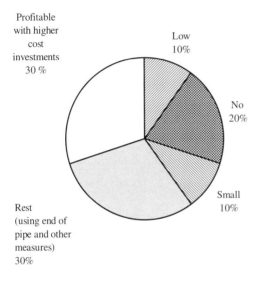

Additional reductions in industrial wastes and emissions with different types of investment

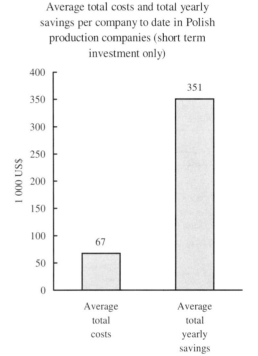

Average total costs and total yearly savings per company to date in Polish production companies (short term investment only)

Notes:

"No" means no hardware investments (only education, management training, process monitoring, etc.).

"Small" and "low" profitable investments have usually been implemented without external loans (i.e. financed from enterprise's own budget).

"Low" is less than US$ 10 000. "Small" is between US$ 10 000-40 000.

"Profitable" investments require external loans and have only been

Figure 2: Options for Waste Minimisation

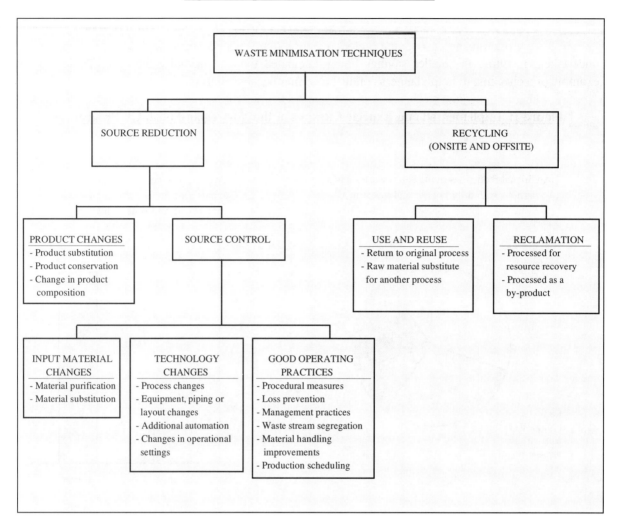

Table 2: Economic Information Checklist

Capital costs	Operating costs/revenue items
Purchased process equipment	Change in direct treatment, disposal cost
Materials	Change in raw materials cost
Utility connections	Change in materials handling and transport costs
Additional equipment	Change in utilities cost
Site preparation	Change in catalysts and chemicals
Installation	Change in operation-maintenance labour costs
Engineering and procurement	Change in operation-maintenance supplies
Start-up costs	Change in insurance costs
Training costs	Change in other operating costs
Permitting costs	Incremental revenues from increased (decreased) production
Initial charge for catalysts/ chemicals	Incremental revenues from marketable by-products
Fixed capital investment	Net operating cost savings
Working capital	
Total capital investment	
Salvage value	
Net capital investment	

2.3   Profitability Analysis

If a CP option has no significant capital costs, the project's profitability can be judged by whether savings in operating costs occur or not. If such a project reduces overall annual operating costs, it should normally be implemented as soon as practical. For projects with low, small or high capital costs, a more detailed profitability analysis is necessary. The two most commonly used profitability measures are the payback period and the internal rate of return on investment.

If the payback period is less than one to two years for low or small investments (up to US$40,000) with low risk, it is usually considered acceptable in those CEECs that have several years' experience with cleaner production. In CEECs such projects will usually be implemented within a period of not more than two to three years. With payback periods of a few weeks to six months, a project will usually be implemented as soon as practicable.

If large capital expenditures are involved, more detailed economic analysis is usually necessary, using internal rate of return (IRR) or net present value (NPV) calculations. Both IRR and NPV are discounted cash flow techniques for determining profitability (i.e. both methods recognise the time value of money by discounting the projected future net cash flows to the present). Companies participating in western-sponsored CP programmes in CEECs use these methods to rank capital projects that are competing for funds. For investments with a low level of risks, an IRR of 4-6 per cent above normal interest rates on bank loans is usually considered acceptable. In some CEECs, however, the local bank interest rate may be 30-40 per cent per year. Then companies will usually require IRR to be 10-15 per cent points higher (i.e. 40-55 per cent). When a CP project is predicted to reduce the environmental, health and safety risks and liabilities of a company, but the value of this reduction cannot be calculated, the profitability requirements of a CP project are sometimes reduced by setting lower IRR requirements.

3.0   Practical Experience from CEECs

The average emission reductions and economic savings from a review of the first 150 production companies that participated in the Norwegian-sponsored joint venture programme between the Norwegian Society of Chartered Engineers and its sister organisation in Poland are shown in Figure 1. Most of these companies completed a CP assessment in all production lines during a period of two to two and a half years, and most of them have started repeat assessments. More than 20 industrial branches are represented.

From the experience to date, the following results may be expected in CEECs seven to ten years after the start-up of a programme designed and operated according to OECD's "Best Practices Guide for Cleaner Production Programmes":

- completion of CP assessments by all relevant industries;

- a 40 per cent reduction in industrial emissions in more than 20 highly polluting industrial branches, without the need for external end-of-pipe treatment and with no or minor investments, financed without loans (i.e. from the company's operating budget);

- average savings per year per large company of US$250,000.

202

Provided the main barriers to financing the large (but profitable) CP investments are reduced to an acceptable level, we may expect:

- major restructuring of the industry sector (away from large-scale, resource-intensive plants to smaller, more resource- and energy-efficient plants);

- a reduction in total industrial emissions of 60-70 per cent in more than 20 highly polluting branches;

- increased profitability and productivity in industry.

In CEECs, this is expected to be achieved based on an initial seed money grant from some OECD countries of about US$1-3 million per CEEC, including the start-up costs of CP centres. After an initial period of one to two years with donor support, the local government should finance the CP programmes from domestic environmental funds but encourage a progressively increasing share of self-financing from industry.

There are, of course, differences in results between industrial branches and from company to company, depending, *inter alia*, on the degree of modernisation and what type of production processes are involved. Industrial branches that exhibit high potential for the introduction of CP programmes are listed in Table 3. The list is not exhaustive, but reflects areas where results in CEECs and in OECD countries have been extremely good.

Table 3: Industrial Branches with High Potential for CP

pulp and paper	wallboard
wood impregnating shops	packaging
chemicals	pharmaceuticals
plastics production	petrochemicals
refineries	paint manufacturing
food processing	breweries and mineral water production
printing shops (including metal printing)	textiles
pesticide production	printed circuit board manufacturing
fabricated metal products	metal casting (foundry)
metal coating (plating)	metallurgical plants
leather tanning	cement production
dry cleaning	insulating materials manufacturing
large photo laboratories	

Annex I provides some examples of emission reduction, CP investments, annual savings and payback periods from the most common groups of source reduction measures (good operating practices, input material change, and technology change) and from recycling. All good housekeeping options, and also small or low investments in technology and material changes, have usually been implemented immediately or within a few months to two years, while many of the high-investment recycling and technology change options remain to be implemented, due to financing difficulties. Each company has normally implemented or planned actions drawing on different approaches, i.e. good housekeeping, material change, technology change and recycling.

4.0   Major Obstacles to Implementing Cleaner Production

4.1   Finance

The most severe obstacle in most CEECs is that, having exhausted good housekeeping options, most companies are not able to obtain loans to finance investments in CP equipment. Even extremely good projects, with payback periods of a few months, are often not implemented for one or more of the following reasons:

- Local banks are not willing to provide loans due to a lack of confidence in the company's ability to pay the loan back and/or lack of government guarantees;

- The investments do not fall within the loan criteria established by foreign banks or international financing institutions; for example, EBRD, the World Bank. Usually the size of the investments is too small (less than US$50,000);

- There is a lack of information in companies about financing options;

- There is a lack of understanding of the economic benefits of CP in financing institutions;

- Complicated loan or grant application procedures deter companies from submitting a proposal.

4.2   Poor Management Motivation to Adopt CP

Insufficient senior company management motivation to become informed about waste minimisation assessment procedures or to obtain external advice, even after having seen examples of the economic savings and environmental benefits achieved by similar companies, is a major obstacle. Even in Poland, where several hundred production companies from 25 different industrial branches have participated in intensive CP education and assessment programmes, with impressive economic and environmental results, the interest of more companies in joining similar programmes is moderate. Intensive marketing of CP benefits, together with free participation in CP/waste minimisation educational programmes with free advice, has yielded good results in overcoming this barrier.

4.3   Subsidies and Poor Economic Incentives

Although subsidies for energy and other inputs are in general being lowered in many CEECs, in others they endure as a major obstacle to economic reform and to the restructuring of industry. Similarly, low pollution charges and emission fees reduce the economic incentive for companies to change their behaviour in the direction of less pollution-intensive, more resource-efficient production.

5.0   Conclusions

The experience of several CEECs, as well as that of OECD countries, has led us to conclude that the above obstacles could be addressed by adopting a mix of actions:

- Governments should promote investments in CP ahead of end-of-pipe treatment.

- Consideration should be given to the Ministry of Environment and Ministry of Industry jointly developing a CP policy paper and issuing a "Cleaner Production Declaration" that, on a voluntary basis, encourages industry to regularly undertake waste minimisation audits and to implement profitable cleaner production options.

- There could be a legal requirement for production companies to complete and periodically update waste minimisation assessments according to established procedures. As a minimum, such requirements should be included in the periodic renewal of permits. A requirement to submit an annual report to the pollution control authorities should be considered.

- Permits should specify goals of discharge (not discharge limits), combined with pollution charges. The pollution charge should be higher than the yearly costs (including interest and depreciation) of the equivalent end-of-pipe treatment that at any time is required to meet the goal.

- Government grants for pilot testing of new CP technologies and for demonstration plants should be provided.

- Local financing sources and insurance companies should be informed about CP concepts to assist their evaluations of loan applications and risk analysis/liability.

- Clear procedures for loan applications for financing larger investments in CP equipment should be established by government working with industry.

- Free-of-charge or subsidised independent auditors should be available to carry out an initial waste minimisation assessment in companies participating in a CP programme. The auditors should also be available to carry out, for a charge, periodic reviews. This might be implemented as part of an education and training programme for 15 to 30 "trial" companies. Government-subsidised training programmes to educate advisors in waste minimisation assessments, as part of industrial "learning-by-doing" training, should be a high priority.

- Governments should stimulate relevant non-governmental organisations that have credibility with industry to run such training programmes. External teachers/advisors should only be used in the start-up phase of such programmes, and should be replaced by trained local advisors as soon as they have acquired the necessary skills and experience.

- Official certification of auditors, and government-approved education and training programmes with exams for auditors, should be established.

- A National Cleaner Production Center, and possibly local CP centres, should be set up.

BIBLIOGRAPHY

OECD, 1995: *Best Practices Guide for Cleaner Production Programmes in Central and Eastern Europe*. OCDE/GD(95)98. Paris.

UNEP, 1994a: *Government Strategies and Policies for Cleaner Production.* Paris.

UNEP, 1994b: *Policy Initiatives to Promote Cleaner Production, Poland and Central Europe.* Paper prepared by Olav Nedenes for the Third High Level Advisory Seminar on Cleaner Production, Warsaw, Poland, 12-14 October, 1994.

US EPA, 1994: *Facility Pollution Prevention Guide.* Washington, D.C.

Annex I: Selected Results from the Norwegian-Polish CP Programme in Poland

Industry	Methods	Waste reduced	Investment*	Savings*
Good housekeeping				
Meat processing *Dabrowna Gornicza*	Elimination of water leaks Cut-off valve in water supply line Continuous control of water line Cleaning procedure change Collection of reused water with NaCl in separate containers Changes in chemical use Collection of solid waste Instruction and responsibility charts Education of operators	NaCl: 67% Wastewater: 30%	None	48
Metallurgical *Huta Cynku "Miasteczko"*	Air-tight sealing of exhaust system Regular cleaning of exhaust piping Water pressure control in Venturi B Removal of Venturi tube in exhaust system	Exhaust gas: 20% Dust: 2.0 mg/yr Zinc: 0.8 mg/yr	4.6	60

*US$000

(continued next page)

207

Material and technology changes

	Material and technology changes			
Zinc sulphate plant *Tarnowsky Gory*	Increase of acid in production procedure Washing and drying of the sludge on filter press Storing the sludge and transporting it by truck to zinc smelter for reuse	100% elimination of sludge disposal	2.9	19
Fabricated metal products *"O.F.N.E. Emalia"*	Cascade rinsing system (pickling and degreasing) Multi-stream settling tank to precipitate iron oxides Reuse of waste pickling solution	Wastewater: 20% HC1:15 mg/yr $Ca(OH)_2$: 11mg/yr Sludge vol.: 30 mg/yr	3.2	27
Metal plating *"F.S.M. Sosnowiec"* Car parts manufacture	Lower concentration of CrO_3 in passifying bath Additional quantity of nitric and acetic acids	CrO_3: 97% Sludge quantity: 78% Air emissions: 97%	None	
Recycling and reuse				
Paint components production *"Zakkady Chemiczne"* *Tarnowsky Gory*	Lump separation from the sludge and recycling to the process as barite substitute Sludge reclamation Recycle SO_2 to rotary kiln	Solid waste: 6,000 tonnes/yr Dust: 90-98% SO_2 emissions: 60-95% Energy savings	185	255
Pulp and paper *"Zahtady Celulozy i Papieru SWIECIE"*	Recycling of 55% of process waters and 61% recovery of suspended solids	Water savings: 11,500 m^3/day Fibre discharge: 14.4 tonnes/day	55	146

PART IV:

THE INTERNATIONAL DIMENSION

MANAGEMENT OF HAZARDOUS WASTES AND CONTROL OF THEIR TRANSFRONTIER MOVEMENTS

Pierre Lieben
Environmental Consultant, France

1.0 Wastes and their Management

Wastes are materials intended for disposal; they are disposed by various means such as burial, incineration, spreading onto land, etc. Hazardous wastes are wastes which, if improperly managed and disposed, could harm man and/or the environment because they are toxic, corrosive, explosive, combustible, etc. Often, regulatory authorities judge wastes potentially hazardous in view of certain of their constituents, such as heavy metals. Lists of hazardous wastes have been issued by many countries. Policies and practices concerning hazardous waste management differ in each country as compared to the others.

Policies for dealing with wastes have evolved over time in many countries. There is general agreement that the management options, ranked in order of desirability from the point of view of environmental amenity, are as follows:

- reduce generation of wastes, for example by more efficient processes in manufacturing, reduction of disposable material in consumer goods, or increase of durability in products;

- separate usable components of the waste at their source, for example by more efficient control of effluents from the manufacturing process, separation of paper, glass, plastic and metals by householders, or concentration of used tyres or oil at collection centres;

- reuse of waste products directly if possible, for example return of an effluent to the production process as in steelmaking or cement kiln operations or exchange of material which is a waste from one process but may be a feedstock for another process:

- transformation or other physical or chemical treatment in order to recycle usable materials from waste, for example burning of household wastes to recover energy, magnetic separation of ferrous scrap from household waste and subsequent use of the material to prepare ferrous products, reclamation of non-ferrous metals from mixed industrial wastes by thermal processes, re-refining of waste lubricating oils, or distillation and regeneration of spent solvents;

- destruction of the waste by physico-chemical treatment or incineration, for example neutralisation by mixing alkaline and acid wastes or burning of pumpable liquid waste or solid wastes;

- permanent storage of the waste in or on land.

These principles, which are now universally recognised as the waste management hierarchy, were first established in a Recommendation adopted by the OECD Council in September 1976 [Recommendation on a Comprehensive Waste Management Policy, C(76)175].

Economic, social, technical and institutional issues will clearly affect how a specific region or country chooses specific policies with respect to waste management. Industrial activity inevitably generates by-products or wastes in addition to the goods and services which are directly demanded. Since industrial growth is a goal of most countries, the question of how to deal with these wastes will eventually arise. Many countries have experienced adverse consequences resulting from improper management of certain potentially hazardous wastes; there is an abundance of data concerning many sites where such wastes were deposited inappropriately. Costs of remedial action are extremely high, and the threat of adverse health and environmental effects is never completely removed.

A number of countries have established national systems for monitoring and control of hazardous wastes. The central goal of such systems is to ensure that discarded substances which are viewed as potentially harmful are managed so as to minimise the possibility for adverse effects to occur. Certain features are common to all existing monitoring and control systems for hazardous wastes. This list includes:

- definition of "wastes", "disposal" and the setting of a boundary (which may be sharp or fuzzy) between wastes destined for disposal and "material" destined for recycling, resource recovery, reuse or reclamation.

- designation of a list of wastes which will constitute "hazardous wastes".

- compilation of a list of probable sources (generators) of hazardous wastes. This list may be general, for example industries X, Y, Z, hospitals, etc. or specific, for example firms A, B, C, etc. Many countries use both.

- assessment of the quantity of each type of hazardous waste to be controlled. This result depends entirely upon the list of wastes deemed to be hazardous, coupled with the existing sources.

- provision of treatment, storage and disposal facilities to match the quantities of each type of hazardous waste produced. The goal is to provide sufficient capacity (sites) to protect man and/or the environment at lowest practicable cost.

- implementation of a monitoring scheme which will afford the competent authorities the means to track the wastes "from cradle to grave" and perhaps beyond.

- means to respond quickly and accurately to any emergencies caused by accident, failure of the system, or discovery of abandoned hazardous wastes which pose a threat to man and/or the environment.

- a regimen for assigning responsibility and liability with respect to the management of hazardous wastes. Ease of settling questions of financial responsibility and insurance increases as clarity in this context increases, and vice versa.

- adequate resources for setting standards of compliance with the regimen selected to control hazardous wastes, and for enforcing the rules in case of non-compliance.

- a longer-term approach meant to induce as much of the waste as possible to move upward in the "order of desirability" or "waste management hierarchy" indicated above. Clearly, this approach must specifically show what benefits are to be expected from any proposed policy changes. Flexibility to react to changing conditions is needed as well.

In one form or another, and with certain national (or local) variations, these items form the foundation for all active systems of hazardous waste management. A number of factors bear on how individual countries choose to emphasise various elements; these factors include costs, geography, industrial mix, public awareness, legislative mandate and many others.

2.0 Transfrontier Movements of Hazardous Wastes

Millions of tonnes of potentially hazardous waste cross national frontiers each year on their way for recycling or to disposal because there is no local disposal capacity for these wastes, or because legal disposal in a foreign country may be more environmentally sound (i.e. recycling in the foreign country as compared to disposal at home), or managing the wastes in the foreign country may be less expensive than at home. While most of this traffic takes place among OECD countries, certain quantities of hazardous wastes are exported from the OECD area. In 1988, there were many articles in the press throughout the world reporting the shipment or proposed shipment of large amounts of wastes to countries with developing economies.

There are a number of potential stimuli for causing generators of waste to consider export as a means of dealing with these wastes. This list includes, but may not be limited to, the following:

- rising costs of disposal in the home country;

- diminishing capacity for disposal of certain types of wastes in the home country;

- potential future liability for any damages caused by wastes disposed into or onto land in the home country;

- tightening of laws, regulations and policies concerning disposal of certain types of wastes, for example prescriptive disposal routes such as incineration being required for liquids containing certain organic constituents;

- tightening of laws, regulations and policies governing on-site waste disposal operations performed by a generator on his own premises;

- general economic growth which may result in more total generation of wastes;

- existence of disposal facilities which may serve several countries;

- market opportunities for materials which can be recovered, reclaimed or recycled from wastes otherwise destined for "final" disposal;

- existence of an appropriate disposal facility in a foreign country which is closer than a similar facility in the home country.

Today, costs for legal disposal of hazardous wastes are high and increasing in most countries. Capacity for legally disposing hazardous wastes into or onto land is becoming more scarce. Regulations in some countries require that certain types of wastes be destroyed by incineration. Simultaneously, the siting and bringing into service of new disposal capacity is becoming more difficult A generator will normally seek least-cost legal disposal for his wastes. If export is available, legal and less costly than disposal in the home country, then export is a likely choice.

3.0   Monitoring and Control of Transfrontier Movements of Hazardous Wastes

In the beginning of the 1980s many OECD countries had adopted or were in the process of developing regulatory measures to enable their authorities to monitor the management of hazardous wastes from the place of generation to the place of disposal. It became rapidly clear, however, that in the case of transfrontier movements such national monitoring systems were not totally adequate since countries had generally insufficient knowledge about consignments of wastes imported into their territory to exercise proper control. On 1st February, 1984, the OECD Council decided that "Member countries shall control the transfrontier movements of hazardous wastes and, for this purpose, shall ensure that the competent authorities of the countries concerned are provided with adequate and timely information concerning such movements" [OECD Council Decision and Recommendation C(83)180(Final)]. Moreover, a comprehensive set of guiding principles concerning the basic policy strategies needed in order to properly monitor and control international traffic in potentially hazardous wastes was recommended to governments.

These principles provided the foundations for European Community legislation in this area [Directive 84/631/EEC of 8 December, 1984]. They were reinforced at a Ministerial Conference that the OECD convened in March 1985 in Basel, Switzerland, in order to provide Ministers and other senior policy-makers, international organisations and non-governmental organisations with an opportunity to discuss the major issues and to recommend what international co-operation is required in order to achieve effective monitoring and control[1] of hazardous wastes moving across national frontiers.

The Conference reaffirmed that the basic principles for the management of wastes (including hazardous wastes) must be first to prevent and reduce, so far as possible, the generation of wastes; and second to increase the proportion of wastes recycled or reused. It considered that efficient and

---

[1]   Monitoring means that the whereabouts of hazardous wastes are known "from cradle to grave" and that the wastes are directed to an appropriate facility for treatment and disposal. Control means that authorities are aware of waste flows and can act rapidly to ensure that the possibility for inappropriate handling of the wastes is minimized.

environmentally sound management of hazardous wastes may, however, justify some transfrontier movements of such wastes; and that, in all cases, the wastes should be directed to adequate disposal facilities.

The Conference also recommended that an effective international system for the control of transfrontier movements of hazardous wastes should be developed by OECD. This system was to address issues concerning the definition and classification of hazardous wastes; their notification, identification and control; the harmonization of technical standards for their management and control; relations with non-Member countries; and the legal and regulatory framework.

The OECD Environment Committee meeting on 20 June 1985 at Ministerial level heeded the outcomes of the Basel Conference and declared that Member country governments would: "Strengthen control of the generation and disposal of hazardous wastes and establish an effective and legally binding system for control of their transfrontier movements, including movements to non-Member countries."

4.0 Identification and Classification of Hazardous Wastes

In 1985, lists of potentially hazardous wastes had been issued by many countries and in a number of international agreements governing the disposal of waste into marine bodies or the transport of hazardous materials. No two of these lists are identical.

The existence of these diverse lists prompted OECD governments to explicitly call for development of "an agreed list of hazardous wastes for all transfrontier movements of such wastes between OECD Member countries" as part of the action programme undertaken in response to the Ministerial Declaration of 20 June 1985. This task was begun by simply determining which items appeared most frequently on all of the national and international lists of hazardous wastes. This process clearly indicated that wastes containing some proportion of one or more of 27 constituents were proscribed by all or almost all of the national and international lists. In addition, certain types of generic wastes (waste streams) are often legally defined or considered to be hazardous to man and/or the environment.

Consideration, discussion and negotiation extending over nearly three years among representatives of OECD countries resulted in adoption by the OECD Council, on 27 May 1988, of a Decision [C(88)90(Final] including a "Core List" of wastes for which consensus was reached that they require control when proposed for disposal following transfrontier movement (see Table 1[2]). This Core List contains 18 generic waste types and 27 constituents. It has been included, almost textually, in the Basel Convention on the Control of Transboundary Movements of Hazardous Wastes and their Disposal, for which negotiations started in June 1987

There are no concentration limits or levels included with the Core List. What decides if a waste listed in the Core List is subject to control is whether that waste does indeed exhibit one or more characteristics which could harm man and/or the environment. These characteristics are listed in Table 2, which was also incorporated as Annex III to the Basel Convention. The note appended to this table makes clear that "absolute" conclusions concerning whether a waste presents a hazard and, if so, the degree of hazard are difficult to achieve given the present state of knowledge. This situation prompted consensus that concentration limits which implied both qualitative and *accurate* quantitative

---

[2]   The tables and figures referred to in the text are at the end of this paper.

analysis of waste batches would be time-consuming and expensive to obtain and, moreover, the results would *not* provide any better protection against harm for man and/or the environment. In practice, only a few countries include concentration as a criterion for deciding whether a waste should be considered as potentially hazardous. The Core List coverage is such that control is flexible; wastes which do not exhibit a hazardous characteristic can be excluded. Hence, the decision not to incorporate strict concentration thresholds provides a brake against unnecessary "overcontrol" while seeking to ensure that hazardous wastes crossing frontiers are indeed subject to suitable control.

The OECD Council Decision C(88)90(Final) also provides for a definition of the terms "wastes" and "disposal" for purposes of control of transfrontier movements. In practical terms, "wastes" are any materials which are subject to any of the "disposal" operations listed in a table annexed to that Council Decision (see Table 3). But any "wastes" destined for operations which may lead to resource recovery, recycling, reclamation, direct reuse or alternative uses are only deemed to be "hazardous wastes" if they are considered to be or are legally defined as hazardous wastes in either the country where they are generated or the country where they are to be disposed or both.

Because many countries have differing definitions, lists and methods of describing wastes considered to be or legally defined as hazardous wastes, Council Decision C(88)90(Final) provides for a uniform classification system referred to as the International Waste Identification Code (IWIC). The use of a coded description for wastes, i.e. the IWIC, allows virtually all wastes deemed to be hazardous by most countries to be described satisfactorily in terms of potential hazard, activity generating the wastes, physical form (liquid, sludge, solid), generic descriptor (contaminated soil, etc.), and constituents. In addition, the IWIC indicates reasons why the materials were intended for disposal (see Table 4) and the disposal operation to which the wastes will be subjected. The IWIC provides a coded cradle-to-grave dossier which fully describes any batch of wastes undergoing transfrontier movement. When included within a notification system for exports of hazardous wastes, the coding scheme of the IWIC will make the system more amenable to modern communications and information transfer technologies as well as to computer-based statistical evaluation.

5.0   Control of Transfers of Hazardous Wastes to Non-OECD Countries, Especially Developing Countries

The OECD was the first international body to take legal action to monitor and control exports of hazardous wastes towards non-members, having acted in Spring 1986. Requirements for exports of hazardous wastes from the OECD area are set out in the Decision/Recommendation of the Council of 5 June 1986 [C(86)64(Final)]. OECD countries must apply no less strict controls on transfrontier movements of hazardous wastes involving non-member countries than would be applied on movements involving only Member countries. Obligations placed upon Member country governments[3] are as follows. They must:

- monitor and control exports of hazardous wastes to a final destination which is outside the OECD area (it follows that the competent authorities of the exporting country must be informed of any such prospective export);

- ensure that their competent authorities have the power to legally prohibit these exports in appropriate instances

---

[3]   Decisions of the OECD Council are legally binding on Member countries.

- prohibit movements of hazardous wastes to a final destination in a non-member country without the consent of that country;

- ensure that any countries of transit are notified in advance of the proposed transfrontier movement(s); and

- prohibit movements of hazardous wastes to a non-member country unless the wastes are directed to an "adequate" disposal facility in that country.

It should be noted that for the OECD Member countries who are also European Community members, Directive 86/279/EEC of 12 June 1986 contained precisely these same requirements concerning control of exports of hazardous wastes outside the European Community.

The Decision of the Council of 27 May 1988 [C(88)90(Final)] defines the terms "wastes" and "disposal", and delineates what must be considered "hazardous wastes" for purposes of control of transfrontier movements. The requirements of Council Act C(86)64(Final) apply therefore to any wastes which are legally defined as or considered to be hazardous wastes in the country of exportation or the country of importation or both.

6.0   The Basel Convention

In June 1987, the Governing Council of the United Nations Environment Programme (UNEP) decided to proceed with development of a global Convention concerning the control of transboundary movements of hazardous wastes. Similar work in OECD was specifically mentioned by the Governing Council; results achieved at OECD were to provide a foundation insofar as practicable for the UNEP efforts. The UNEP Secretariat adopted a very ambitious schedule; a Convention was to be proposed for adoption by late March 1989.

On 22 March 1989, the Basel Convention on the Control of Transboundary Movements of Hazardous Wastes and their Disposal was adopted. This Convention contains the basis for a method of identification, notification and control of transfrontier movements of certain wastes. Management of these wastes is also the subject of the Convention since both generation rates and disposal are taken into account. The goals of the Convention are that the generation of wastes subject to the Convention should be minimised, that transboundary movements of such wastes should also be minimised, and that disposal of these wastes be performed so that man and the environment will be protected from "the adverse effects which may result from such wastes".

In keeping with the instructions of the UNEP Governing Council, some portions of the Basel Convention are taken verbatim or are close paraphrases of the relevant OECD initiatives. For example, wastes subject to control are essentially those of the OECD Core List of Council Decision C(88)90(Final).[4] The obligations placed upon generators, exporters, importers and disposers are founded upon the OECD text as well. There are, in addition, a number of requirements concerning generation and management of hazardous wastes, provisions for aid and assistance to developing countries, as well as a delineation of illegal traffic in hazardous wastes.

---

[4]   The OECD Core List was amended in July 1994 to make it conform to Annex I of the Basel Convention.

OECD Member country governments wholeheartedly supported the UNEP efforts from the inception of UNEP work in mid-1987. OECD Council Resolutions C(89)1(Final) and C(89)112(Final) clearly reflect this support. The extension and amplification of the basic OECD efforts to the global level was encouraged by Member country governments and the Secretariat since all sovereign states could participate in such global negotiations.

Nevertheless, the OECD Council instructed its Environment Committee to keep under review progress towards the implementation of the Basel Convention and the possibility that further action by OECD concerning control of transfrontier movements of hazardous wastes might be necessary. To achieve these aims, it was agreed that certain steps should be taken within the OECD in advance of the entry into force of the Basel Convention.[5]

In January 1991, a Decision-Recommendation concerning the Reduction of Transfrontier Movements of Wastes[C(90)178/FINAL] was adopted by the OECD Council. This calls for delineation of such controls as may be appropriate for the transfrontier movements of wastes destined for recovery operations, clarification of the definition of such wastes, and characterisation of those wastes which may require different levels of control. The Decision requires that wastes not destined for recovery operations should, to the extent possible, consistent with environmentally sound and efficient management practices, be disposed of within the Member country in which the waste is generated. The Decision provides that OECD countries should develop disposal capacity for wastes which currently cannot be managed within their own territory. Alternatively, where this is not possible, countries should enter into bilateral or regional agreements conducted and approved at governmental level which provide for environmentally sound management of such wastes.

7.0   Movements of Wastes Destined for Recovery Operations

In March 1992, Member countries of OECD resolved to create and fully implement an international mechanism to control transfrontier movements of wastes destined for recovery operations within the OECD area. The Decision concerning the Control of Transfrontier Movements of Wastes Destined for Recovery Operations, C(92)39/FINAL, contains provisions to allow what is now referred to as the "OECD Control System" to be developed. This System identifies wastes destined for recovery operations; it classes these wastes in Green, Amber and Red lists depending on their overall environmental risk and their management practices; and it establishes different levels of control for each list of wastes, ranging from regular commercial control (green) to stricter controls (amber and red). It ensures that sufficient information is provided, in advance, to all countries involved in a transfrontier movement of wastes (exporting and importing countries and any countries of transit) in order that they may decide to allow or forbid the intended movement.

The OECD Control System applies only to OECD Member countries. It concerns all wastes involved in transfrontier movements and destined for recovery within the OECD area. A Review Mechanism has been established in order to evaluate the current placement of some wastes on the green, amber or red lists, to assess the placement of "new" wastes on one of these three lists, and to make any proposals deemed necessary for revisions of the control system. The lists of wastes established by the OECD Council Decision C(92)39 in March 1992 were revised for the first time in July 1993, and again in July 1994.

---

[5]   The Basel Convention entered into force in May 1992.

A detailed description of the OECD Control System is contained in the next section.

8.0 The OECD Control System for Transfrontier Movements of Wastes Destined for Recovery Operations

8.1 General Description of the System

The OECD System is applicable to all transfrontier movements of wastes destined for recovery operations within the OECD area. The System does *not* apply to wastes destined for disposal, and applies only to OECD Member countries. The wastes destined for recovery operations must go to a facility which is operating or is authorised to operate in the importing country under applicable domestic law. All such transfrontier movements shall be carried out under the terms of applicable international transport agreements.

The OECD System does not apply to the movement of hazardous wastes outside of the OECD area. However, any such movements shall be subject to all relevant international and national laws and regulations (for example, Basel Convention), as well as the OECD Decision C(86)64 mentioned in the previous section.

The OECD System has created three lists of wastes which are intended to be exclusive and which have been set up according to the degree of hazard they could present. Hence, if a waste is listed as "Green" it is considered not to be hazardous and thus is not controlled by the OECD System. Green listed wastes are only subject to existing controls for commercial transactions.

If a waste is listed "Amber" or "Red", it is considered to be hazardous, and thus is subject to the Control System. In such cases all parties involved in the movement have prescribed responsibilities that must be met for the movement to be approved by the countries concerned. The parties that may be affected include: waste generators, waste exporters and importers, waste transporters, operators of recovery facilities, competent authorities for waste of exporting, importing and transit countries, and the OECD Secretariat.

Specific details relating to planned transfrontier movement of Amber or Red listed waste to recovery facilities must be transmitted to the appropriate competent authorities of concerned countries using the OECD notification form. This form requires information, in particular, on:

- the nature of the waste;
- details regarding the generator and the notifier;
- details regarding the waste recipient;
- the proposed fate of the waste; and
- the existence of a legal contract between parties, including arrangements for any required insurance or financial guarantees.

The competent authorities can use this information to identify the parties involved in the shipment and to decide whether the proposed transfrontier movement is in accord with existing national legislation. If no difficulties are identified, then either tacit or written consent may be granted for the movement. However, if an objection is raised by one of the competent authorities of the concerned countries, the transfrontier movement cannot legally be carried out until the objection is satisfactorily resolved.

If the transfrontier movement is approved by the competent authorities of the concerned countries, then shipment may proceed. A tracking form which contains specific details relating to the consignment must accompany it until it reaches the recovery facility. The tracking form is used to confirm that wastes that have been shipped actually arrive at the designated recovery facility.

Upon acceptance of the consignment by the recovery facility, an authorised representative has the responsibility of sending the completed and signed tracking form to all competent authorities and the notifier. This provides them with a record of the fate of all hazardous wastes legally exported from, transported through, or imported into their country.

A simplified procedure for pre-consent has also been established for designated recovery facilities which regularly receive a specific type of waste. In this case, movements of this particular type of waste to the designated facility can proceed without any further consent from the importing country. A notification form must, however, be received by the competent authorities of all concerned countries prior to dispatch of the consignment. Authorisation for this "pre-consent" procedure may be granted by the competent authority of any importing country.

Parties Affected by the OECD System

Those persons or parties within the jurisdiction of an OECD Member country which are involved with a transfrontier movement of waste destined for recovery are legally bound to comply with national laws which reflect the requirements of the OECD System and all other applicable laws and regulations.

The **generator or original producer**[*] whose activities create waste intended for transfrontier movement going to recovery is the first party that may be subject to the System. If two or more batches of waste are mixed before being moved and recovered, and/or otherwise subjected to physical or chemical operations which render the original wastes indistinguishable or inseparable in the resulting mixture, the party or parties who perform(s) these operations is (are) considered to be the generator of the new wastes resulting from these operations.

The **notifier or exporter**[*] is regarded as the key party under the OECD System. The notifier, who must be under the legal jurisdiction of the state or country of export or dispatch,[*] is the person who has or will have at the time that the planned transfrontier movement commences, possession or other forms of legal control of the wastes. The notifier is the party who proposes transfrontier movement of wastes for the ultimate purpose of submitting them to recovery operations in another OECD country.

The **consignee or importer**[*] is the party to whom possession or some other form of legal control of the waste is assigned at the time the waste is received in the state or country of import or destination.[*] The consignee arranges for hazardous wastes to be imported and must be under the legal jurisdiction of the country of import. The consignee may also be the operator of a recovery facility.

A **recognised trader** is the party which, with appropriate authorisation of concerned countries, acts in the role of principal to purchase and subsequently sell wastes. This party has legal control of such wastes and may act to arrange and facilitate transfrontier movements of wastes destined

---

[*]   The OECD Council Decision, the Basel Convention and the European Community Regulation sometimes use different words to designate the same entity.

for recovery operations. A recognised trader may act as the notifier, the carrier (the party that transports hazardous wastes), or the consignee and must comply with the respective procedural requirements.

The **competent authorities** of the exporting, importing and transit countries are the regulatory authorities appointed by national governments, which have jurisdiction over transfrontier movements of wastes destined for recovery operations in their respective countries. The competent authorities will receive and process the notification forms, and object to any movements that are contrary to their national legislation. The competent authority of the country of import has the extra responsibility of returning an acknowledgement of receipt of the duly completed notification form to the notifier and the competent authorities of the countries of export and transit.

The **Review Mechanism** is a body made up of representatives of Member countries that is charged with recommending possible modifications to the Green, Amber and Red lists of wastes. This includes the reassignment of wastes that are already listed and the addition of new wastes to these lists.

The **OECD Secretariat** acts as a repository and a distributor of information regarding the System.

The OECD Document for the Transfrontier Movement of Wastes

The OECD System requires prior notification of each movement of hazardous waste that is destined for recovery within the OECD area. The OECD Document for Transfrontier Movement of Wastes is to be used to notify competent authorities in concerned OECD Member countries of all such movements and, subsequently, to accompany the movement. Competent authorities in countries will issue this document, which consists of two forms: the notification form and the movement/tracking form (hereafter referred to as the tracking form).

The notification form and its annexes are designed to provide detailed, accurate and complete information on the parties involved with the movement, on the waste itself, on the recovery operations to be performed, and on other details relating to the proposed movement. This information will allow the competent authorities to make informed judgement on whether to object or consent to the movement according to their national legislation.

Contracts

The OECD System requires the existence of a valid written contract or chain of contracts, starting with the notifier and terminating at the recovery facility, prior to any transfrontier movement of hazardous waste. Contracts should confirm that the transporters, traders, and recovery facilities operate under the legal jurisdiction of OECD Member countries and have appropriate legal status. They must be licensed or otherwise authorised, approved, or "recognised" by the competent authorities in those OECD Member countries to transport, trade, or perform required recovery operations on the waste.

The parties to a contract must ensure that the contract complies with the minimum OECD and national requirements. The assignment of legal responsibility and liability in contracts for any adverse consequences resulting from mishandling, accidents, or any other unforeseen events assists the competent authorities in identifying the responsible parties at any given moment, in accordance with national and international regulations. The contract should also specify which party shall assume responsibility for alternative management in cases where the original terms of the contract are not fulfilled. Such alternative management could include alternate transport, recycling, disposal, or other means for environmentally sound management of the waste.

Contracts shall include provisions for financial guarantees in accordance with applicable national and international law requirements. These guarantees are intended to provide funds for alternative management of the waste in cases where shipment and recovery cannot be carried out as originally intended. These guarantees may take the form of an insurance policy, bank letters, bonds, or other promise of compensation for damage.

International Shipping Standards

For all wastes subject to the OECD System, packing, labelling, and transport of the wastes must be arranged in accordance with generally accepted and recognised international rules, standards and practices, and any applicable international transport agreements. The UN publication, *Recommendations of the United Nations Concerning Transport of Dangerous Goods* (the so-called Orange Book), provides basic details on these requirements.

Movements which Cannot be Completed as Intended

In cases where the movement cannot be completed as intended, the party that has possession of the waste must immediately inform the notifier and the competent authorities of the countries of import and export. If the consignment is located in a country of transit, then the competent authority of that country must also to be immediately informed.

In such cases, alternative management and control arrangements, or return of the wastes to the generator if necessary, must be arranged. The basic principle is to hold the generator responsible for his or her waste until recovery takes place. However, there may be a chain of responsible parties specified in the contract for such alternative management.

On a case-by-case basis, the competent authorities of the concerned countries shall co-operate to ensure that all necessary arrangements are made, transport documents are obtained, and action taken, within a limited time period, in order to ensure the best alternative management of the waste. Concerned countries must not oppose, hinder, or prevent the return of the consignment to the country of export.

8.2 Identification of Wastes Subject to Control by the OECD System

The OECD System separates wastes into three tiers of progressively prescriptive procedures for transfrontier movements. They are referred to as the Green, Amber and Red Tiers. The choice to classify these wastes in one of these "tiers" is based on the examination by the Review Mechanism of specific criteria such as the physical and chemical properties of the waste, its hazardous characteristics and hence the management regime required (see Table 5 and Figure 1).

Green Tier wastes destined for recovery operations typically do not show hazardous characteristics and no control is required from the OECD System, which establishes procedures only for transfrontier movements of *hazardous* wastes.

On the other hand, both Amber and Red Tier wastes have been determined by OECD Member countries typically to exhibit characteristics which are regarded as hazardous. Consequently, they are subject to the OECD Control System and their transfrontier movements have to be notified to the competent authorities of concerned countries. Amber Tier wastes, however, are treated less stringently than Red Tier wastes by the OECD System; this is due to the fact that Amber Tier wastes present a lower degree of risk than Red Tier wastes. Also, considerable experience in recovery operations has been gained for Amber Tier wastes, which are frequently subject to transfrontier movements.

For waste not appearing on any list, national legislation of the concerned countries shall regulate the transfrontier movement. However, if the waste is considered hazardous by the competent authorities of any of the concerned countries, then any movements of that waste will fall under the control of the Red Tier of the OECD System until it has been evaluated and listed by the OECD Review Mechanism.

Procedures for Modifying Green, Amber and Red Tier Lists – The OECD Review Mechanism

A Review Mechanism has been established by the OECD in order to evaluate the current placement of some wastes on the Green, Amber or Red lists, and to assess the placement of "new" wastes to one of these three lists. An ad hoc OECD working party reviews applications for listing modifications. Detailed information in support of such modifications is submitted to the OECD by Member governments, or by any interested party if supported by a Member government, preferably on a specific application form. This form is based on the criteria set out in Decision C(92)39. Modifications to the lists of wastes are effective when approved by the OECD Council.

8.3   Operation of the System

Green Tier wastes destined for recovery operations typically do not exhibit hazardous characteristics and have been deemed to pose negligible risks during transfrontier movement. Also, Green Tier wastes must not be contaminated by other materials at a concentration which would cause them to exhibit hazardous characteristics and thereby require that they be handled under Amber or Red Tier procedures. Green Tier wastes therefore are not controlled directly under the OECD System, which establishes procedures only for transfrontier movements of *hazardous* wastes. However, Green Tier wastes must go only to a facility which, under applicable national law, is operating or is authorised to operate in the importing country. Their movement is also subject to terms of applicable international transport agreements and other existing controls normally applied in commercial transactions.

Within the OECD area, all transfrontier movements of Amber Tier wastes require written notification of the competent authorities of all concerned countries (see Figure 2). This notification procedure allows national competent authorities to object to a transfrontier movement in accordance with their domestic laws.

Two "cases" exist within the Amber control system:

- **Case 1:** movement requiring specific consent; and

- **Case 2:** movement for which pre-consent has already been granted (pre-authorised facility).

For each case, the notification can be a single one if it covers a single shipment, or a general one if it covers a series of shipments of wastes which have similar physical and chemical characteristics, which are sent by the same notifier, and which are destined for the same recovery facility. These two main cases are illustrated in the figures.

Before the transfrontier movement can take place, the notifier must have provided written notification of the proposed movement to the competent authorities of the concerned countries. The competent authority of the importing country must transmit an acknowledgement of receipt of the duly completed notification form to the notifier, with copies to the competent authorities of the other concerned countries, within three working days of receiving the notification.

A movement may proceed only if it has received consent from the competent authorities of all concerned countries. This consent may be given in one of the following two ways for Amber Tier wastes. Either:

Tacit Consent

If no objection has been lodged by any of the concerned countries within 30 days, this is referred to as "tacit consent". This 30-day period begins with the date of the issuance of the acknowledgement by the importing country.

Written Consent

If written authorisation is received from all concerned countries within the 30-day period, this is referred to as "written consent". Written consent is effected by the competent authority returning a copy of the notification form with the appropriate block completed, thus indicating a consent to the proposed movement.

If competent authorities decide to prohibit a movement of an Amber Tier waste, they MUST submit a written objection to the notifier within 30 days of the date that the acknowledgement was returned. If a written objection to the movement has been lodged by any of the concerned countries during the 30-day period, shipment may not proceed until this objection has been lifted or, in the case of an objection by a transit country, an alternative route is found and accepted.

Once the necessary consent has been granted, shipment may proceed after the notifier completes the tracking form. The tracking form must accompany the consignment at all times until it reaches the recovery facility. If more than one carrier is used for a shipment, transfer of the consignment to the new carrier must be recorded on the tracking form.

On receipt of a consignment at the designated recovery facility, a duly authorised representative of the facility must acknowledge receipt of the consignment by completing the tracking form which accompanies the waste. A signed copy of the completed form must be handed to the last carrier. Within three working days of receipt of the consignment, individually signed copies of the tracking form must be forwarded to the notifier and the competent authorities of concerned countries.

For multiple shipments of similar wastes from the same notifier, going to the same recovery facility, a simplified notification procedure has been produced. In such cases several shipments may be notified at the same time using one notification form. This procedure is called general notification. In this case the notification procedure is the same as that described above. However, each consignment for shipment must be accompanied by its own tracking form.

The competent authority in an importing country may grant pre-consent for quantities of certain wastes to be accepted by one or more designated recovery facilities within its jurisdiction. Under such an authorisation a consignment may be transported directly to a recovery facility, thus avoiding the required time delays for consent which are built into the OECD notification procedure (see Figure 3). The competent authorities of importing countries that elect to adopt this option for certain recovery facilities must inform the OECD Secretariat of any such consent they grant. Although case-by-case consent is not required, the notifier must i) enter into a valid written contract or chain of contracts with the consignee or recovery facility; and ii) submit a notification form to the competent authorities of concerned countries. Notification must be received by all competent authorities before the dispatch of any consignments to a pre-authorised facility can take place.

All the rules of the notification procedure for Amber Tier wastes (single or multiple shipments) apply to Red Tier wastes, except that the importing country and any countries of transit must provide written consent prior to transfrontier movement. Pre-consent cannot be granted to facilities to recover Red Tier wastes.

8.4   Conclusion

OECD Council Decision C(92)39 was adopted on 30 March 1992 prior to entry into force of the Basel Convention. It organises the control of transboundary movements of wastes destined for recovery operations (reflecting Annex IV B of the Basel Convention) within the OECD area. This Decision classifies wastes to be recovered into one of three categories – Green, Amber and Red lists – and specifies the control regime which should apply for each.

Red list wastes are subject to similar control procedures as applied to hazardous wastes under the Basel Convention, although the time limit for prior written consent of the importing and transit countries has been set at 30 days, based on experience of such procedures within OECD.

Amber list wastes are subject to a somewhat simplified control procedure, because they have been considered to present a lower overall risk when such wastes are destined for recovery operations than do red list wastes. All movements of amber list wastes must be notified in advance to all countries concerned (exporting, importing and transit countries); there is a 30-day time limit for responding to a notification, and consent is assumed if no objection to the movement has been lodged by any of the concerned countries within the time limit.

The green list covers wastes destined for recovery operations which do not exhibit any of the hazardous characteristics set forth in Annex III of the Basel Convention. Wastes on the green list are therefore permitted to be moved across borders within the OECD area, to authorised recovery facilities, subject to all existing controls normally applied in commercial transactions. Such a procedure does not prejudice the right of Member countries to control certain wastes which have been assigned to the Green list as if those wastes had been assigned to one of the other lists, in conformity with domestic legislation and the rules of international law, in order to protect human health and the environment.

In the first instance, wastes have been assigned to one or another list in accordance with a number of criteria referring to environmental considerations, the properties of the material, and the method of management and recovery. A Review Mechanism has been established to consider, where necessary, the placement of a particular waste in the different lists, or to propose any modification to the control system based on practical experience or technical progress.

The main features of the OECD System are the following:

- It applies to transfrontier movements of all wastes subject to control under Article 1 of the Basel Convention (minor historical differences having been totally resolved);

- It prohibits exports of hazardous wastes for final disposal to non-OECD countries without consent of the importing country and requires OECD countries to take action to reduce to a minimum the transfrontier movements of such wastes;

- The provisions relating to wastes destined for recovery apply only to movements to authorised facilities within the OECD area (they do not apply to movements to or through non-OECD countries); they classify wastes subject to control according to environmental considerations, the properties of the waste itself, and the management method;

- It identifies competent authorities responsible for transfrontier movements of wastes in each Member country, and establishes a set of control measures including prior notification of all countries concerned and prohibition of any movement for which the consent (written or tacit) has not been obtained; each authorised movement must be accompanied by tracking documentation, and the completion of the movement must be notified to all countries concerned;

- it stipulates that any movement must be covered by a contract or a chain of contracts, starting with the notifier and terminating at the recovery facility, which specifies who is responsible for alternate management of the wastes if the operation cannot be concluded as foreseen.

The Basel Convention and the OECD Council Decision C(92)39 have been translated into European Union legislation through the adoption of Regulation 259/93 on the Supervision and Control of Shipments of Wastes within, into and out of the European Community. This Regulation became effective on 6 May 1994.

The EC Regulation 259/93 embodies the notion that differential risks to human health and the environment should be differentially managed. Different procedures are thus prescribed depending on the type of waste and its destination, including whether it is destined for disposal or recovery. For recovery-bound wastes, the OECD three-tier (Green, Amber, Red) waste classification scheme is fully adopted. The Regulation further states that these lists of wastes shall be adapted by the Commission only to reflect changes already agreed under the Review Mechanism of OECD.

Figure 1: Identification of Wastes to be Controlled by the OECD System

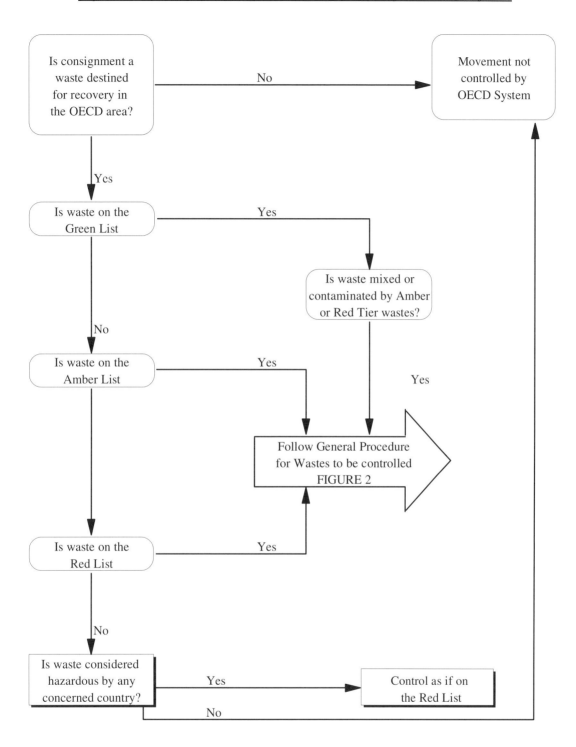

Figure 2: General Procedure for Notification of Wastes to be Controlled

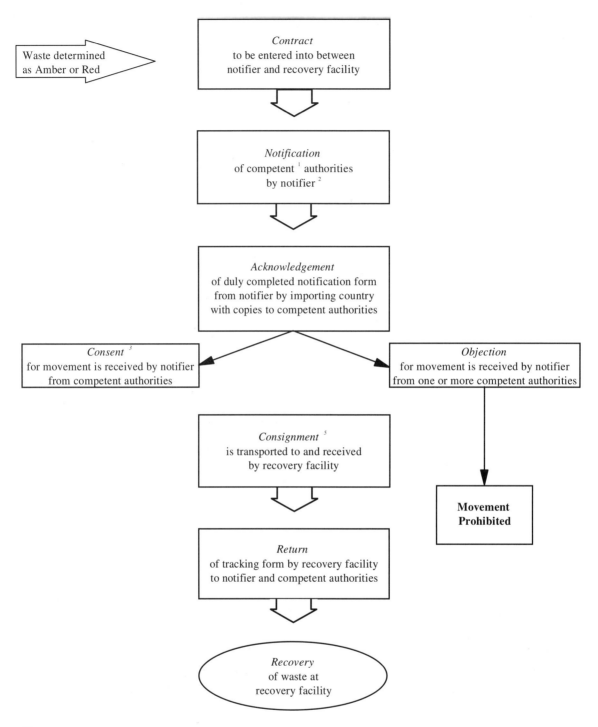

Notes:
1) Authorities of importing, exporting, and possibly transit countries.
2) In some Member countries the competent authority may transmit notification form in lieu of the notifier.
3) Tacit or written consent for Amber Waste. Written only for Red Waste.
4) Until objection is lifted or an alternative route is found in case of objection by a transit country.
5) Accompanied by a tracking form.

Figure 3: Procedure for Notification of Amber Wastes Destined for a Pre-authorised Recovery Facility

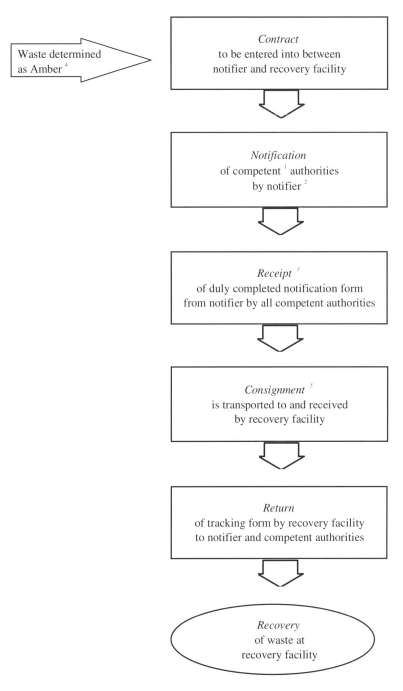

Notes:
1) Authorities of importing, exporting, and possibly transit countries.
2) In some Member countries the competent authority may transmit notification form in lieu of the notifier.
3) In some Member countries a seven day contract review period may be required prior to movement.
4) Pre-consent procedure is not applicable for Red Tier wastes.

Table 1: Core List of Wastes to be Controlled

Waste streams:

Y1   Clinical wastes from medical care in hospitals, medical centres and clinics

Y2   Wastes from the production and preparation of pharmaceutical products

Y3   Waste pharmaceuticals, drugs and medicines

Y4   Wastes from the production, formulation and use of biocides and phytopharmaceuticals

Y5   Wastes from the manufacture, formulation and use of wood preserving chemicals

Y6   Wastes from the production, formulation and use of organic solvents

Y7   Wastes from heat treatment and tempering operations containing cyanides

Y8   Waste mineral oils unfit for their originally intended use

Y9   Waste oil/water, hydrocarbon/water mixtures, emulsions

Y10 Waste substances and articles containing or contaminated with polychlorinated biphenyls (PCBs) and/or polychlorinated terphenyls (PCTs) and/or polybrominated biphenyls (PBBs)

Y11 Waste tarry residues arising from refining, distillation and any pyrolytic treatment

Y12 Wastes from production, formulation and use of inks, dyes, pigments, paints, lacquers, varnish

Y13 Wastes from production, formulation and use of resins, latex, plasticizers, glues/adhesives

Y14 Waste chemical substances arising from research and development or teaching activities which are not identified and/or are new and whose affects on man and/or the environment are not known

Y15 Wastes of an explosive nature not subject to other legislation

Y16 Wastes from production, formulation and use of photographic chemicals and processing materials

Y17   Wastes resulting from surface treatment of metals and plastics

Y18   Residues arising from industrial waste disposal operations

Wastes having as constituents:

Y19   Metal carbonyls

Y20   Beryllium; beryllium compounds

Y21   Hexavalent chromium compounds

Y22   Copper compounds

Y23   Zinc compounds

Y24   Arsenic; arsenic compounds

Y25   Selenium; selenium compounds

Y26   Cadmium; cadmium compounds

Y27   Antimony; antimony compounds

Y28   Tellurium; tellurium compounds

Y29   Mercury; mercury compounds

Y30   Thallium; thallium compounds

Y31   Lead; lead compounds

Y32   Inorganic fluorine compounds excluding calcium fluoride

Y33   Inorganic cyanides

Y34   Acidic solutions or acids in solid form

Y35   Basic solutions or bases in solid form

Y36   Asbestos (dust and fibres)

Y37   Organic phosphorous compounds

Y38   Organic cyanides

Y39   Phenols; phenol compounds including chlorophenols

Y40   Ethers

Y41   Halogenated organic solvents

Y42   Organic solvents excluding halogenated solvents

Y43   Any congenor of polychlorinated dibenzo-furan

Y44   Any congenor of polychlorinated dibenzo-p-dioxin

Y45   Organohalogen compounds other than substances referred to in this table
       (e.g. Y39, Y41, Y42, Y43, Y44)

Table 2: List of Hazardous Characteristics

Code Number[*]   **Characteristics**

H1   **Explosive.** An explosive substance or waste is a solid or liquid substance or waste (or mixture of substances or wastes) which is in itself capable by chemical reaction of producing gas at such a temperature and pressure and at such a speed as to cause damage to the surroundings.

H3   **Flammable Liquids.** The word "flammable" has the same meaning as "inflammable". Flammable liquids are liquids, or mixtures of liquids, or liquids containing solids in solution or suspension (for example, paints, varnishes, lacquers, etc. but not including substances or wastes otherwise classified on account of their dangerous characteristics) which give off a flammable vapour at temperatures of not more than 60.5°C, closed-cup test, or not more than 65.6°C, open-cup test. (Since the results of open-cup tests and of closed-cup tests are not strictly comparable and even individual results by the same test are often variable, regulations varying from the above figures to make allowance for such differences would be within the spirit of this definition.)

H4.1   **Flammable Solids**. Solids, or waste solids, other than those classed as explosives, which under conditions encountered in transport are readily combustible, or may cause or contribute to fire through friction.

H4.2   **Substances or Wastes Liable to Spontaneous Combustion**. Substances or wastes which are liable to spontaneous heating under normal conditions encountered in transport, or to heating up in contact with air, and being liable to catch fire.

H4.3   **Substances or Wastes which, in Contact with Water, Emit Flammable Gases.** Substances or wastes which, by interaction with water, are liable to become spontaneously flammable or to give off flammable gases in dangerous quantities.

H5.1   **Oxidizing.** Substances or wastes which, while in themselves not necessarily combustible, may, generally by yielding oxygen cause, or contribute to, the combustion of other materials.

H5.2   **Organic Peroxides.** Organic substances or wastes which contain the bivalent-0-0-structure are thermally unstable substances which may undergo exothermic self-accelerating decomposition.

H6.1   **Poisonous (Acute).** Substances or wastes liable either to cause death or serious injury or to harm human health if swallowed or inhaled or by skin contact.

---

[*]   Corresponds to hazard class numbering system included in the United Nations Recommendations on the Transport of Dangerous Goods (Orange Book) for H1 through H9; omissions of H2, H7 and H9 are deliberate.

H6.2   **Infectious Substances.** Substances or wastes containing viable micro organisms or their toxins which are known or suspected to cause disease in animals or humans.

H8   **Corrosives.** Substances or wastes which, by chemical action, will cause severe damage when in contact with living tissue, or, in the case of leakage, will materially damage, or even destroy, other goods or the means of transport; they may also cause other hazards.

H10   **Liberation of Toxic Gases in Contact with Air or Water.** Substances or wastes which, by interaction with air or water, are liable to give off toxic gases in dangerous quantities.

H11   **Toxic (Delayed or Chronic).** Substances or wastes which, if they are inhaled or ingested or if they penetrate the skin, may involve delayed or chronic effects, including carcinogenicity.

H12   **Ecotoxic.** Substances or wastes which if released present or may present immediate or delayed adverse impacts to the environment by means of bioaccumulation and/or toxic effects upon biotic systems.

H13   Capable, by any means, after disposal, of yielding another material, e.g., leachate, which possesses any of the characteristics listed above.

The potential hazards posed by certain types of wastes are not yet fully documented; objective tests to define quantitatively these hazards do not exist. Further research is necessary in order to develop means to characterise potential hazards posed to man and/or the environment by these wastes. Standardised tests have been derived with respect to pure substances and materials. Many Member countries have developed tests which can be applied to materials destined for disposal by means of operations listed in Table 3 in order to decide if these materials exhibit any of the characteristics listed in Table 2.

Table 3: Disposal Operations

(A) **OPERATIONS WHICH DO NOT LEAD TO THE POSSIBILITY OF RESOURCE RECOVERY, RECYCLING, RECLAMATION, DIRECT RE-USE OR ALTERNATIVE USES**

Table A is meant to encompass all such disposal operations which occur in practice, whether or not they are adequate from the point of view of environmental protection.

D1   Deposit into or onto land [e.g., landfill, etc.]

D2   Land treatment [e.g., biodegradation of liquid or sludgy discards in soils, etc.]

D3   Deep injection [e.g., injection of pumpable discards into wells, salt domes or naturally occurring repositories, etc.]

D4   Surface impoundment [e.g., placement of liquid or sludge discards into pits, ponds or lagoons, etc.]

D5   Specially engineered landfill [e.g., placement into lined discrete cells which are capped and isolated from one another and the environment, etc.]

D6   Release into a water body except seas/oceans

D7   Release into seas/oceans including sea-bed insertion

D8   Biological treatment not specified elsewhere in the Table which results in final compounds or mixtures which are discarded by means of any of the operations in Table A

D9   Physico chemical treatment not specified elsewhere in this Table which results in final compounds or mixtures which are discarded by means of any of the operations in Table A [e.g., evaporation, drying, calcination, etc.]

D10   Incineration on land

D11   Incineration at sea

D12   Permanent storage [e.g., emplacement of containers in a mine, etc.]

D13   Blending or mixing prior to submission to any of the operations in Table A

D 14   Repackaging prior to submission to any of the operations in Table A

D15   Storage pending any of the operations in Table A

(B) **OPERATIONS WHICH MAY LEAD TO RESOURCE RECOVERY, RECYCLING, RECLAMATION, DIRECT RE-USE OR ALTERNATIVE USES**

Table B is meant to encompass all such operations with respect to materials considered to be or legally defined as hazardous wastes and which otherwise would have been destined for operations included in Table A.

R1   Use as a fuel (other than in direct incineration) or other means to generate energy

R2   Solvent reclamation/regeneration

R3   Recycling/reclamation of organic substances which are not used as solvents

R4   Recycling/reclamation of metals and metal compounds

R5   Recycling/reclamation of other inorganic materials

R6   Regeneration of acids or bases

R7   Recovery of components used for pollution abatement

R8   Recovery of components from catalysts

R9   Used oil re-refining or other reuses of previously used oil

R10   Land treatment resulting in benefit to agriculture or ecological improvement

R11   Uses of residual materials obtained from any of the operations numbered R1-R10

R12   Exchange of wastes for submission to any of the operations numbered R1-R11

R13   Accumulation of material intended for any operation in Table B

Table 4: Reasons Why Materials are Intended for Disposal

Q1   Production residues not otherwise specified below

Q2   Off-specification products

Q3   Products whose date for appropriate use has expired

Q4   Materials spilled, lost or having undergone other mishap including any materials, equipment etc. contaminated as result of the mishap

Q5   Materials contaminated or soiled as a result of planned actions [e.g., residues from cleaning operations, packing materials, containers, etc.]

Q6   Unusable parts [e.g., reject batteries, exhausted catalyst, etc.]

Q7   Substances which no longer perform satisfactorily [e.g., contaminated acid, contaminated solvents, exhausted tempering salts, etc.]

Q8   Residues of industrial processes [e.g., slags, still bottoms, etc.]

Q9   Residues from pollution abatement processes [e.g., scrubber sludges, baghouse dusts, spent filters, etc.]

Q10   Machining/finishing residues [e.g., lathe turnings, mill scales, etc.]

Q11   Residues from raw materials processing [e.g., mining residues, oil field slops, etc.]

Q12   Adulterated materials [e.g., oils contaminated with PCB, etc.]

Q13   Any materials, substances or products whose use has been banned by law in the country of exportation

Q14   Products for which there is no further use [e.g., agriculture, household, office, commercial and shop discards, etc.]

Q15   Materials, substances or products resulting from remedial actions with respect to contaminated land

Q16   Any materials, substances or products which the generator or exporter declares to be wastes and which are not contained in the above categories.

Table 5: Identification of Wastes Subject to Control by the OECD System

CRITERIA

A)   Properties

1)   Does the waste normally exhibit any of the hazardous characteristics listed in Table 5 of OECD Council Decision C(88)90(Final)? Furthermore, it is useful to know if the waste is legally defined as or considered to be a hazardous waste in one or more Member countries.

2)   Is the waste typically contaminated?

3)   What is the physical state of the waste?

4)   What is the degree of difficulty of cleanup in the case of accidental spillage or mismanagement?

5)   What is the economic value of the waste bearing in mind historical price fluctuations?

B)   Management

6)   Is there technological capability to recover the waste?

7)   Is there a history of adverse environmental incidents arising from transfrontier movements of the waste or associated recovery operations?

8)   Is the waste routinely traded through established channels and is that evidenced by commercial classification?

9)   Is the waste usually moved internationally under the terms of a valid contract or chain of contracts?

10)   What is the extent of reuse and recovery of the waste and how is any portion separated from the waste but not subject to recovery managed?

11)   What are the overall environmental benefits arising from the recovery operations?

CONTROL MEASURES CONCERNING THE IMPORT OF HAZARDOUS WASTES INTO CHINA

Youfu Xia
China Institute of Trade and Environment, and
University of International Business and Economics, China

1.0   Introduction

Since opening to the outside world in 1978, China has made great achievements in foreign trade development. Imports in 1995 amounted to US$132.08 billion (an increase of 1212.86 per cent compared with 1978). In 1995 China ranked eleventh in the world in total imports. The value of imports in 1996 was US$138.84 billion. With the rapid increase in goods imports, increased volumes of hazardous wastes have been illegally imported into China and the number of cases discovered by China's customs authorities has risen rapidly.

Illegal imports of hazardous wastes to China have a major impact on her environment. In this paper we first attempt to estimate the total quantity of wastes, especially hazardous wastes, imported into China. Control measures presently being taken are then analysed. Finally, recommendations are made concerning the prevention and control of the illegal import of hazardous wastes.

2.0   Quantity of Wastes Imported

Many incidents involving the illegal import of hazardous wastes have been discovered and reported in recent years. For example, 1,353 tonnes of hazardous wastes, mainly non-ferrous wastes and batteries from disused automobiles, was reportedly imported from the United Kingdom in 1991. In 1992 and 1993, this amount was 7,315 tonnes and 4,186 tonnes, respectively. In October 1993, 1,228 tonnes of hazardous chemical wastes was illegally imported from Korea as "other fuel oil". On 3 March 1994, Jiangxi Hualong Chemical Co., Ltd. imported from Germany 3,109 tonnes of wastes of biological origin. It imported 5,700 tonnes of the same wastes on 18 and 21 April, and a certain amount of mixed biological and industrial wastes in May. In June 1994, 500 tonnes of waste electrical machinery with industrial hazardous wastes from Japan was discovered by Ningbo Customs. On 5 June 1994, Shanghai Customs seized 100 tonnes of waste telephone sets from the United States. In July 1994, 70 sets of waste transformers containing PCBs, imported from the United States by a packaging company, were discovered by the Xiamen customs authority. In 1995, a variety of illegal waste imports were discovered by local customs authority's in several provinces. The most common illegal imports found were biological wastes, agri-chemical wastes, slag and mine ash, sludge and waste plastics. The quantities concerned ranged from 18 tonnes to 678 tonnes.

Although many cases of hazardous waste import have been discovered, no study has yet tried to estimate the total quantity of such wastes coming into China. Based on very incomplete customs statistics, we calculated the import quantity and value of more than 120 wastes. We found that large quantities of wastes, including hazardous wastes, have been imported into China in recent years. Table 1 shows that the quantity and value of imported wastes in 1993 reached 8,285,361 tonnes and US$1,575 million, an increase of 735.6 and 505.6 per cent, respectively, compared with 1990.

The quantity and value of wastes imported in 1994 decreased by 19.50 per cent and 13.58 per cent, respectively, compared with 1993. The main reasons for this decline were the sharp decreases in imports of steel scrap and of ships to be disassembled. The quantity of these two wastes imported in 1994 decreased by 28.81 per cent and 53.96 per cent, while the import value decreased by 33.1 per cent and 53.96 per cent. In 1995, the quantity of wastes imported decreased by 145,460 tonnes compared to 1994; the import value of these wastes was US$1,730 million, an increase of 27.13 per cent compared to 1994.

Based on the waste classification system used in the European Union, China divides wastes into five groups: normal green wastes (NGW) which can be imported without limitation; restricted green wastes (RGW) which can be imported only with the approval of certain government authorities; prohibited green wastes (PGW) which cannot be imported; amber wastes (AW); and red wastes which are not allowed to be imported. Table 2 shows four groups of wastes imported between 1990 and 1995. In the table, the percentage of NGW decreased from 77 in 1990 to 49 in 1995, while the percentage of RGW increased from 8 to 40. The quantity and value of PGW increased rapidly over the period 1990-1995, from 11,533 tonnes to 108,213 tonnes and from US$1.69 million to US$31.82 million. The quantity and value of AW rose from 137,239 tonnes to 469,105 tonnes and from US$12.23 million to US$84.49 million. The quantity and value of restricted and prohibited wastes between 1992-1995 is shown in Table 3.

In 1996, an Interim Regulation on the Import and Management of Wastes, and a Catalogue of Wastes Subject to Import Restrictions were promulgated. The Catalogue divides wastes into nine categories: animal wastes, refuse, wood waste and wood scrap, waste paper and paperboard, textiles waste, scrap metal, electrical and electronics waste, waste from equipment used in transport, and special wastes. Wastes not listed in the Catalogue are prohibited from being imported.

In 1993-1994, more than 50 per cent of total imported wastes came from OECD countries, more than 13 per cent came from five Asian economies, and the rest from other countries and regions (see Table 4). Large quantities of wastes have also been imported from OECD countries through Hong Kong.

Table 5 shows the percentage of total wastes imported from 22 OECD countries between 1993 and 1994. Japan, the United States, Germany, Sweden, the United Kingdom and the Netherlands are shown to be the largest waste exporters.

Tables 6 and 7 show the quantity and value of the main restricted and prohibited wastes imported from OECD countries in 1994, and of four groups of wastes imported from Japan and the United States in 1993-1994.

Table 1: China's Importation of Wastes, 1990-1995
(unit: tonnes; value: US$10,000)

	Imported Wastes			
	Total Import Value	**Quantity**	**Value**	**% TIV**
1990	5,334,500	991,542	25,999.2	0.49
1991	7,379,100	2,114,410	60,610.5	0.95
1992	8,058,500	5,715,823	134,326.0	1.67
1993	10,395,900	8,285,361	157,448.7	1.50
1994	11,561,400	6,668,963	136,067.4	1.18
1995	13,208,354	6,523,505	172,987.0	1.31

Note: TIV = Total Import Value

Source: Calculated on the basis of data in *Statistics Yearbook of China's Customs, 1990-1995.*

Table 2: Classification of Wastes Imported into China, 1990-1995
(unit: tonnes; value: US$10,000)

		NGW	**RGW**	**PGW**	**AW**	**Total**
1990	Quantity	763,540	79,230	11,533	137,239	991,542
	%	77.01	7.99	1.16	13.84	100
	Value	20,080	4,528	169	1,223	25,999
	%	77.23	17.42	0.65	4.70	100
1991	Quantity	1,671,111	367,039	9,866	66,394	2,114,410
	%	79.03	17.36	0.47	3.14	100
	Value	45,425	13,555	534	1,096	60,611
	%	74.95	22.36	0.88	1.81	100
1992	Quantity	2,979,045	2,237,217	42,964	456,597	5,715,823
	%	52.12	39.14	0.75	7.99	100
	Value	72,972	53,896	1,194	6,264	134,326
	%	54.32	40.12	0.89	4.66	100
1993	Quantity	4,360,824	3,314,595	50,040	559,902	8,285,361
	%	52.63	40.12	0.89	4.66	100
	Value	84,071	66,964	1,328	5,357	157,449
	%	53.40	42.53	0.84	3.40	100
1994	Quantity	3,794,476	2,315,218	90,164	469,105	6,668,963
	%	56.90	34.72	1.35	7.03	100
	Value	76,179	52,450	2,436	5,002	136,067
	%	55.99	38.55	1.79	3.68	100
1995	Quantity	3,162,853	2,583,284	108,213	669,155	6,523,505
	%	48.48	39.60	1.66	10.26	100
	Value	72,525	88,831	3,182	8,449	172,987
	%	41.93	51.35	1.84	4.84	100

Note: NGW = Normal Green Wastes; RGW = Restricted Green Wastes; PGW = Prohibited Green Wastes;
AW = Amber Wastes

Source: Calculated from data in the *Statistics Yearbook of China's Customs, 1990-1995*

Table 3: Imports of Some Restricted and Prohibited Wastes, 1992-1995
(unit: 10,000 tonnes; value: US$ 10,000)

Restricted Wastes

	1992		1993		1994		1995	
	Q	V	Q	V	Q	V	Q	V
Waste copper	49.1	24,226	57	21,872	77.4	23,239	118.9	49,260
Scrap iron and steel	124.3	18,326	298	45,816	212.2	30,651	133.5	17,542
Ships for disassembly	262	18,606	2,051	32,804	375	15,104	213	4,754
Aluminium waste and scrap	4.5	1,672	6.1	2,008	10.9	2,714	35.7	14,916
Refuse and other wastes from the manufacture of iron and steel	7.3	29.7	6.5	57.1	8.2	27.6	5.8	26.1
Waste paper or paperboard	79	10,525	60.4	7,476	71.1	9,356	90.6	17,241
Wood waste	12.3	1,135	8	503.7	6.7	262	8.1	344
Cotton waste	2.4	335.7	2.4	262.2	2.7	411.7	2.6	415.3

Note: Q = quantity; V = value

Source: Calculated from data in the *Statistics Yearbook of China's Customs, 1992-1995*

Prohibited Wastes

	1992		1993		1994		1995	
	Q	V	Q	V	Q	V	Q	V
Waste from petroleum refining	10.1	1,877	15.7	2,399	13.8	2,050	34.8	5,448
Waste plastics	30.7	8,165	37.4	8,755	45.7	10,265	56	11,447
Used rags; scrap twine, cordage, cables and rope, etc.	1.9	161	1	224	2.1	361	4.2	810
Metal ash and slag and associated chemical compounds	4.8	1,891	6	1,168	4.3	820	3.6	830
Other slag and mine ash	18.4	123	24.1	17	17.5	33.8	14.6	9.2
Waste rubber	0.48	95.9	0.53	92.7	0.51	94.2	3.73	284.4
Leather scraps	4.9	2,256	2.7	1,606	1.8	1,687	1.9	1,803

Notes: Q = quantity; V = value
Based on classification adopted in 1996.

Source: Calculated from data in the *Statistics Yearbook of China's Customs, 1992-1995*.

Table 4: Wastes Imported from Different Economies and Regions, 1993-1994
(unit: 10,000 tonnes; value: US$ 1,000,000)

	1993				1994			
	Q	**%***	**V**	**%****		**%***	**V**	**%****
Total	829	100	1575	100	667	100	1361	100
OECD	470	56.7	878	55.8	347	52.1	682	50.1
NICs	150	18.2	243	15.3	105	15.7	181	13.3
Hong Kong	89	10.7	118	7.5	76	11.5	106	7.8
Singapore	11	1.3	65	4.1	10	1.6	17	1.3
Korea	7	0.8	21	1.4	11	1.7	26	1.9
Chinese Taipei	10	1.2	43	2.8	14	2.1	52	3.8
Macao	4	0.4	3	0.2	3	0.4	3	0.2
Others	209	25.1	454	28.9	215	32.2	498	36.6
Russia	69	8.3	125	7.9	75	11.3	126	9.3

Note: Q = quantity; V = value

*   percentage of total quantity of imported wastes
** percentage of total value of imported wastes

Source: Calculated from data in the *Statistics Yearbook of China's Customs, 1993-1994*

Table 5: Percentage of Total Wastes Imported into China
Originating from 22 OECD Countries, 1993-1994

Country	1993			1994		
	Q	V	%*	Q	V	%*
Japan	26.98	23.41	1.58	18.49	15.98	1.07
United States	14.24	16.59	2.44	21.29	21.19	2.08
Germany	3.59	3.32	0.87	2.15	1.87	0.36
Sweden	2.66	2.33	5.48	0.80	0.62	1.01
United Kingdom	1.81	1.93	1.84	1.26	1.21	0.93
Netherlands	1.61	1.74	3.85	1.92	1.98	3.80
Italy	0.98	0.88	0.51	0.28	1.05	0.46
France	0.70	0.58	0.55	0.49	0.39	0.27
Canada	0.48	0.57	0.65	0.32	0.55	0.41
Norway	0.61	0.53	6.28	0.50	0.37	3.38
Spain	1.10	0.93	3.09	1.38	1.06	1.60
Greece	0.35	0.31	23.41			
Belgium	0.34	0.41	0.82	0.64	0.76	0.99
New Zealand	0.10	0.17	0.99	0.17	0.19	0.83
Australia	0.26	0.50	0.40	0.65	0.84	0.47
Portugal	0.01	0.01	0.51			
Denmark	0.03	0.03	0.33	0.01	0.01	0.04
Austria	0.002	0.01	0.06	0.003	0.003	0.02
Switzerland	0.01	0.02	0.03	0.002	0.01	0.01
Finland	0.03	0.12	0.57	0.06	0.08	0.23
Mexico	0.01	0.01	0.08	0.002	0.01	0.12
Turkey				0.01	0.03	0.10

Note: Q = quantity; V = value

* percentage of country's total exports to China

Source: Calculated from data in the *Statistics Yearbook of China's Customs, 1993-1994*

Table 6: Selected Restricted and Prohibited Wastes Imported from OECD Countries in 1994
(unit: 10,000 tonnes; value: US$10,000)

Restricted Wastes

	Quantity	%*	Value	%*
Ships for disassembly	263	70.13	11,493	77.99
Copper scrap	59.1	76.41	16,276	70.04
Waste paper and paperboard	35.4	49.73	4,548	48.62
Scrap iron and steel	105.5	49.71	15,861	51.75

Prohibited Wastes

	Quantity	% *	Value	% **
Other slag and mine ash	2.4	13.81	2.9	8.61
Wastes from petroleum refining	3.6	25.73	522	25.47
Waste plastics	34.3	75.16	7,611	74.14
Metal ash and slag and associated chemical compounds	1.7	38.95	296	36.78
Leather waste	1.1	61.80	901	53.40
Used rags, scrap twine, etc.	0.4	16.89	83	23.00

*   percentage of total quantity of these wastes imported
** percentage of total value of these wastes imported

Source: Calculated on data from *Statistics Yearbook of China's Customs, 1992-1994*

Table 7: Classification of Imported Wastes from Two OECD Countries, 1993-1994
(unit: 10,000 tonnes; value: US$1,000,000)

	United States						Japan					
	Q	PUQ	PTQ	V	PUV	PTV	Q	PUQ	PTQ	V	PUV	PTV
1993												
NGW	69.9	59.2	8.4	118	45.1	7.5	73.8	33.0	8.9	133	35.9	8.4
RGW	44.9	38.1	5.4	135	51.6	8.6	137.8	61.7	16.6	232	63.0	14.8
PGW	0.2	0.2	0.03	2	0.6	0.1	0.7	0.3	0.08	1	0.3	0.08
AW	3.0	2.5	0.4	7	2.7	0.5	11.3	5.1	1.4	3	0.7	0.2
Total	118	100	14.2	262	100	16.7	223.6	100	27	369	100	23.5
1994												
NGW	87.8	61.8	13.2	120	41.6	8.8	52.1	42.3	7.8	82	37.9	6.1
RGW	52	36.6	7.8	161	55.9	11.8	66.5	54	10	126	57.9	9.3
PGW	0.3	0.2	0.04	2	0.6	0.1	0.7	0.6	0.1	3	1.2	0.2
AW	1.9	1.4	0.3	6	2.1	0.5	4.0	3.2	0.6	7	3.1	0.5
Total	142	100	21.3	288	100	21.2	123.3	100	18.5	217	100	16.1

Note: NGW = Normal Green Wastes; RGW = Restricted Green Wastes; PGW = Prohibited Green Wastes; AW = Amber Wastes; Q = quantity; V = value; PUQ = percentage of the total quantity of wastes imported from this country; PTQ = quantity of wastes imported from this country as a percentage of total quantity of imported wastes; PUV = percentage of the total value of wastes imported from this country; PTV = value of wastes imported from this country as a percentage of total value of imported wastes

Source: Calculated from data in the *Statistics Yearbook of China's Customs, 1993-1994*

The illegal import of hazardous wastes into China has the following characteristics:

- Most of the wastes are biological wastes, chemical wastes, mine slag and ash, chemical compounds, wastes from petroleum refining, and waste plastics.

- OECD countries are the main exporters. Some of the hazardous wastes have been exported to China directly, others indirectly through Hong Kong, Macao and Chinese Taipei. Table 8 shows the imports of four types of waste from Hong Kong in the period 1993-1994.

- Exporters seldom pre-notify and receive the permission of the designated competent national authority, the National Environmental Protection Agency (NEPA), as required by the Basel Convention. Moreover, importers may incorrectly identify imported wastes, for example waste electrical equipment containing hazardous materials or hazardous biological and industrial wastes. When some importers obtain permission to import wastes, the first parts of a shipment may be in accordance with the permit but later shipments may contain a mix of permitted and non-permitted hazardous wastes.

- Some foreign enterprises established in China are involved in illegal imports of hazardous wastes.

- Most users of the hazardous wastes are township enterprises located on China's eastern seaboard, and individuals. These users almost never consider the negative impact of illegal hazardous waste imports on China's environment.

- China has made some improvements in environmental protection but the overall environmental situation remains serious. Economic development has been affected by the seriousness of environmental damage and pollution. The illegal import of hazardous wastes worsens China's environmental problems: many people contract skin diseases when using old imported garments; the storage, processing and disposal of illegally imported hazardous wastes seriously pollutes air, water and land resources in many regions and poses threats to public health. For example, 30,000 tonnes of hazardous wastes imported by the Hualong Chemical Co. seriously contaminated 20 hectares of cultivated land. Contact with the hazardous wastes caused many workers and peasants to suffer from serious illness.

Table 8: Wastes Imported from Hong Kong, 1993-1994

	Q	PUQ	PTQ	V	PUV	PTV
1993						
NGW	50.72	57.3	11.6	63	53	7.4
RGW	18.34	20.7	5.5	48	40.8	7.2
PGW	0.84	1.0	16.7	2.0	1.4	12.6
AW	18.66	21.1	33.3	6.0	4.8	10.6
Total	88.56	100.1	67.1	119	100	37.8
1994						
NGW	46.94	61.4	12.4	58	54.3	7.6
RGW	17.93	23.5	7.8	40	37.7	7.6
PGW	0.85	1.1	9.4	4	3.5	15.2
AW	10.67	14	22.8	5	4.5	9.6
Total	76.39	100	52.4	107	100	40

Note: NGW = Normal Green Wastes; RGW = Restricted Green Wastes, PGW = Prohibited Green Wastes; AW = Amber Wastes; Q = Quantity; V = Value; PUQ = percentage of the total quantity of wastes imported from Hong Kong; PTQ = quantity of wastes imported from Hong Kong as a percentage of the total quantity of imported wastes; PUV = percentage of the total value of wastes imported from Hong Kong; PTV = value of wastes imported from Hong Kong as a percentage of total value of imported wastes.

Source: Calculated from data in the *Statistics Yearbook of China's Customs, 1993-1994*.

3.0 Legislation Concerning the Import of Hazardous Wastes

The government of China is ever vigilant against the illegal import of hazardous wastes into the country. On the international front, China became a party to the Basel Convention in 1991. In 1994, China and many other developing countries were instrumental in promoting the Geneva Agreement amending the Basel Convention, which specifies that the export of all hazardous wastes will be forbidden after 1998.

China has established more than 20 laws and regulations to prevent and control the import of hazardous wastes. These legislative initiatives include:

- Regulations of the People's Republic of China on the administration of dumping of hazardous wastes into the sea (1985);

- Circular of the Ministry of Foreign Economic Relations and Trade prohibiting the importation of old garments (1985);

- Provisional rules on environmental management in the open regions (1986);

- Regulations on the prevention of environmental pollution from the disassembly of ships (1988);

- Provisional measures for the management of the importation of toxic chemicals (1989).

Five pieces of legislation directly control or prohibit the import of hazardous wastes:

- Notice on the strict control of the import of hazardous wastes to China (this notice, jointly adopted by NEPA and the Customs General Administration in 1991, forbids the importation of wastes containing 23 types of hazardous matter and establishes strict prevention and control measures);

- Provisional rules on the strict control of wastes imported form EU countries (enacted by NEPA in 1994, the rules classify five groups of wastes and specify the different control measures applying);

- Law of the People's Republic of China on the prevention and control of solid waste pollution (adopted by the People's Congress on 30 October 1995, this law has eight articles concerning the prevention and control of the importation of hazardous solid wastes);

- Draft Notice on Controlling the Import of Hazardous Wastes to China (issued by the General Office of the State Council on 7 November 1995); and

- Interim Regulation on the Import and Management of Wastes and a Catalogue of Wastes Subject to Import Restrictions.

The main principles and measures to prevent and control the illegal import of hazardous waste are:

- the dumping, storage and disposal of imported hazardous wastes is prohibited;
- solid wastes which can be used as raw materials should be imported under strict controls, including mandatory inspection. Such wastes are listed in the Catalogue of Wastes Subject to Import Restrictions. The import of other wastes is prohibited;
- the transit of hazardous wastes through China is prohibited;
- penalties for transgressions depending on the particular circumstances include: fines of US$6,000 to US$120,000 and the return of the waste to the exporting country; disciplinary sanctions; criminal proceedings.

The Chinese government has rejected many applications by foreign businesses to export hazardous wastes to China. Both NEPA and some local authorities, such as Weihai, have been in the forefront of action. Nonetheless, it remains very difficult to prevent and control the illegal import of hazardous wastes into China.

4.0   Recommendations

Increased efforts should be made to raise environmental awareness, especially among businesses engaged in trade with China. It is very important to reinforce the position that the illegal import of hazardous wastes will endanger China's environment and the health of her people. Short-term economic gains should not be at the expense of the Chinese people's long-term environmental and public health interests.

A combination of factors such as the much higher environmental awareness of people in the developed countries, the very strict environmental laws and regulations on disposing wastes in those countries and the very high cost of waste disposal may tempt some businesses to try to export hazardous wastes to developing countries. They sometimes export these wastes at a very cheap price by offering subsidies to the importers. This was the case for an importer of biological wastes from Hong Kong to Fuzhou. The average import price of 240,000 tonnes of slag and ash in 1995 was only US$0.63 per tonne; the average import price of 180,000 tonnes of such waste coming from Hong Kong was US$0.17; and for 38,000 tonnes of this waste coming from Japan, the average import price was US$0.18. At such a low price, the exporters cannot cover the transportation cost. Therefore, some other factor is likely to exist behind the contracts.

In order to increase the public's environmental awareness, they should be encouraged to take part in preventing and controlling the illegal import of hazardous wastes. The press should have the right to thoroughly report on the cases that are discovered.

Further adjustments should be made to guidelines affecting foreign direct investment projects. In principle, foreign enterprises are not allowed to invest in industries which use imported restricted and prohibited green, amber and red wastes.

Refinements should be made to the the Catalogue of Wastes Subject to Import Restrictions. In compiling the list of wastes in the Catalogue, account should be taken of their present and potential environmental and economic impact. Consolidation of waste groups into three categories could also be undertaken: strictly controlled wastes, normal green wastes allowed to be imported, and prohibited wastes. Wastes from the dismantlement of obsolete equipment and technologies that culd seriously pollute the environment should be included in the group of prohibited wastes.

Environmental management could be strengthened in the following ways:

- An administrative mechanism should be set up to organise and co-ordinate all related governmental organisations. Under the leadership of the State Council, a co-ordinating and administrative team should be established with the participation of NEPA, the General Customs Administration, the Ministry of Foreign Trade and Economic Co-operation, and other related industrial ministries.

- NEPA should become a Ministry of Environmental Protection or a State Commission of Ecological and Environmental Protection. Similar to the General Customs Administration, it should delegate authority to competent lower levels of government, e.g. provincial environmental protection bureaus.

- Several major harbours should be designated as official entry points for waste imports. The customs authority and environmental protection bureau should have the resources to examine the cargo.

- Several major import corporations and large users only should be given permission to import restricted wastes.

- The scope of users should be restricted. Only users with the ability to prevent and eliminate pollution by wastes should have the right to use imported restricted wastes.

- An environmental pollution tax or import duty should be levied on the use of imported restricted wastes in order to protect the environment. The revenue collected could be used to strengthen the ability of relevant institutions and their staff in preventing and controlling illegal imports of hazardous wastes.

Environmental laws, their regulations and their enforcement should be revised, including:

- Pollution from the importation of hazardous wastes should be considered a serious crime committed against society as a whole. Those who break the relevant laws and pollute the environment should be severely punished. Enterprises which break the laws should be closed down or their rights to import waste rescinded, and those in charge should be considered responsible for environmental crime.

- severe financial penalties should be imposed on those who break the law.

International co-operation could be strengthened through:

- Further amendments to the Basel Convention. On the one hand, provisions covering the transfer of pollution-intensive industries through foreign direct investment might be included in the Convention; on the other hand, developed countries and newly industrialised economies should adopt effective national measures to enforce the provisions of the Convention.

- Exporting countries should be responsible for punishing illegal exporters of hazardous wastes. The approach of sending-back illegally transferred wastes does not always punish the exporter.

- A fund to compensate countries that suffer damages from the illegal export of hazardous wastes could be established.

- In WTO work on trade and environment, the national treatment principle should be redefined, and domestically prohibited and restricted products should be specified in any future understanding covering trade, investment and environment.

THE ISO 14000 SERIES OF ENVIRONMENTAL MANAGEMENT STANDARDS[1]

Philippe Bergeron
Regional Institute of Environmental Technology, Singapore

1.0   Background: Technical Committee TC 207

Following the work and recommendations of the Strategic Advisory Group on the Environment (SAGE) in preparation for the 1992 UNCED (Rio) Conference, the International Organization for Standardization (ISO) created TC 207 to develop a series of standards to address a need for international voluntary environmental management standards, in response to fears that environmental issues were being, or could be, used as barriers to international trade. The work of TC 207 started in 1993 and has been divided among six Sub-Committees as follows:

1.1   Sub-Committees

SC-1   Environmental Management Systems (EMS)
SC-2   Environmental Auditing (EA)
SC-3   Environmental Labelling (EL)
SC-4   Environmental Performance Evaluation (EPE)
SC-5   Life Cycle Assessment (LCA);
SC-6   Terms and Definitions (T and D)

A Working Group has been established to examine the Environmental Aspects of Product Standards (EAPS) and another focusing on forest management.

All the standards are being developed through an iterative process of international consensus and will create a voluntary set of qualitative specifications, general principles and guidelines as opposed to prescriptive technical standards.

The cornerstone of the series is the Environmental Management System (EMS), which aims to assist organisations on a voluntary basis to address environmental concerns and balance economic and environmental interests through a coherent allocation of resources, assignment of responsibilities, and an ongoing evaluation of practices, procedures and processes. All other standards can be seen as

---

[1]   This is an updated version of the paper presented in the workshop.

supportive guidelines or complementary instruments to be used to assist in developing and implementing an EMS. Environmental Auditing (EA) and Environmental Performance Evaluation (EPE) are more management-oriented tools, while Environmental Labelling (EL) and Life Cycle Assessment (LCA) are more product and process-oriented (see Figure 1).

2.0   Environmental Management Systems (EMS)

The EMS standard follows the core management system elements of the ISO 9000 quality standard. It uses the tried and tested methodology of "understanding issues, setting targets, monitoring progress and reviewing performance".

It differs significantly, however, by requiring organisations to commit to continual environmental improvement through a process of enhancing the EMS. Although it does not itself state specific environmental performance criteria, it requires an organisation to define environmental improvement objectives and targets, taking into account information about significant environmental impacts.

Taken simply, an EMS is a management tool made up of organisational structures, responsibilities, practices, procedures, processes and resources which enables an organisation to achieve and systematically control the level of environmental performance which it sets itself. The system enables organisations to i) identify the significant environmental impacts arising from existing or planned activities; ii) establish an environmental policy; iii) set appropriate environmental improvement objectives; iv) establish a programme to achieve targets; and v) facilitate control, monitoring, auditing and review of activities to ensure that the policy is complied with and remains relevant.

An EMS helps organisations to plan and document environmental improvement by means of recurring management reviews and verification audits against objectives and targets. New goals and targets are periodically set, enabling an upward spiral of continuous improvement (see Figure 2).

Considering the increasing environmental awareness in the general community, and the fact that carrying out a project in an environmentally correct way is already a cost of doing business today, it is expected that implementing an EMS will readily win acceptance by many organisations and companies. Most environmentally conscious firms will view it as being in their enlightened self-interest to build awareness about environmental concerns, understand the impact of business activities, and learn how to profit from environmental improvement. Some will see it as good business sense and will want to put an EMS in place to minimise environmental risk liabilities, maximise the efficient use of resources, reduce waste, and use it as a decision-making tool for planning investment in cleaner technology. Others will also consider the clear marketing advantages in portraying a clean and green public image of their organisation as one that takes its environmental responsibilities seriously.

As with ISO 9000, enterprises reliant on international trade will view certification to the international standard as a prime objective to secure or enhance market share.

With major financial stakeholders such as banks, insurance companies or pension funds taking an increasing interest in the environmental performance of their clients and lenders, and building environmental considerations into their lending policy, EMS will probably also influence the capacity of organisations and industry to raise finance, negotiate loans, or attract investment.

ISO 14001, which was adopted as an international standard in 1996, specifies the core elements of an EMS that may be objectively audited for certification, registration or self-declaration purposes. ISO 14004, also adopted in 1996, serves as the overall guidance document for the establishment of an EMS and include general guidelines, principles, systems and support techniques that an organisation may consider.

Figure 1: Inter-relationship of ISO 14000 Standards

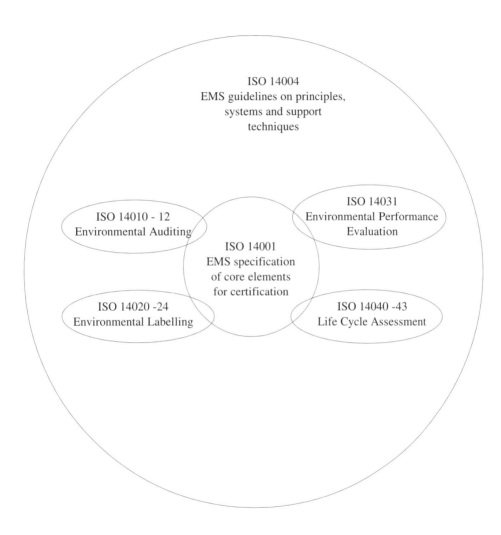

Figure 2: The EMS Spiral for Continuous Improvement

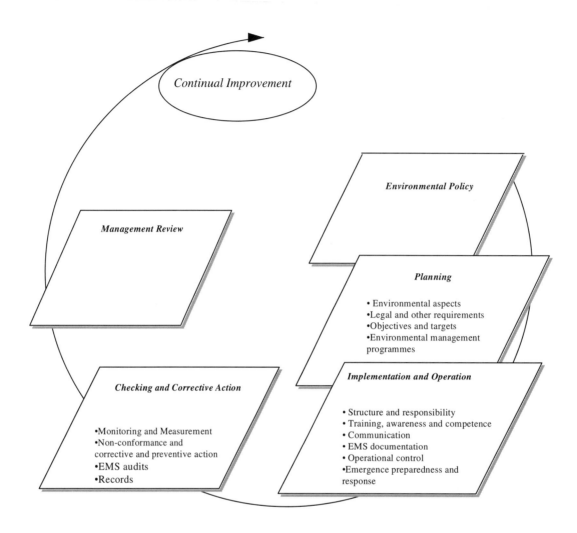

Compared with other already existing environmental management systems, in particular the BS 7750 or the European EMAS Regulation, ISO 14001 exhibits subtle differences.

While, for example, the British and European systems explicitly require an organisation to make a commitment to continual improvement in environmental performance, the ISO standard defines continual improvement in terms of "enhancing the environmental management system with the purpose of achieving improvement in overall environmental performance". This could be seen as a somewhat less stringent requirement. Indeed, the establishment and operation of an EMS will not, in itself, necessarily result in an immediate reduction of adverse environmental impact.

Other differences which suggest that the ISO standard is less stringent that its British and European cousins include the freedom in the ISO approach to set up an EMS for an entire organisation or only a specific operating unit thereof (it is a "site" or "an organisation" in the two other systems), the non-mention of a need to maintain an internal register of significant environmental impacts and legislative and regulatory requirements (a must in the two other systems), and the non-requirement of making environmental objectives and/or environmental statements publicly available in the ISO standard (an implied or overt requirement in the British and European systems).

3.0   Environmental Auditing (EA)

An Environmental Audit is the systematic, documented verification process of objectively obtaining and evaluating evidence to determine whether specified environmental activities, systems or information conform with audit criteria. In the ISO 14001 standard, auditing the EMS is a specific requirement for certification.

The following standards relating to environmental auditing were all adopted in 1996. ISO 14010 establishes general guidelines and principles for environmental auditing. ISO 14011 provides specific guidelines and procedures for the planning and performance of an EMS audit and ISO 14012 covers the qualification criteria for environmental auditors and lead auditors who will perform EMS audits as described in ISO 14011.

4.0   Environmental Labelling (EL)

Work continues on developing standards in this work area under the guidance of three working groups. The first working group is developing guiding principles, practices and certification procedures for environmental labelling (ISO 14024). A second working group is focusing on "self-declaration environmental claims" made by organisations supplying and marketing goods and services (ISO 14021), environmental labelling symbols (ISO 14022), and testing and verification methodologies (ISO 14023). The third working group is working on basic principles for all environmental labelling (ISO 14020)

5.0   Environmental Performance Evaluation (EPE)

With the Environmental Performance Evaluation Standard (ISO 14031), expected to be adopted in 1998, an organisation will have access to an internal process and supporting tool to assist its management to determine how its environmental objectives are met and how well its economic and environmental interests are aligned.

It represents a four-step iterative process (planning; applying; describing; reviewing and improving) to help an organisation focus on trends and change in environmental performance as needed to implement and review an EMS. It is not intended for use as a specification standard for certification purposes. It is expected to play an instrumental part in the process of continual improvement, by assisting in the selection and validation of relevant environmental performance indicators and ensuring that those are aligned with the organisation's objectives, especially in the area of management systems, operational systems, or the state of the environment.

6.0   Life Cycle Assessment (LCA)

In 1997, ISO 14040 was adopted. ISO 14040 provides principles and guidelines for conducting and reporting the results of an LCA as a systematic tool for assessing the environmental impacts associated with a product or service along the continuum of its life (cradle to crave). Other standards under consideration are planned to cover the various phases of an LCA, in particular the Life Cycle Inventory Analysis (ISO 14041), the Life Cycle Impact Assessment (ISO 14042) and Life Cycle Improvement Assessment (ISO 14043). All three of these standards are expected to be adopted in 1998. The slower pace of development of the LCA standards reflects the fact that this environmental management tool is still in its infancy and requires further research and development to become a practical instrument for industry and business.

7.0   Terms and Definitions

A standard called Environmental Management Vocabulary (ISO 14050) aims at developing a comprehensive and self-consistent set of terms and definitions. It is being developed and refined through an iterative process of consultation with all other Sub-Committees, and is expected to be adopted in 1998.

8.0   ISO 14000 EMS as a Tool to Improve Competitiveness

The logic of the ISO 14000 series is clearly to assist companies and organisations to look beyond mere legal environmental compliance to the economic benefits associated with production efficiency and increased market acceptability. In this way, the motivation for industry is competitiveness and the outcome is environmental performance.

The ISO 14000 series and, in particular, the EMS standards provide in fact a strategic and systematic approach to environmental management towards the corporate goals of efficiency, resource maximisation, product and process differentiation, regulatory compliance, and risk management.

By avoiding prescriptive technical specifications which place organisations in less developed countries at a disadvantage, and focusing instead on simple and verifiable environmental improvement systems which can start at any level, the ISO 14000 EMS standards have the potential to assist any industry move towards greater competitiveness. With large and small companies from less or more developed countries all qualified to structure an EMS whatever their initial environmental performance, it also helps level the global playing field needed by industries to demonstrate environmental commitment. ISO 14001 and its drive for continuous environmental improvement may in the early stages, in fact, place companies with a genuine environmental track record at a disadvantage.

In practice, however, and not least because of the effort, expertise and resources needed to move through the various steps of implementing an EMS (Initial Environmental Review, Identification and Evaluation of Environmental Impacts, Planning of Environmental Objectives and Targets, Establishment of Environmental Management Programmes, Measurement and Evaluation), organisations from less developed countries and SMEs may have more difficulties in putting the resources together to develop an EMS and benefiting from it.

Considering that the spirit of an EMS is rooted in providing a competitive advantage to environmentally committed companies, it is important that application of an environmental management system within the framework of ISO 14001 remains open and affordable to all interested companies or organisations whatever the country, the sector, or company size.

Possibilities for resource-strapped organisations to develop an EMS consistent with the broad aim of ISO 14000 may include: i) stepped development and implementation over an extended period; ii) collaboration with other companies for information and know-how access; iii) pooling of resources for necessary external consultancy; and iv) progressive accreditation to the standard through self-declaration, second party recognition, and finally third party certification.

9.0   ISO 14000 EMS and Cleaner Production

As indicated, the key motivation for an EMS under ISO 14000 is competitiveness, enabling industry to lower production costs and increasing the acceptability of processes and products in the market. The long-term outcome is greater profitability from "greener" products and processes.

It is clear that early environmental improvement will focus on better housekeeping and the systematic elimination of losses and wastes through optimised operational procedures. However, once improvement of environmental performance has been maximised through efficient utilisation of resources, further improvement almost certainly will require process changes and investment in cleaner production technology.

By providing a systematic approach and framework to identify waste streams and propose prioritised recommendations to lower or eliminate them through the application of cleaner production technology, an EMS can play an instrumental role in helping industry cut or eliminate water, energy and material consumption and enhance productivity and profitability. An EMS stimulates a gradual shift away from "cost only" end-of-pipe pollution treatment towards clean technologies and improved process and product designs that involve more efficient resource utilisation.

10.0   ISO 14000 EMS and SMEs

SMEs worldwide contribute very significantly to national economies. They may account for up to 70 per cent of world products, although this may vary considerably from country to country. In East and Southeast Asia there are more than 1.1 million SMEs in the manufacturing sector alone. It is clear that SMEs have limited financial resources and staff to deal with environmental management issues. Studies confirm that the smaller the enterprise, the less money it will spend on environmental protection and the fewer environmental staff, if any, are employed. On the other hand, although an SME alone may not appear to cause significant impacts, the cumulative effects of SMEs on a global scale are undoubtedly immense.

Recognising the global importance of SMEs and their limited resources, it is important that assistance to SMEs in implementing EMS addresses the needs and constraints of SME managers by minimising additional burdens on them.

After all, the motivation of the standard is to enable competitive advantage, and this should also apply to SMEs. Most smaller firms work on an ad hoc basis with little or no long-term corporate objectives except to survive week after week, to minimise costs, and to maximise profits. Rather than encouraging strategic environmental planning, EMS for SMEs would help focus attention on day-to-day operations to enable recycling, energy saving, and improved waste management.

Arguably, the less stringent requirements of ISO 14001 when compared with the two European systems, such as the non-necessity of a formal register of legislation and environmental effects, which have been driven by some advanced countries, may incidentally benefit the interests of SMEs by reducing the paperwork to the absolute minimum.

To facilitate the acceptance of ISO 14000 EMS by SMEs, it is clear, however, that external support and mechanisms for collaboration among SMEs will be needed.

Potential objectives for co-operation might include sharing access to information, co-operating on know-how and technology, collaborating on waste management and reuse, collaborating on training, pooling resources, and collective lobbying.

Another interesting approach to overcome the financial strains faced by SMEs may be "environmental performance contracting". In such a concept, an external consultancy may suggest energy or environmental savings, manage the changes, and then charge for its services as a percentage of the profits resulting from the energy or environmental savings.

11.0   ISO 14000 EMS and International Trade

According to WTO rules, there are essentially "no constraints for a country to protect its own environment, by doing anything to imports or exports that it does to its own products". Also according to this rule, a country cannot use trade policy to protect its environment from foreign production or to protect the environment outside its own jurisdiction.

One perspective on the trade-environment debate is that trade liberalisation will generate economic growth, providing the resources needed to satisfy the growing demand for environmental protection and improved living standards. In practice, however, the principal purpose of trade liberalisation is the expansion of output, and the expansion of output and its trade has a direct impact on the environment.

It is, for example, increasingly obvious that the strategy of some successful newly industrialised economies of "economic growth first, environmental protection later" may require rethinking in light of the economic costs of pollution and the loss of, or damage to, productive natural resources.

Without doubt trade also contributes to energy-related environmental concerns. Transportation as a precondition and factor of trade is today responsible for up to one-eighth of world oil consumption.

In the European Union (EU), environmental and trade issues have proved to be intimately linked. One widely publicised case involved the import of a German-produced beer which was prohibited by the Danish authorities because the beer containers were non-recyclable under the schemes operating in Denmark. On appeal to the European Court of Justice, the case was rejected on the grounds that action taken in the best interests of environmental protection could override EU trade agreements.

Progress in advancing the trade and environment work in international institutions such as the WTO has been slow. The experience to date suggests that it could be some time before the world trading system adopts a framework in which environmental sustainability is an integral element. In the absence of such a framework, ISO 14000 EMS, as a market-based instrument, may play an important role in supporting the emergence of environmentally sound trade.

Experience with ISO 9000 has demonstrated that a voluntary, third party-verifiable management standard can gain popularity on a global basis provided that it delivers tangible benefits to users. In Europe, where it has been widely adopted across a broad range of businesses, many companies have discovered that it is becoming increasingly difficult to do business as a supplier to larger firms, or to obtain government contracts, unless your firm has ISO 9000 certification. Certified industries are less and less willing to jeopardise their own annual certification process by working with non-certified firms. The same may happen in the case of ISO 14000, with industry requiring contractors along the global supply chain to demonstrate greater environmental stewardship and adopt their standards.

In a world which is seeing a decline in the internalisation of company operations and an increase in contracting and sub-contracting activities, trade may increasingly be predicated on the attainment of standards such as ISO 9000 and ISO 14000.

12.0   Implications of ISO 14000 in the Asia Region

The most significant implication of ISO 14000 for the Asian region concerns human resources. EMS implementation, and the periodic environmental reviews and audits required to support it, will need competent professionals throughout organisations.

At company level, personnel will need to be trained to undertake environmental reviews, possibly with external assistance; this role is almost certainly to fall to the plant engineers, the health and safety officer, or the quality manager. They will need to be backed up by other in-house staff trained in auditing company operations they are not involved with on a day-to-day basis. There will also be a strong demand for external consultancy services for EMS implementation and auditing, particularly in the vital task of assisting companies to assess their environmental impacts and to help set realistic objectives and targets for improvement in close consultation with company management.

Certification bodies will also need to staff-up with high calibre specialists who not only understand the principles and auditing of management systems but also have the necessary environmental expertise needed to understand whether environmental targets really have been achieved, and to understand the monitoring systems by which this can be demonstrated. Before certification bodies can be authorised to certify that a company meets the requirement of the standard, they will need to be accredited by an appropriate accreditation authority or council in each country. In most countries these bodies do not yet exist. When they do, they will need to have competent environmental personnel capable of judging whether the certification bodies have sufficient expertise and qualified personnel to undertake environmental certification activities.

MAIN SALES OUTLETS OF OECD PUBLICATIONS
PRINCIPAUX POINTS DE VENTE DES PUBLICATIONS DE L'OCDE

AUSTRALIA – AUSTRALIE
D.A. Information Services
648 Whitehorse Road, P.O.B 163
Mitcham, Victoria 3132   Tel. (03) 9210.7777
                            Fax: (03) 9210.7788

AUSTRIA – AUTRICHE
Gerold & Co.
Graben 31
Wien I   Tel. (0222) 533.50.14
                            Fax: (0222) 512.47.31.29

BELGIUM – BELGIQUE
Jean De Lannoy
Avenue du Roi, Koningslaan 202
B-1060 Bruxelles   Tel. (02) 538.51.69/538.08.41
                            Fax: (02) 538.08.41

CANADA
Renouf Publishing Company Ltd.
5369 Canotek Road
Unit 1
Ottawa, Ont. K1J 9J3   Tel. (613) 745.2665
                            Fax: (613) 745.7660

Stores:
71 1/2 Sparks Street
Ottawa, Ont. K1P 5R1   Tel. (613) 238.8985
                            Fax: (613) 238.6041

12 Adelaide Street West
Toronto, QN M5H 1L6   Tel. (416) 363.3171
                            Fax: (416) 363.5963

Les Éditions La Liberté Inc.
3020 Chemin Sainte-Foy
Sainte-Foy, PQ G1X 3V6   Tel. (418) 658.3763
                            Fax: (418) 658.3763

Federal Publications Inc.
165 University Avenue, Suite 701
Toronto, ON M5H 3B8   Tel. (416) 860.1611
                            Fax: (416) 860.1608

Les Publications Fédérales
1185 Université
Montréal, QC H3B 3A7   Tel. (514) 954.1633
                            Fax: (514) 954.1635

CHINA – CHINE
Book Dept., China National Publications
Import and Export Corporation (CNPIEC)
16 Gongti E. Road, Chaoyang District
Beijing 100020   Tel. (10) 6506-6688 Ext. 8402
                            (10) 6506-3101

CHINESE TAIPEI – TAIPEI CHINOIS
Good Faith Worldwide Int'l. Co. Ltd.
9th Floor, No. 118, Sec. 2
Chung Hsiao E. Road
Taipei   Tel. (02) 391.7396/391.7397
                            Fax: (02) 394.9176

**CZECH REPUBLIC –
RÉPUBLIQUE TCHÈQUE**
National Information Centre
NIS – prodejna
Konviktská 5
Praha 1 – 113 57   Tel. (02) 24.23.09.07
                            Fax: (02) 24.22.94.33
E-mail: nkposp@dec.niz.cz
Internet: http://www.nis.cz

DENMARK – DANEMARK
Munksgaard Book and Subscription Service
35, Nørre Søgade, P.O. Box 2148
DK-1016 København K   Tel. (33) 12.85.70
                            Fax: (33) 12.93.87

J. H. Schultz Information A/S,
Herstedvang 12,
DK – 2620 Albertslung   Tel. 43 63 23 00
                            Fax: 43 63 19 69

Internet: s-info@inet.uni-c.dk

EGYPT – ÉGYPTE
The Middle East Observer
41 Sherif Street
Cairo   Tel. (2) 392.6919
                            Fax: (2) 360.6804

FINLAND – FINLANDE
Akateeminen Kirjakauppa
Keskuskatu 1, P.O. Box 128
00100 Helsinki

Subscription Services/Agence d'abonnements :
P.O. Box 23
00100 Helsinki   Tel. (358) 9.121.4403
                            Fax: (358) 9.121.4450

*FRANCE
OECD/OCDE
Mail Orders/Commandes par correspondance :
2, rue André-Pascal
75775 Paris Cedex 16   Tel. 33 (0)1.45.24.82.00
                        Fax: 33 (0)1.49.10.42.76
                        Telex: 640048 OCDE
Internet: Compte.PUBSINQ@oecd.org

Orders via Minitel, France only/
Commandes par Minitel, France exclusivement :
36 15 OCDE

OECD Bookshop/Librairie de l'OCDE :
33, rue Octave-Feuillet
75016 Paris   Tel. 33 (0)1.45.24.81.81
                        33 (0)1.45.24.81.67

Dawson
B.P. 40
91121 Palaiseau Cedex   Tel. 01.89.10.47.00
                            Fax: 01.64.54.83.26

Documentation Française
29, quai Voltaire
75007 Paris   Tel. 01.40.15.70.00

Economica
49, rue Héricart
75015 Paris   Tel. 01.45.78.12.92
                            Fax: 01.45.75.05.67

Gibert Jeune (Droit-Économie)
6, place Saint-Michel
75006 Paris   Tel. 01.43.25.91.19

Librairie du Commerce International
10, avenue d'Iéna
75016 Paris   Tel. 01.40.73.34.60

Librairie Dunod
Université Paris-Dauphine
Place du Maréchal-de-Lattre-de-Tassigny
75016 Paris   Tel. 01.44.05.40.13

Librairie Lavoisier
11, rue Lavoisier
75008 Paris   Tel. 01.42.65.39.95

Librairie des Sciences Politiques
30, rue Saint-Guillaume
75007 Paris   Tel. 01.45.48.36.02

P.U.F.
49, boulevard Saint-Michel
75005 Paris   Tel. 01.43.25.83.40

Librairie de l'Université
12a, rue Nazareth
13100 Aix-en-Provence   Tel. 04.42.26.18.08

Documentation Française
165, rue Garibaldi
69003 Lyon   Tel. 04.78.63.32.23

Librairie Decitre
29, place Bellecour
69002 Lyon   Tel. 04.72.40.54.54

Librairie Sauramps
Le Triangle
34967 Montpellier Cedex 2   Tel. 04.67.58.85.15
                            Fax: 04.67.58.27.36

A la Sorbonne Actual
23, rue de l'Hôtel-des-Postes
06000 Nice   Tel. 04.93.13.77.75
                            Fax: 04.93.80.75.69

GERMANY – ALLEMAGNE
OECD Bonn Centre
August-Bebel-Allee 6
D-53175 Bonn   Tel. (0228) 959.120
                            Fax: (0228) 959.12.17

GREECE – GRÈCE
Librairie Kauffmann
Stadiou 28
10564 Athens   Tel. (01) 32.55.321
                            Fax: (01) 32.30.320

HONG-KONG
Swindon Book Co. Ltd.
Astoria Bldg. 3F
34 Ashley Road, Tsimshatsui
Kowloon, Hong Kong   Tel. 2376.2062
                            Fax: 2376.0685

HUNGARY – HONGRIE
Euro Info Service
Margitsziget, Európa Ház
1138 Budapest   Tel. (1) 111.60.61
                            Fax: (1) 302.50.35
E-mail: euroinfo@mail.matav.hu
Internet: http://www.euroinfo.hu//index.html

ICELAND – ISLANDE
Mál og Menning
Laugavegi 18, Pósthólf 392
121 Reykjavik   Tel. (1) 552.4240
                            Fax: (1) 562.3523

INDIA – INDE
Oxford Book and Stationery Co.
Scindia House
New Delhi 110001   Tel. (11) 331.5896/5308
                            Fax: (11) 332.2639
E-mail: oxford.publ@axcess.net.in

17 Park Street
Calcutta 700016   Tel. 240832

INDONESIA – INDONÉSIE
Pdii-Lipi
P.O. Box 4298
Jakarta 12042   Tel. (21) 573.34.67
                            Fax: (21) 573.34.67

IRELAND – IRLANDE
Government Supplies Agency
Publications Section
4/5 Harcourt Road
Dublin 2   Tel. 661.31.11
                            Fax: 475.27.60

ISRAEL – ISRAËL
Praedicta
5 Shatner Street
P.O. Box 34030
Jerusalem 91430   Tel. (2) 652.84.90/1/2
                            Fax: (2) 652.84.93

R.O.Y. International
P.O. Box 13056
Tel Aviv 61130   Tel. (3) 546 1423
                            Fax: (3) 546 1442
E-mail: royil@netvision.net.il

Palestinian Authority/Middle East:
INDEX Information Services
P.O.B. 19502
Jerusalem   Tel. (2) 627.16.34
                            Fax: (2) 627.12.19

ITALY – ITALIE
Libreria Commissionaria Sansoni
Via Duca di Calabria, 1/1
50125 Firenze   Tel. (055) 64.54.15
                            Fax: (055) 64.12.57
E-mail: licosa@ftbcc.it

Via Bartolini 29
20155 Milano   Tel. (02) 36.50.83

Editrice e Libreria Herder
Piazza Montecitorio 120
00186 Roma   Tel. 679.46.28
                            Fax: 678.47.51

Libreria Hoepli
Via Hoepli 5
20121 Milano   Tel. (02) 86.54.46
                            Fax: (02) 805.28.86

Libreria Scientifica
Dott. Lucio de Biasio 'Aeiou'
Via Coronelli, 6
20146 Milano   Tel. (02) 48.95.45.52
                                Fax: (02) 48.95.45.48

JAPAN – JAPON
OECD Tokyo Centre
Landic Akasaka Building
2-3-4 Akasaka, Minato-ku
Tokyo 107   Tel. (81.3) 3586.2016
                                Fax: (81.3) 3584.7929

KOREA – CORÉE
Kyobo Book Centre Co. Ltd.
P.O. Box 1658, Kwang Hwa Moon
Seoul   Tel. 730.78.91
                                Fax: 735.00.30

MALAYSIA – MALAISIE
University of Malaya Bookshop
University of Malaya
P.O. Box 1127, Jalan Pantai Baru
59700 Kuala Lumpur
Malaysia   Tel. 756.5000/756.5425
                                Fax: 756.3246

MEXICO – MEXIQUE
OECD Mexico Centre
Edificio INFOTEC
Av. San Fernando no. 37
Col. Toriello Guerra
Tlalpan C.P. 14050
Mexico D.F.   Tel. (525) 528.10.38
                                Fax: (525) 606.13.07
E-mail: ocde@rtn.net.mx

NETHERLANDS – PAYS-BAS
SDU Uitgeverij Plantijnstraat
Externe Fondsen
Postbus 20014
2500 EA's-Gravenhage   Tel. (070) 37.89.880
Voor bestellingen: Fax: (070) 34.75.778

Subscription Agency/   Agence d'abonnements :
SWETS & ZEITLINGER BV
Heereweg 347B
P.O. Box 830
2160 SZ Lisse   Tel. 252.435.111
                                Fax: 252.415.888

**NEW ZEALAND –
NOUVELLE-ZÉLANDE**
GPLegislation Services
P.O. Box 12418
Thorndon, Wellington   Tel. (04) 496.5655
                                Fax: (04) 496.5698

NORWAY – NORVÈGE
NIC INFO A/S
Ostensjoveien 18
P.O. Box 6512 Etterstad
0606 Oslo   Tel. (22) 97.45.00
                                Fax: (22) 97.45.45

PAKISTAN
Mirza Book Agency
65 Shahrah Quaid-E-Azam
Lahore 54000   Tel. (42) 735.36.01
                                Fax: (42) 576.37.14

PHILIPPINE – PHILIPPINES
International Booksource Center Inc.
Rm 179/920 Cityland 10 Condo Tower 2
HV dela Costa Ext cor Valero St.
Makati Metro Manila   Tel. (632) 817 9676
                                Fax: (632) 817 1741

POLAND – POLOGNE
Ars Polona
00-950 Warszawa
Krakowskie Prezdmiescie 7   Tel. (22) 264760
                                Fax: (22) 265334

PORTUGAL
Livraria Portugal
Rua do Carmo 70-74
Apart. 2681
1200 Lisboa   Tel. (01) 347.49.82/5
                                Fax: (01) 347.02.64

SINGAPORE – SINGAPOUR
Ashgate Publishing
Asia Pacific Pte. Ltd
Golden Wheel Building, 04-03
41, Kallang Pudding Road
Singapore 349316   Tel. 741.5166
                                Fax: 742.9356

SPAIN – ESPAGNE
Mundi-Prensa Libros S.A.
Castelló 37, Apartado 1223
Madrid 28001   Tel. (91) 431.33.99
                                Fax: (91) 575.39.98
E-mail: mundiprensa@tsai.es
Internet: http://www.mundiprensa.es

Mundi-Prensa Barcelona
Consell de Cent No. 391
08009 – Barcelona   Tel. (93) 488.34.92
                                Fax: (93) 487.76.59

Libreria de la Generalitat
Palau Moja
Rambla dels Estudis, 118
08002 – Barcelona
                 (Suscripciones) Tel. (93) 318.80.12
                 (Publicaciones) Tel. (93) 302.67.23
                                 Fax: (93) 412.18.54

SRI LANKA
Centre for Policy Research
c/o Colombo Agencies Ltd.
No. 300-304, Galle Road
Colombo 3   Tel. (1) 574240, 573551-2
                           Fax: (1) 575394, 510711

SWEDEN – SUÈDE
CE Fritzes AB
S–106 47 Stockholm   Tel. (08) 690.90.90
                                Fax: (08) 20.50.21

For electronic publications only/
Publications électroniques seulement
STATISTICS SWEDEN
Informationsservice
S-115 81 Stockholm   Tel. 8 783 5066
                                Fax: 8 783 4045

Subscription Agency/Agence d'abonnements :
Wennergren-Williams Info AB
P.O. Box 1305
171 25 Solna   Tel. (08) 705.97.50
                                Fax: (08) 27.00.71

Liber distribution
Internatial organizations
Fagerstagatan 21
S-163 52 Spanga

SWITZERLAND – SUISSE
Maditec S.A. (Books and Periodicals/Livres
et périodiques)
Chemin des Palettes 4
Case postale 266
1020 Renens VD 1   Tel. (021) 635.08.65
                                Fax: (021) 635.07.80

Librairie Payot S.A.
4, place Pépinet
CP 3212
1002 Lausanne   Tel. (021) 320.25.11
                                Fax: (021) 320.25.14

Librairie Unilivres
6, rue de Candolle
1205 Genève   Tel. (022) 320.26.23
                                Fax: (022) 329.73.18

Subscription Agency/Agence d'abonnements :
Dynapresse Marketing S.A.
38, avenue Vibert
1227 Carouge   Tel. (022) 308.08.70
                                Fax: (022) 308.07.99

See also – Voir aussi :
OECD Bonn Centre
August-Bebel-Allee 6
D-53175 Bonn (Germany)   Tel. (0228) 959.120
                                Fax: (0228) 959.12.17

THAILAND – THAÏLANDE
Suksit Siam Co. Ltd.
113, 115 Fuang Nakhon Rd.
Opp. Wat Rajbopith
Bangkok 10200   Tel. (662) 225.9531/2
                                Fax: (662) 222.5188

**TRINIDAD & TOBAGO, CARIBBEAN
TRINITÉ-ET-TOBAGO, CARAÏBES**
Systematics Studies Limited
9 Watts Street
Curepe
Trinidad & Tobago, W.I.   Tel. (1809) 645.3475
                                Fax: (1809) 662.5654
E-mail: tobe@trinidad.net

TUNISIA – TUNISIE
Grande Librairie Spécialisée
Fendri Ali
Avenue Haffouz Imm El-Intilaka
Bloc B 1 Sfax 3000   Tel. (216-4) 296 855
                                Fax: (216-4) 298.270

TURKEY – TURQUIE
Kültür Yayinlari Is-Türk Ltd.
Atatürk Bulvari No. 191/Kat 13
06684 Kavaklidere/Ankara
                         Tel. (312) 428.11.40 Ext. 2458
                         Fax : (312) 417.24.90
Dolmabahce Cad. No. 29
Besiktas/Istanbul   Tel. (212) 260 7188

UNITED KINGDOM – ROYAUME-UNI
The Stationery Office Ltd.
Postal orders only:
P.O. Box 276, London SW8 5DT
Gen. enquiries   Tel. (171) 873 0011
                                Fax: (171) 873 8463

The Stationery Office Ltd.
Postal orders only:
49 High Holborn, London WC1V 6HB
Branches at: Belfast, Birmingham, Bristol,
Edinburgh, Manchester

UNITED STATES – ÉTATS-UNIS
OECD Washington Center
2001 L Street N.W., Suite 650
Washington, D.C. 20036-4922 Tel. (202) 785.6323
                                Fax: (202) 785.0350
Internet: washcont@oecd.org

Subscriptions to OECD periodicals may also be
placed through main subscription agencies.

Les abonnements aux publications périodiques de
l'OCDE peuvent être souscrits auprès des
principales agences d'abonnement.

Orders and inquiries from countries where Distribu-
tors have not yet been appointed should be sent to:
OECD Publications, 2, rue André-Pascal, 75775
Paris Cedex 16, France.

Les commandes provenant de pays où l'OCDE n'a
pas encore désigné de distributeur peuvent être
adressées aux Éditions de l'OCDE, 2, rue André-
Pascal, 75775 Paris Cedex 16, France.

                                        12-1996